THE LIMITS
AND
POSSIBILITIES
OF CONGRESS

THE LIMITS
AND
POSSIBILITIES
OF CONGRESS

Philip Brenner
American University

St. Martin's Press • New York

Acknowledgment
"Almost the Way It Works," by Russell Baker. Copyright © 1978 by The New
York Times Company. Reprinted by permission.

To my parents, Sol and Lillian Brenner

Preface

Every day, in ever new ways, the United States Congress disappoints more people. This is the fault not of Congress but of our expectations. We know intuitively that the structure of our society creates struggles over the production and distribution of the goods and services we need. But we have trouble understanding how this societal structure profoundly limits what Congress can do. We know that what happens in Congress depends on the varying energy, values, venality, resources, political skill, and determination of the people and the groups involved, as well as on flexible features of the legislature such as subcommittees and rules. But we should not expect that changing the personnel or the rules of Congress alone will enable it to do all the things that we wish. The problem is much more complex.

Associated with our system of production and distribution are material and ideological forces that both broadly limit and create possibilities for congressional action. Individual legislators believe that their peculiar goals, interests, resources, capabilities, and histories shape thier behavior, and that the legislature itself limits them. In part, they are correct. But a member of Congress operates in three worlds, worlds defined by his or her personal interests, by the nature of the institution, and by society.

The three worlds limit what members can do and create many possibilities for legislative achievement. To comprehend the limits and possibilities of Congress is to probe its fundamental nature. Without understanding the complex relation between Congress and the larger society, we might ask the impossible of Congress. Worse, the resulting frustration may discourage us from asking even what is possible.

This book explores these limits and possibilities through three case studies (presented in Chapters 3 through 6) that examine the process of congressional foreign and domestic policy making and detail the significant reforms within Congress during the 1970s. These case studies—which analyze congressional policy towards Cuba, higher-education policy, and congressional reform—are based not only on close observations but also on extensive interviews with the legislators who shaped Congress's position in each case. Most of these legislators were unwilling to be identified by name, but this anonymity enabled them to be extraordinarily forthright in their answers to sensitive questions.

The study of Congress's policy towards Cuba is particularly detailed: Cuba has figured prominently in American Foreign-policy considerations, and the changing complexion of this specific policy reflects broader issues of Congress's role in making foreign policy. The study of higher education illustrates Congress's approach to domestic issues and shows how Congress sees higher education as a component of the larger political system. The study of congressional reform indicates how Congress's image of itself reveals the interests of its members and the effect of the external environment on these interests.

Framing the case studies are three chapters that are more generally interpretive. Chapter 1 analyzes and evaluates the assumptions that undergird traditional scholarship in this field. Chapter 2 offers an alternative approach to the study of Congress, which, although it does not wholly reject the prevailing assumptions, departs from them radically to explore congressional behavior in terms of the larger political economy. Chapter 7 reviews the propositions of Chapters 1 and 2 in the light of the case studies.

These framing chapters may help to bridge the gap between Marxist literature on the state and more traditional literature on the institutions of the United States government. Marxist literature has often ignored the nature of particular institutions, because they are seen merely as derivative of larger forces or are at the middle levels of power. Traditional political-science literature, on the other hand, has tended to ignore Marxist state theory, which many scholars consider too global and irrelevant to an understanding of immediate phenomena. The book thus addresses questions of importance to congressional scholars by means of an approach developed by Marxist scholars.

Acknowledgments

Over the years during which I have developed the ideas in this book, I have been fortunate to gain the advice and assistance of many people. Foremost among them has been Betsy Vieth, whose ideas and support have been essential to the development of the book. Our marriage during the course of my work on it is a testament to her love. My parents, Sol and Lillian Brenner, contributed in a special way: not only did they provide research assistance through the assiduous clipping of articles that were particularly important in Chapters 3 and 4, but more importantly, they offered encouragement and nurtured in me a set of values I hope is evident in the book.

I am grateful to the following friends and colleagues for critical commentary and emotional support: Gordon Adams, Morton Baratz, Stephen Boyan, Amy Bridges, Irene Diamond, Lawrence Dodd, Richard Feinberg, Kenneth Fox, David Gold, Paul Goldman, Ira Katznelson, Saul Landau, George LaNoue, William LeoGrande, Margaret Levi, Bruce Oppenheimer, Robert Pastor, Marcus Raskin, Barry Rossinoff, Gary Sellers, Barry Sklar, Susan Strasser (my "book buddy"), Marvin Surkin, Jean Woy, and Erik Olin Wright. Three scholars deserve great thanks: Bertram Gross, Norman Ornstein, and David Vogler.

I owe a special debt to David B. Truman, who guided me into political science when I was an undergraduate and counseled me from afar when I was in graduate school. We parted ways many years ago, but he remains for me the model of a scholar and teacher. In graduate school I was fortunate to study under two men who taught me about Congress and encouraged me to be imaginative in the ways of studying it: Milton Cummings, Jr., and Robert Peabody supervised my dissertation, out of which this book has developed.

Some of the research for Chapters 3 and 4 was done in conjunction with Roger Majak for a paper we wrote together: "Congressmen as Statesmen: The Case of Cuba." The chapters benefit from that work as well as from numerous discussions I have had with him. We were lucky to have the assistance of Anthony Coe, who helped in coding interviews and gathering material. Richard Keller provided important research assistance for Chapter 5.

Colleagues and students at the Institute for Policy Studies, American University, the University of Maryland–Baltimore County, and *Politics & Society* have generated an atmosphere of continuing inquiry and intellectual growth that I have tried to reflect in the book.

My research could not have been conducted without the help of many people in Congress and the Executive Branch who gave freely of their views. One member of Congress—Phillip Burton—was uncommonly helpful in providing me with office space, a telephone, and his time, and he deserves special thanks. His staff, especially Nancy Leong and Frank Kieliger, was also extraordinarily helpful.

In the production of this book I was fortunate to have the services of Ann Wilcox, who combined intelligence with typing skill. At St. Martin's Press I have had the pleasure of working with superb editors whose sensitivity improved both the style and conceptual clarity of the book. My thanks to Bob Woodbury, Michael Weber, and Charles Thurlow for their patience and care.

Philip Brenner

Contents

PART I Introduction: Approaches to the
Study of Congress   1

1 Assumptions About Congress   2
An Analysis of the Five Assumptions   6
  Parochialism   6
  Re-election   7
  Maximizing Other Personal Interests   8
  Internal Institutional Power   9
  Good Public Policy   10
Implications of the Assumptions   11
  The Five Assumptions and the Limits and Possibilities of
    Congress   11
  The Five Assumptions and the Study of Congress   12
Two Caveats   17
  Reifying Congress   17
  Methodology   18

2 Placing Congress in Context   23
A Changing Political and Economic Context   24
  The Material Base   24
  The Ideological Base   28
Interest Groups and the Political-Economic Context   30
The Significance of the Larger Context   33
  Personal Interests and the Larger Context   35
  Institutional Interests and the Larger Context   35

PART II Case Studies   39

3 Foreign Policy: Towards Normal Relations with Cuba—
Congress's Role   40
The Background of American Cuba Policy   40
Congressional Action on Cuba Policy   44
  Congressional Activity, 1971–1975   45
  Congressional Activity, 1976   48
  Congressional Activity, 1977–1978   49
Members' Perceptions   52
  Personal Interests   54

Institutional Interests   56
National Interests   57

4 Foreign Policy: Towards Normal Relations with Cuba—the International Context   67
The Context of Congressional Policy   67
    The International Context, 1971–1975   68
    The International Context, 1976   78
    The International Context, 1977–1978   82
Congress and Foreign Policy   88
    The Limits of Initiative   88
    New Patterns of Policy Initiation   90
    Lessons of the Cuba Case Study   93

5 Domestic Policy: Restructuring Higher Education   100
The Higher Education Act of 1972   101
    Interest Groups, Policy Elites, and the
        Executive Branch   102
    Personal Interests of the Members   107
    An Instrumentalist Explanation Rejected   111
Members' Perceptions   117
The Larger Context: A Legitimacy Crisis   121
Congressional Initiative and the Legitimacy Crisis   128

6 Restructuring Congress: The Context of Reform   134
Personal and Organizational Reforms   135
    Personal Reforms   135
    Organizational Reforms   137
Institutional Consequences of Reform   148
    The Centralizing Potential of Reforms   148
    The Decentralizing Effect of Reforms   151
The Context for Reform   152
Conclusion   157
    Decentralizing Reforms   158
    Centralizing Reforms   158

PART **III** Conclusion   164

7 The Limits and Possibilities of Congress   166
Congressional Reform   166
    Higher Education Act   167
    Normalization of Relations with Cuba   167

A Critique of the Assumptions   *169*
  Members of Congress Are As Nationally Oriented As
    Other Elites   *169*
  Re-election Isn't All That It's Cracked Up to Be   *171*
  The Rich Are Not Omniscient, and Legislators Are Not
    Easily Manipulated   *173*
  Power for a Purpose, Not for Its Own Sake, Is the
    Quest   *174*
  Most Members Care About Making Public Policy—Good
    and Bad   *175*
  Beyond Narrow Limits   *178*
Members of Congress Think What They Think Because They
  Do What They Do   *179*
  How Members See Themselves   *179*
  Rulers of a Weak State   *183*
  The Dialectics of Congressional Decision-Making   *186*
Functions of Congress   *188*
  Contradictions and Possibilities   *191*
Index   *197*

PART I

Introduction:
Approaches to the Study
of Congress

1 Assumptions About Congress

Most Americans know a lot about Congress—probably more than they are aware. Some of this knowledge comes from familiarity with other organizations, and some of it comes from bits and pieces picked up from the media, trips to Washington, and casual conversations. And, of course, some comes from studying Congress in school. We all have an idea about the way Congress works, and even a sense about why it works as it does.

When we hear, for example, that a member of Congress has added an amendment to a tax bill that protects an industry in his or her district, we are unlikely to be surprised. We expect representatives to protect their constituents. When a legislator explains that election year pressures prevent him or her from taking a clear stand on a controversial issue, we might nod understandingly and say, "That's natural for members of Congress." Similarly, many of us have grown immune to shock from revelations about congressional bribes or about the dazzling sums that politicians spend to get re-elected. It may bore us that members fight among themselves for power in Congress, but it is hardly news. Finally, though we might have grown skeptical, we acknowledge that members of Congress also work hard and that many try to fashion good public policy. These likely expectations about Congress embody a general picture of how and why it operates. *New York Times* humorist Russell Baker explored this general picture of Congress in a 1978 column titled "Almost the Way It Works":

> In the beginning God sent a Creation bill to the Congress. It proposed a crash program under which everything from light to man would be created in six days. It ran into trouble almost immediately in the Senate Finance Committee.
>
> The powerful light lobby was unhappy with the bill's language, which said, "Let there be light." This suggested that the light was going to be free, it was observed. Everybody knew there was no such thing as a free lunch. Why deceive people with the notion that there could be free light?
>
> The light lobby demanded that the bill clearly spell out the light industry's right to sell light without divine interference at whatever price the free market would bear. This provoked powerful opposition from consumer lob-

bies, which insisted that the price of light be regulated by God with infinite mercy, and from business groups, which wanted the price of light to be made tax-deductible if it was used for business purposes.

Another fierce struggle developed in the House Firmament Committee about the creation of the dry land. Everybody was dissatisfied with the bill's meager provisions for stocking the dry land after its creation. This passage said, "Let the earth bring forth grass, the herb yielding seed, and the fruit tree yielding fruit after his kind, whose seed is in itself, upon the earth."

While grass, herbs and fruit were all very nice, House members noted, the bill was suspiciously silent on such matters as oil. It was quickly amended to read, "Let there also be oil." The issue of where the oil was to be placed, however, was not so readily settled. Congressmen from Louisiana and Texas wanted the oil created in Texas and Louisiana, while those from New England wanted it created under Route 128 outside Boston.

This impasse might have lasted for years except for the intervention of Senator William Proxmire, chairman of the powerful Public Virtue Committee, who opposed creating the oil anywhere near New York on ground that New York would waste it in sinful pursuits such as driving to Queens political clubs for the purpose of getting idle cousins on the city payroll.

Under the Proxmire compromise, Texas and Louisiana got the oil and New England got the great whales, which were to be created under the original provisions of the bill. This by no means solved God's problems, for the Joint Committee on Man had been paralyzed by contending lobbies fighting over the design characteristics of man.

At the outset, women objected to the committee's name and lobbied to have it changed to The Joint Committee on Person. They won chiefly with the assistance of the medical lobbies, led by A.M.A., which wanted the design to include an appendix and a gall bladder.

Consumer lobbyists argued that the only conceivable purpose for putting in an appendix and gall bladder was to make work for surgeons. When the feminist lobby agreed to support the appendix-and-gall-bladder amendment in return for the A.M.A.'s agreement to support renaming the committee, however, the fight was settled.

There were many more. One of the bitterest was over the language in the original bill proposing that man be created "in the image of God." This was intensely contested by a coalition of foundations and fund-raising groups. Since God was perfect and eternal, they pointed out, a man designed in His image would also have to be perfect and eternal. A Creation peopled exclusively by perfect and eternal persons, they said, would be unbearably dull. They demanded that the bill be modified to have man created imperfect and temporary.

Consumer groups argued that the foundations and fund-raisers were less interested in having an exciting Creation than they were in having a variety of human ailments whose alleviation would provide jobs for the foundation-and-fund-raising industry. The funeral industry, however, sided with the fund-raisers, arguing that by making man temporary instead of eternal Congress would enrich his existence by encouraging him to dwell on philosophy.

The matter was settled when the dental lobby made a deal with the funeral and fund-raising industries about jaw design. The dental lobby had proposed an absurd scheme in which three or four dozen small pieces of bone would be awkwardly planted in the jawbone where they would be subject to quick decay and easy loss. The drawings for this design looked so ridiculous that the Subcommittee on Mastication discarded them after a glance and chose a sensible two-piece cutting-and-grinding device of durable titanium.

The dental lobby carried the day, however, when it formed a coalition with the funeral and fund-raising industries, which is why to this very day we are imperfect, temporary and found at the dentist twice a year. Congressmen are, too, which suggests that justice isn't entirely dead.

Baker's satire suggests a widely shared vision of Congress: members of both houses are buffeted by many pressures and confront scores of obstacles (not the least of which are the legislators' own selfishness and the nature of the institution) in trying to accomplish anything at all; moreover, were they to overcome these limits, any accomplishment—including the creation of the world—might be possible. Baker is not alone in this view. So many journalists and scholars present essentially the same argument, though without Baker's wit, that some might have wondered why Baker called his piece "Almost the Way It Works": he describes what seems to be exactly the way Congress works.

The serious view of Congress that underlies Baker's humor is exaggerated at both ends. As this book argues, the pressures on Congress do not create great obstacles to action: members have fewer limits on them than we have been led to believe. At the other end, the structure of society imposes obstacles that prevent legislators from doing whatever they wish: the ultimate possibilities of congressional action are more limited than we have been led to believe.

Our inaccurate picture of Congress owes its prevalence to five widely articulated assumptions about the members of Congress:[2]

1. members of Congress are parochial and narrow;
2. most members care principally about their own re-election;
3. when they do not focus on re-election, members of Congress attempt to maximize other personal interests;
4. in order to pursue their interests, members of Congress concern themselves with internal institutional power, and this concern may become an end in itself;
5. some members of Congress care most about making good public policy.

Scholars and journalists rely on these assumptions when they describe and explain congressional behavior—even when they focus on interest groups, the executive branch, political parties, the media, constituents, staff, congressional committees, informal caucuses, and the rules of Congress.[3] In some cases congressional analysts depict a member's actions as rooted in all five assumptions: a representative who favors a larger military budget may be shown to care about a local munitions plant, potential charges in an election campaign that he is soft on communism, his ambitions for the Senate, discharging an obligation to another legislator, and the national defense. In other cases only one or two assumptions may be seen to pertain.[4]

Each of the five assumptions has some validity, and together they capture a partial truth about Congress. What distorts the overall picture of Congress that they project is the absence of an important sixth assumption: Congress relates to the domestic and international political and economic contexts in ways that both give members great room to maneuver and define the outer limits of their behavior. The larger contexts, beyond Capitol Hill, are necessary considerations in analyses of Congress's limits and possibilities.

This book is about the nature of the larger contexts, and about the way that their inclusion in descriptions of congressional behavior changes the picture we have of Congress. This chapter examines the picture we have by elaborating the five assumptions. The next chapter explores the sixth assumption—that Congress's link to the larger contexts shapes its behavior.

The three case studies that follow—in Chapters 3 through 6—examine the complexity of the relationship between congressional behavior and the larger system. In each case, the relevant context is explored to clarify the nature of each of the problems that Congress addressed. What Congress did is then analyzed in terms of the problems. From this perspective, that Congress is not isolated from the transformations of society becomes evident. But the cases also reveal that Congress does not merely respond to demands from particular groups in the society: Congress can act with a will of its own in its search for solutions.

Congress appears to act independently when presented with a series of "negative events"—what political scientist Claus Offe has called "the absence or disturbance of an accumulation process."[5] In our society accumulating profit motivates the private decisions to produce the goods and services we need for survival. Without a stable process of profit accumulation, the viability of a capitalist society is weakened, and the government therefore tends to equate the stability of accumulation with the stability of society. When there is a problem in the accumulation process, Congress may become aware of it through complaints and specific demands, but it may act in ways that no particular group has demanded as it attempts to fashion a response to the problem. In such cases, a simple, mechanistic model would misrepresent the reality of congressional behavior.

In the three cases the relevant context is significant because it generated the events that set the agenda for Congress. As members responded to these events, they acted on the basis of options they perceived before them. In part they limited the options by their very definition of the problems they sought to solve, in that they were concerned about disturbances in the process of accumulating profit.

But these limits only set the outer bonds of the possible—they did not determine the outcome of each case. The possibilities in each case reflected the particular people involved and their abilities and interests. Their interests included personal and institutional goals embraced by the five assumptions and interests of the state related to the sixth assumption.

Chapter 7 returns directly to the question of the limits and possibilities of Congress. It draws on the case studies to provide a critique of the five assumptions and to explore how the sixth assumption leads to a less exaggerated view about Congress's limits and possibilities.

An Analysis of the Five Assumptions

Parochialism

Members of Congress tend to be rooted in their districts, to be responsive to local elites and constituents, and to care about specific problems rather than a pattern of problems. Perhaps the most articulate presentation of this assumption was made by Samuel P. Huntington:

> Congressmen have tended to be oriented toward local needs and small-town ways of thought. The leaders of the administration and of the great private national institutions are more likely to think in national terms. . . . The congressman is part of a local consensus of local politicians, local businessmen, local bankers, local trade union leaders, and local newspaper editors.[6]

Huntington writes from a conservative perspective, but this assumption is made by a wide spectrum of scholars, including Marxists, who have argued that Congress attempts to tailor programs "to local and regional interests—the interests of small-scale capital."[7]

At best, according to scholars who accept this assumption, legislators may act on behalf of particular groups that transcend geographic boundaries—such as blacks, Greeks, Jews, steel companies, and so on—but they do so only around the specific interests the groups espouse. As a consequence, Congress does not take a broad view of problems and cannot fashion good general policy because the sum of particular interests is less than the interest of the whole.[8] Instead, it tends to transform broad policies into segmented ones that can distribute clear benefits to the largest number of districts.[9]

There are several sources, these scholars argue, for the parochialism of legislators, including the nature of their recruitment and, accordingly, that of their backgrounds. But the ultimate source of this orientation is the congressional election. Each member of Congress is ultimately tied to a locality—a city, region, or state—by virtue of the need to be re-elected from that locality. In contrast to some parliamentary systems, where a national party selects a candidate and thereby pressures a legislator to take on a national perspective alongside a local one, members of Congress are beholden only to the coalition of supporters they maintain locally. Often they run without significant party support, sometimes they run against the gubernatorial or presidential candidate at the head of the ticket, and they even may run against Congress itself, portraying it as an evildoer that needs the vigilance of the incumbent. Elections force congresspeople to be locally oriented and Congress to be parochial. The first assumption, in turn, leads to the second.

Re-election

A member of Congress may care about many things other than re-election, political scientist Morris Fiorina argues, "but in order to retain the status, excitement, and power (not to mention more tangible things) of office, the congressman must win re-election every two years."[10] The necessity of keeping his or her job prompts a legislator to make re-election the first concern and to examine all behavior in terms of its possible effect on re-election.[11]

This necessity determines the organization of a legislator's time and affects how time is split between Washington and the district. As the costs of elections have risen, members of Congress have devoted increasing efforts to raising money. The need for campaign resources may also lead a member to vote a particular way, to sponsor certain legislation, or to lobby the executive branch in order to benefit large contributors.[12] In part campaign finances explain Congress's unwillingness to take up certain issues—issues that incumbents' benefactors would prefer buried.

Legislators also tend to devote more time than they might otherwise wish to constituent services, such as casework, and to bringing federal largesse to the district, largely because they believe that these activities will benefit them electorally.[13] On issues important to their constituents, members will often vote much as they perceive the active voters in their districts would have them vote, regardless of the members' personal judgments and other pressures.[14] Elected legislators have even developed the organization of Congress and the norms of the institution in ways that enhance the electability of incumbents, by enabling members to shine and claim credit, by allowing a representative to take from the trough for his or her district, and by encouraging segmented rather than broad-based policymaking.[15] While some members may appear to act in ways that do not directly serve their districts, they do so in order to enhance their ability to bargain in the end for district benefits.

The politics of re-election explain much of the work that Congress does vis-à-vis the executive branch. The duties of overseeing the bureaucracy are performed in a determined fashion when such performance can "contribute directly and substantially to political survival."[16] For example, a member would be quick to challenge an executive branch decision to close a district federal facility. Similarly, the links between congressional committees, executive agencies, and interest groups that seem to dominate Washington politics—to the extent that they have been described as an "iron triangle"[17]—are forged by the legislators' drive for re-election. Iron triangle politics enable members "to develop close ties to key interest groups and to key bureaucratic agencies," Lawrence Dodd and Richard Schott observe. "It goes almost without saying that these close ties bring electoral benefits."[18]

Maximizing Other Personal Interests

Though members may concentrate on their re-election in order to gain power or to effect some public policy, their focus on re-election is similar to any worker's concern about job security. In this sense, re-election can be thought of as a *personal* concern of legislators—a concern that legislators have as people and that does not distinguish them from people who are not in positions of power or who do not have the opportunity to shape policy. Of course, job security is not the only personal interest of the members. As with non-elites, they want prestige, respect, status, money, special perquisites, and other jobs that might lead to even more prestige, money, and so on.

C. Wright Mills may have located the Congress at only "the middle levels of power," but for most members it is the center of the world. They revel in the deference that staff, constituents, lobbyists, journalists, scholars, and at times even presidents show them. The "office of congressman," Morris Fiorina notes, "carries with it prestige, excitement and power."[19] Members respond well to the deference they believe is their due, and chafe at treatment they consider beneath their dignity. Such responses can have political impacts, depending on how skillful a lobbyist or president might be.[20]

In part members claim the right to a variety of perquisites—such as subsidized restaurants, free parking, and two bathrooms in their office suites—as symbols of their status.[21] Such concerns with status make it difficult for them to turn away occasional gifts from lobbyists, lavish dinners or paid vacations, and payments for service that may verge on the illegal.[22] Of course, the lust for "benefits" may be no more than a reflection of greed, too.

At one time, election to the House and certainly to the Senate was the cap on a person's political career. Few sought any office beyond. Today ambition is a personal concern of a large number of members. Political scientist Randall Ripley concludes, "If the members are not interested primarily in re-election to their present seats, they may well have their eyes on other elective offices."[23] Ambitious politicians may even seek office in the House or Senate for no reason other than that it offers them opportunities to gain attention, claim credit, and develop reputations.[24]

Seeking higher office may prove contradictory to a member's immediate interests. Such ambition can lessen a representative's chances of gaining power within the House because members tend to punish "disloyalty" to the institution by withholding rewards. Because power in the House can also be an avenue to higher office, as it was for former House Minority Leader Gerald Ford, members may temper their pursuit of personal concerns in order to gain it. This paradox leads to the fourth assumption.

Internal Institutional Power

The quest for power, to use Lawrence Dodd's phrase,[25] may be the defining characteristic of members of Congress if not of all politicians. At the least, some analysts believe, it ranks alongside the compulsion to be re-elected as an animating force of congressional behavior and is an enduring feature of Congress.[26] When they seek information about a bill, for example, members of Congress above all tend to ask about two of its effects: they are interested in its impact on their constituents and how it will affect their position vis-à-vis other members.[27]

The dedicated pursuit of power pervades all aspects of Congress. Members calculate how their power will be affected when they decide whether to fight for a bill, because congressional power often resides in appearances. The appearance of never losing a fight contributes to a "powerful lawmaker" image, which may help the legislator win future fights.[28] Seemingly neutral features of legislative life, such as rules or norms that appear to enable the Congress to operate efficiently, are at base expressions of power that shape the distribution of influence in the legislature.[29] This becomes evident when the institution abandons a set of rules or a norm in response to a shift in power. The increase in northern liberal Democrats in the Senate since 1958, for example, appears to have discouraged apprenticeship, a norm that tended to benefit senior conservative southern Democrats.[30] Formal positions of authority within Congress—committee chairs or party leaderships—do not always carry with them a degree of power commensurate to the stature of the position.[31] Power is a behavioral phenomenon and is not fixed on an organization chart. It shifts as members struggle for it, and the continual struggle defines what Congress does.

Members may seek power for many reasons. One explanation, which borrows from a rich literature in psychology, is that they attempt to fulfill a psychological need. Without power they may feel "short-changed" or deprived.[32] Those who have power enjoy it and want to maintain it.[33] Some may struggle for power in order to gain "access to considerable financial support in re-election campaigns . . . ; status and deference from key political actors . . . ; and the personal knowledge that one could help mold key public policy in areas of personal constituency interest."[34] In their pursuit, some members may come to dwell on power so much that they see it as an end in itself, and may even see the legislature as a game unrelated to the world. But most associate power with the pursuit of other ends, which might include the institution of new public policies or the preservation of existing policy directions.[35] This concern with public policy relates to the fifth assumption about members of Congress.

Good Public Policy

Some members of Congress have "genuine policy commitments"[36] and have chosen a congressional career in order to fulfill these commitments. Legislators who focus on making policy, it is said, gravitate to committees that are concerned with broad policy areas, such as the House Education and Labor Committee or House Foreign Affairs Committee. Members choose these committees because they "deal with 'interesting,' 'exciting,' 'controversial,' and 'important' subjects," not because they expect to gain any electoral benefit or power in Congress.[37]

To effect their policy goals, these legislators will rely necessarily on members whose principal interests do not involve policy but rather lie in re-election, other personal interests such as wealth or ambition, or power. In fashioning coalitions to secure their policy ends, the policy-oriented members will address these interests of the other members.[38] Through this process, their policies in the end will have a democratic cast to them, because the coalitions will include those who are sensitive to constituent concerns and those who are linked closely to interest groups.

Implications of the Assumptions

The Five Assumptions and the Limits and Possibilities of Congress

To repeat an earlier point, few scholars focus on only one of the five assumptions. Most rely on a few, if not all, of them to probe for data that explain congressional behavior. Within each assumption lies an implicit expectation about the limits and possibilities of Congress. Taken together, the five suggest that the limits on a member of Congress are enormous, but paradoxically that the possibilities for action are unbounded.

Consider briefly the limits and possibilities indicated by each assumption.

Members of Congress are parochial and narrow. The orientation of Congress will lead it to resist change that might benefit national and international enterprises at the expense of local ones, or change that takes resources from one area to help another. But it also encourages members of Congress to be sensitive to disruptions in people's lives and to mitigate dislocation.

Most members of Congress care principally about their own re-election. Legislators will not undertake tasks necessary to make sound policy, will avoid difficult decisions that might hurt them electorally, and will serve the interests of campaign contributors instead of the public interest. But if people want major changes, the electoral link will force a legislator to support them, even if he or she would have acted differently otherwise. Furthermore, members from "marginal" districts might pursue policy innovation as a way of strengthening their voter support.

When they do not focus on re-election, members of Congress attempt to maximize other personal interests. The lure of prestige and lucrative benefits discourages members from rocking the boat and leads them to support policies that benefit those who can provide prestige, wealth, and support in campaigns for higher office. But these beneficiaries of Congress are often associated with national enterprises, and members' connection with such "leaders" counteracts their parochialism and makes Congress responsive to national interests.

In order to pursue their interests, members of Congress concern themselves with internal institutional power, and this concern may become an end in itself. The struggle for power absorbs the energies of members and leads them to worry more about an action's effects on their own degree of influence than about its policy implications. Yet the distribution of influence is unequal, and this feature makes possible situations in which enough powerful members intent on major change might effect any change they wished.

Some members of Congress care most about making good public policy. There is no ideological consistency or policy agreement among those who see themselves as policymakers, and this political spectrum prevents Congress from consensus. But because some members care about making good laws, they could fashion any well-developed policy they desired were they in agreement.

Arguments about Congress that derive from the five assumptions have an air of apology about them, a tone of rationalizing and justifying that echoes the language used to assuage anger or contempt. In effect, by accepting the five assumptions, one excuses Congress for its behavior, because it is acting in accord with human nature or in accord with the selfish demands of constituents. There is not much anyone can do to tinker with such a "natural" phenomenon. Nor should anyone want to tinker, because the ingredients are already there to enable Congress to create the best of all possible worlds.

From the perspective of the five assumptions, the ultimate limit, as it should be, is the electorate. "In large degree," political scientist William Keefe argues, "government mirrors society. As the nation's representative body, Congress is especially sensitive to popular currents of thought. No barriers insulate it from the people. . . . Congress is an extension of the people. That is both its strength and its weakness."[39] Great leaps in public policy, such as aid to education or civil rights protection, demonstrate that policies that were seen previously as unattainable are achievable.[40]

Most congressional scholars would agree with this conclusion, even though they have developed analyses that can provide critiques of the assumptions on which it is based. Despite their analyses, the assumptions live on because the dominant analysis of Congress turns on the relationship between members and the institution and excludes the larger context. This framework for analysis has emerged during the last thirty years, and it is important to appreciate how it affects the questions we might ask about congressional behavior.

The Five Assumptions and the Study of Congress

In the early part of what Robert Peabody has called the period of "behavioral-empirical studies,"[41] scholars emphasized the way in which the institution shaped the behavior of the members of Congress. At first glance there appear to be some obvious organizational constraints on the participants. These constraints include the size of the two chambers and the very fact that there are two houses of Congress; the control that committees exercise over legislation, which limits what individual members can influence; the continuity of the membership, which means that a senator or representative must work with many of the same colleagues year after year; and the social nature of producing legislation—members must learn to work with other members.

Related to these organizational characteristics of Congress are other, less obvious constraints on the individual member. There are centers of power, rooted in the organization, with which each legislator must deal. Some members are more influential than others in passing legislation, in part because of the particular committee on which they sit, their position in the leadership of one chamber, their political party, or the number of years they have served continuously on a committee. In turn, these more influential legislators may themselves act as constraints on the less influential members.[42]

There is little question that the organizational emphasis has been useful in sensitizing scholars to see members of Congress in this context in order to explain congressional behavior. Because scholars have recognized that the organizational emphasis can lead to partial explanations, they have also focused on the other half of the everyday world of Congress—the personal inclinations and aspirations of the members.

Here scholars have started with the individual legislator. Senators and representatives ultimately owe their elections only to their constituents, the voters in their districts. This is their source of being a member of Congress; it is the basis of their status. This central fact weakens the hold that a party or Congress itself has on each member. Yet districts themselves seem to have little hold on the legislator. Seminal work in the 1960s by Warren Miller and Donald Stokes[43] indicated that representatives (if not senators) were not greatly influenced by constituency pressures on most issues. Roger Davidson found that members of Congress sometimes acted as "delegates" from their districts, but also assumed a Burkean "trustee" posture.[44] They felt free at times to ignore the district.

While scholars found that constituents might not influence a member's voting, the thrust of these studies was to push the focus of scholarship towards the personal motivations of the legislators. In this regard, re-election seemed to remain the most important personal motivation. David Mayhew's widely respected contention that the re-election motive shapes all other congressional behavior contributed to a shift in the emphasis of congressional studies towards examining the volitional quality of members' actions.[45] For example, scholars began to look at the members' ambitions for higher office and their drive for power. These studies emphasized legislators' personal frustrations, desire for recognition, and anger at disrespect. In part, events encouraged such investigations, as the Senate became the launching pad for myriad presidential campaigns, and there were several challenges to the party leadership in both the House and the Senate. Notably, these events were often explained by reference to the personal goals of the members.

In relating such changes to personal motivations, scholars importantly link the two worlds of a legislator. They in effect describe the way in which the personal world affects the institutional world, and they emphasize the possibilities of change. Norman Ornstein, for example, argues that members may have altered the committee system because of the frustration several experienced with their lack of power.[46] Richard Fenno found that members of the House tended to choose their committees in accord with three different sets of personal goals and that there were three different types of committees associated with these goals.[47] He implied that members maintain the orientations of these committees because of their personal goals. This suggestion reversed the thrust of his previous work, where he had emphasized the way in which the committees affect the members.[48]

To start with the fact that Congress is an organization—as much earlier work did—is to emphasize the restraints on the personal behavior of individuals in Congress. In looking at the organization first, and then at the legislators' places within the organization, scholars underestimated the possibility of change. The organization persisted and members adapted to it; the organization engendered behavior necessary for its maintenance, and members fit themselves into appropriate roles. From that perspective, personal needs and desires were adjusted to fit into the organizational mold. Conversely, scholars have recently emphasized the possibilities of Congress and the apparent free will with which members seem to make decisions. An emphasis on personal motivations leads to the belief that anything would be possible given the right mix of members.

In short, congressional scholarship of the last thirty years has examined the links between the personal and institutional worlds of the legislator, regardless of whether scholars emphasized the importance of the institution or the "freedom" of the legislator. In both cases it has been focused narrowly on Congress itself. The context within which congressional behavior has been described is Capitol Hill.[49] Close contact, the behavioral revolution, and pluralism have led political scientists to take this view.

Close contact. In contrast to Woodrow Wilson, who wrote his famous *Congressional Government* without once visiting the Congress (though he lived only forty miles away in Baltimore), many contemporary students of Congress have logged untold hours in Washington, D.C. Some have worked for members as regular staffers, or through the American Political Science Association Congressional Fellowship Program. Many have learned about Congress through interviews with members and other participants. Others have been called in as consultants.

Close contact with Congress encourages observers to see the legislature as the legislators see it. Abstract categories and theories that seem sensible away from Capitol Hill are often met with ridicule among legislators. John Kingdon reports one member's remarks: "I actually taught political science years ago, and I didn't know a thing about Congress until I came here. . . . You sure got an inaccurate picture." Professor Kingdon responded, "That's why some of us recently have been coming here to find out how congressmen behave."[50] To members of Congress, the "accurate" picture is the world that they immediately perceive—namely, the personal and institutional aspects of Congress.

Behaviorism. Close contact with participants in Congress encourages political scientists to describe what exists as if it necessarily must exist, or to pose only those alternatives and to examine only those changes that the participants determine are within an acceptable range of reform. The process of choosing data for investigation becomes similar to what sociologist Lewis Coser describes in his discipline:

> To the extent that the sociologist works within a business or governmental framework, a change in audience as well as a change in the relation between the sociologist and the audience occurs. . . . Two consequences follow from this: (1) the sociologist . . . will be expected to deal with problems that decision-makers pose for him; and (2) those problems are likely to concern primarily, as Lerner and Merton have argued, "the preservation of existing institutional arrangements."[51]

The emphasis in political science on describing what is rather than what ought to be, the determination to develop an empirical science rather than a normative one, received nourishment in this way from the experiences of congressional scholars. This emphasis is at the heart of what Robert Dahl has called the "behavioral revolution."[52] Congressional research became part of the revolution and propelled it, as political scientists focused their investigations on observable data. To do so, they took their cues from the members of Congress. To be "realistic," they let members of Congress guide them to the "relevant" data to be observed, such as interest groups, the executive, party leaders and staffs.

This tendency was further encouraged by material incentives, as the Carnegie Institution and the Social Science Research Council, among others, awarded grants to political scientists who studied Congress from the behavioral persuasion. Grants provided opportunities for research and writing, which facilitated publication. By the 1960s, the major political science journals had enshrined behaviorism as the principal methodology in the study of Congress.

The behavioral persuasion became dominant even for those who were not in close contact with the "Hill." At a distance the most readily available significant evidence of observable behavior is roll call votes. These votes became important material for study, and they have been explained in terms of observable variables that might influence a legislator's decision.[53]

Pluralism. As congressional scholars developed a behavioral approach to the study of Congress, they were able to conceptualize their findings well because these were in accord with the pluralist model of the governmental process.[54] They found that the most evident source of external pressure was interest groups, and pluralism offers a way of seeing the world in terms of groups.

The pluralist model provides a clear agenda of research for the congressional scholar. In theory, what the government does can be described in large part by the demands of interest groups. The government is assumed to be a synthesizing mechanism that processes demands into policy. Thus the links between groups and Congress, through elections, personal contacts, and formal mechanisms such as hearings, become important subjects for study. However, to the extent that the government's actions do not reflect group demands, an investigator must examine how the internal machinery of government—that is, personal motivations of the participants and organizational factors—has prevented inputs from being resolved into outputs. It is this investigation that has consumed the energies of congressional scholars.

In the study of Congress, behaviorism and pluralism further meshed well, because Congress made decisions that could be observed. Discrete decisions are important in terms of pluralist analysis, and the fact that they are both observable and objective satisfied two behavioral criteria.

Though a pluralist analysis emphasizes group behavior, it is rooted in an individualist perspective. Individual self-interest explains group preferences: a group's interest is the sum of the interests of the individual members.[55] Scholars who write from a pluralist perspective emphasize the interaction between discrete actors, be they groups or individuals. Pluralism is not a mode of interpreting the world that can comprehend broad social forces, or even structures within a society. The focus is on the individual units, not on patterns established by aggregates of units. For example, when Robert Dahl discusses the question of power, he asks who has power, or does actor A have power over actor B. Power, he argues, is a relationship between actors.[56] An alternative conception, though, might emphasize the way in which a set of conditions favors certain groups instead of others. That the favored groups gain their ends against the disfavored groups would not indicate that they are more powerful in this situation, but that the structure places them in a favorable position.[57]

Viewed from Capitol Hill, the behavior of Congress seems to confirm the pluralist model. Members of Congress daily interact with interest groups and with other people in Congress. It is difficult to see aggregates and patterns. Members think in terms of people who have power and those who do not have power. In this way, the same intuitive sense that scholars experience in close contact with the Hill is affirmed intellectually by behaviorism and by pluralism.

This study steps away from Capitol Hill to look at Congress from afar and place it in a larger context. This study also examines the immediate context of congressional decisions, and in doing so explores assumptions related to behaviorism and pluralism. In order to appreciate the larger context, however, this analysis relies on Marxist assumptions that do not enter into traditional studies of Congress.

Two Caveats

Just as Congress has limits and possibilities, so has this book: first, there is the question of whether Congress acts, decides, or accomplishes anything as a whole; second, there is the question of methodology.

Reifying Congress

One might argue that Congress rarely acts as a whole. It may speak as "Congress" when it votes—and then usually only a majority of the members agree on the position that the Congress takes, not the whole body. (The same could be said of the House and Senate.) This study often refers to Congress as a single actor, as if the whole body has a will and a being. Is this language a distortion of reality? Does it give life to an inanimate institution that would be better described only by reference to the real people who work there? Yes, and that is a disadvantage of such language, but there are several advantages that warrant its use.

First, members of Congress register their disposition in more ways than a vote. Speeches are obvious examples of this phenomenon and, as discussed in Chapter 4, speeches often send signals to other governments and in this way involve members of Congress in policymaking. Significantly, the legislators indicate their positions in many cases when they permit a minority to act and do nothing to thwart the minority's behavior. An advantage of the artificial language here is that it implicitly assigns responsibility to all members for the behavior of the few. Members are responsible and should be held accountable for what Congress does. They are neither drawn along blindly by "natural instincts" to secure personal interests or by organizational imperatives, nor are they helpless to change decisions of the whole body. Most members of Congress during the 1940s and 1950s were responsible for the excesses of the House Un-American Activities Committee and the Senate Internal Security Subcommittee. They may not have participated directly in the actions that abused citizens' liberties, but they acquiesced in those actions by allowing them to continue.[58] By tacit agreement the body as a whole acts, and we can speak of Congress doing this and that, though only a few may be the active participants.

Similarly, by referring to Congress as a unitary actor, the experience of the members themselves is echoed. They may not believe that they are their colleagues' keepers, but they recognize that they share a title in common, that the sins and virtues of one may be visited upon another, and that they have common responsibilities for the institution as a whole. They think of themselves as members of Congress, and for them the institution has a meaning apart from their own identities. This meaning is partly conveyed by speaking of Congress as a unitary actor.

In a related and final instance, the language offers the advantage of directing our attention to an institution that is a single part of the state. In the United States, distinguishing between institutions of the state is more useful than trying to conceive of a state embracing a single interest or consistent set of functions. Although the constitutional division between branches of the federal government may not illuminate the functional differences between parts of the state that act in a contradictory fashion, to assume at this point that Congress has its own set of interests and functional dynamics is reasonable. The inability of the state to act in a concerted and forceful manner, in pursuit of interests that may be uniquely state interests, is an important phenomenon that demands continued investigation.[59]

Methodology

The thrust of this study is to focus on Congress as a whole and to place it in a larger context, although the method of inquiry in parts of the book might seem to move in the opposite direction—down to the individual member. Much of the data here comes from interviews with representatives, senators, and staff.

This apparent anomaly is in fact not a problem for the analysis here, but it should caution the reader to limit the sorts of inferences that can be drawn from the interviews. The focus on individual members provides two pieces of important information. First, it reveals the extent to which legislators are aware of systemic problems and interests and consciously consider them when they make policy. Second, it reveals other factors that they take into account—factors related to the larger political economy. For example, a member's apparent concern about re-election, at a time when other legislators are also sensing an anti-incumbent electorate, reflects the impact that the "legitimacy crisis" had on major institutions. As it is examined in Chapter 5, the legitimacy crisis of the 1970s involved citizens questioning the right of major institutions to govern their lives. The crisis stemmed partly from a breakdown in the dominant ideology. Members' sensitivity to their own legitimacy can be related to a general phenomenon.

Information about the larger political economy is also linked to decisions that Congress as a whole has made. To know that Senator So-and-So made a particular decision for narrow reasons, which might not relate to the larger political economy, is important. Little decisions often shape a congressional decision. Congressional decisions are not only affected by the larger society, but also affect it.

Ultimately, this study searches to identify patterns of behavior. To be sure, the members of Congress were not "held constant," and there was a dramatic turnover of membership during the period covered by the case studies, but this study is more suggestive than experimental. In addition, its focus is more on Congress than on the members themselves, and on the relation between Congress and its changing external environment. One fortunate, though unintended, consequence of the methodology is that despite the institutional and systemic focus of the book, our method of inquiry always reminds us of the people who are the institution.

NOTES

1. Russell Baker, "Almost the Way It Works," *New York Times,* 29 April 1978, op ed page.
2. The five assumptions do not include two important constraints on members of Congress: tradition and constitutional limitations and obligations. At one time, these constraints were the focus of most congressional scholarship. But contemporary scholars tend to focus on members' intentionality, on their "free choices," and have de-emphasized tradition and constitutional proscriptions. For a good review of the earlier literature, see Robert L. Peabody, "Research on Congress: A Coming of Age," in Ralph K. Huitt and Robert L. Peabody, *Congress: Two Decades of Analysis* (New York: Harper & Row, 1969). For a recent study that emphasizes the constitutional perspective, see Louis Fisher, *The Constitution Between Friends* (New York: St. Martin's, 1978).
3. Examples of this can be found in the leading textbooks on Congress, such as David J. Vogler, *The Politics of Congress,* 3rd ed. (Boston: Allyn and Bacon, 1980); William J. Keefe, *Congress and the American People* (Englewood Cliffs, N.J.: Prentice-Hall,

1980); Randall B. Ripley, *Congress: Process and Policy*, 2nd ed. (New York: Norton, 1978).

4. Richard Fenno addressed this point directly when he wrote: "We have assumed that most members of Congress develop, over time, a mix of personal goals. We particularly assume that most members will trade off some of their personal commitment to re-election in order to satisfy a personal desire for institutional or policy influence." Richard F. Fenno, Jr., *Home Style: House Members in Their Districts* (Boston: Little, Brown, 1978), p. 221. Similarly, Lynette P. Perkins found that members of the House Judiciary Committee evidenced at least three of the five characteristics listed here. See "Influences of Members' Goals on Their Committee Behavior: The U.S. House Judiciary Committee," *Legislative Studies Quarterly*, 3 (1980), 373–392.

5. "The Theory of the Capitalist State and the Problem of Policy Formation," in Leon Lindberg, et al., *Stress and Contradiction in Modern Capitalism* (Lexington, Mass.: D.C. Heath, 1975), p. 133.

6. Samuel P. Huntington, "Congressional Responses to the Twentieth Century," in David B. Truman, ed., *The Congress and America's Future*, 2nd ed. (Englewood Cliffs, N.J.: Prentice-Hall, 1973), pp. 17–18. For similar statements, see: Ripley, *Congress: Process and Policy*, p. 5; Keefe, *Congress and the American People*, p. 12; James L. Sundquist, "Congress and the President: Enemies or Partners?" in Lawrence C. Dodd and Bruce I. Oppenheimer, eds., *Congress Reconsidered* (New York: Praeger, 1977), pp. 230–231.

7. James O'Connor, *The Fiscal Crisis of the State* (New York: St. Martin's Press, 1973), p. 81. Also see C. Wright Mills, *The Power Elite* (New York: Oxford University Press, 1959), pp. 251–256.

8. Morris P. Fiorina, "Congressional Control of the Bureaucracy: A Mismatch of Incentives and Capabilities," in Lawrence C. Dodd and Bruce I. Oppenheimer, eds., *Congress Reconsidered*, 2nd ed. (Washington, D.C.: CQ Press, 1981), pp. 336–337.

9. Vogler, *The Politics of Congress*, pp. 308–309.

10. Morris P. Fiorina, *Congress: Keystone of the Washington Establishment* (New Haven: Yale University Press, 1977), p. 39.

11. David R. Mayhew writes, for example: "[The electoral goal] has to be the *proximate* goal of everyone, the goal that must be achieved over and over if other ends are to be entertained. . . . Reelection underlies everything else." *Congress: The Electoral Connection* (New Haven: Yale University Press, 1974), p. 16.

12. Mark Green, *Who Runs Congress?*, 3rd ed. (New York: Bantam, 1979), Chapter 1.

13. Ripley, *Congress: Process and Policy*, p. 109; Green, *Who Runs Congress?*, p. 239.

14. John W. Kingdon, *Congressmen's Voting Decisions*, 2nd ed. (New York: Harper & Row, 1981), pp. 60–68.

15. Barbara Hinckley, *Stability and Change in Congress*, 2nd ed. (New York: Harper & Row, 1978), pp. 69–70. Also, Mayhew, *Congress: The Electoral Connection*, pp. 81–105.

16. Morris S. Ogul, "Congressional Oversight: Structures and Incentives," in Dodd and Oppenheimer, *Congress Reconsidered*, 2nd ed., p. 327.

17. Gordon Adams, *The Iron Triangle: The Politics of Defense Contracting* (New York: Council on Economic Priorities, 1981).

18. Lawrence C. Dodd and Richard L. Schott, *Congress and the Administrative State* (New York: Wiley, 1979), p. 125. Also, Fiorina, "Congressional Control of the Bureaucracy," pp. 339–340.

19. Fiorina, *Congress: Keystone of the Washington Establishment*, p. 39. Also, Green, *Who Runs Congress?*, pp. 206–207.

20. Elizabeth Wehr, "Reputation as Smooth Professionals: Reagan's Team on the Hill Getting Members' Praise for Hard Work, Experience," *Congressional Quarterly Weekly Report*, 2 May 1981, p. 747.

21. Green, *Who Runs Congress?*, pp. 223–230.

22. Dodd and Schott, *Congress and the Administrative State*, p. 103; Green, *Who Runs Congress?*, Chapter 5; Warren Weaver, Jr., *Both Your Houses: The Truth About Congress* (New York: Praeger, 1972), pp. 233–242.

23. Ripley, *Congress: Process and Policy*, p. 9.

24. Norman J. Ornstein, Robert L. Peabody, and David W. Rohde, "The Contemporary Senate: Into the 1980s," in Dodd and Oppenheimer, *Congress Reconsidered*, 2nd ed., pp. 27–28.
25. Lawrence C. Dodd, "Congress and the Quest for Power," in Dodd and Oppenheimer, *Congress Reconsidered*, 1st ed., pp. 270–283.
26. Lawrence C. Dodd, "Congress, the Constitution, and the Crisis of Legitimation," in Dodd and Oppenheimer, *Congress Reconsidered*, 2nd ed., pp. 410–411.
27. Kingdon, *Congressmen's Voting Decisions*, 2nd ed., p. 232.
28. Philip Brenner, "An Examination of Conflict in the U.S. House of Representatives" (Ph.D. diss., Johns Hopkins University, 1975), p. 39. Also, Charles L. Clapp, *The Congressman: His Work as He Sees It* (Washington, D.C.: Brookings Institution, 1964), p. 30.
29. Ted Siff and Alan Weil, *Ruling Congress* (New York: Penguin, 1977), p. 203; Lewis A. Froman, Jr., *The Congressional Process* (Boston: Little, Brown, 1967), p. xi. For a discussion of the way in which power underlies the norm of reciprocity, see Alvin W. Gouldner, "The Norm of Reciprocity: A Preliminary Statement," *American Sociological Review*, 25, No. 2 (April 1960).
30. Ornstein, Peabody, and Rohde, "The Contemporary Senate: Into the 1980s," p. 18.
31. Robert L. Peabody, *Leadership in Congress: Stability, Succession and Change* (Boston: Little, Brown, 1976), p. 29. Also, Richard F. Fenno, Jr., "The Internal Distribution of Influence: The House," in Truman, *The Congress and America's Future*, 2nd ed., pp. 64–83.
32. Norman J. Ornstein, "Causes and Consequences of Congressional Change: Subcommittee Reforms in the House of Representatives, 1970–73," in Norman J. Ornstein, ed., *Congress in Change: Evolution and Reform* (New York: Praeger, 1975), p. 89.
33. Dodd and Schott, *Congress and the Administrative State*, p. 127.
34. Ibid., pp. 100–101.
35. Ornstein, "Causes and Consequences of Congressional Change," pp. 95–96.
36. Dodd and Schott, *Congress and the Administrative State*, p. 126.
37. Richard F. Fenno, Jr., *Congressmen in Committees* (Boston: Little, Brown, 1973), p. 9.
38. For example, see: Philip Brenner, "Congress Watch: The Shifting Alliances," *The Nation;* 4 November 1978; Eric Redman, *The Dance of Legislation* (New York: Simon and Schuster, 1974); Norman J. Ornstein and Shirley Elder, *Interest Groups, Lobbying and Policymaking* (Washington, D.C.: CQ Press, 1978), Chapter 7.
39. Keefe, *Congress and the American People*, pp. 170–171.
40. Gary Orfield, *Congressional Power: Congress and Social Change* (New York: Harcourt Brace Jovanovich, 1975), Chapters 5–9. Also: Eugene Eidenberg and Roy D. Morey, *An Act of Congress* (New York: Norton, 1969); Philip Meranto, *The Politics of Federal Aid to Education in 1965: A Study in Political Innovation* (Syracuse: Syracuse University Press, 1967).
41. Peabody, "Research on Congress: A Coming of Age," p. 10.
42. Richard F. Fenno, Jr., "The Internal Distribution of Influence: The House," in Truman, *Congress and America's Future*, 2nd ed. Also see, Ralph K. Huitt, "The Internal Distribution of Influence: The Senate," in Truman, *Congress and America's Future*, 2nd ed.
43. Warren E. Miller and Donald E. Stokes, "Constituency Influence in Congress," *American Political Science Review*, LVII, No. 1 (1963).
44. Roger H. Davidson, *The Role of the Congressman* (New York: Pegasus, 1969), pp. 121–139.
45. Mayhew, *Congress: The Electoral Connection*.
46. Ornstein, "Causes and Consequences of Committee Change," p. 89.
47. Fenno, *Congressmen in Committees*, Chapter 1.
48. Richard F. Fenno, Jr., *The Power of the Purse: Appropriations Politics in Congress* (Boston: Little, Brown, 1966), Chapters 1, 3, 5.
49. An important exception to this is the more recent work of Richard Fenno. See Fenno, *Home Style*.
50. Kingdon, *Congressmen's Voting Decisions*, 2nd ed., p. 3.

51. Lewis A. Coser, *The Functions of Social Conflict* (New York: Free Press, 1964), p. 27.
52. Robert A. Dahl, "The Behavioral Approach in Political Science: Epitaph for a Monument to a Successful Protest," *American Political Science Review,* LV, No. 3 (1961).
53. See, for example, Donald R. Matthews and James A. Stimson, *Yeas and Nays: Normal Decision-Making in the U.S. House of Representatives* (New York: Wiley, 1975); Aage R. Clausen, *How Congressmen Decide: A Policy Focus* (New York: St. Martin's Press, 1973).
54. See, for example, Robert A. Dahl, *Pluralist Democracy in the United States* (Chicago: Rand McNally, 1967); David B. Truman, *The Governmental Process: Political Interests and Public Opinion* (New York: Alfred A. Knopf, 1951); Bertram M. Gross, *The Legislative Struggle: A Study in Social Combat* (New York: McGraw-Hill, 1953).
55. Mancur Olson, Jr., *The Logic of Collective Action* (New York: Schocken Books, 1968), pp. 126–127.
56. Robert A. Dahl, "The Concept of Power," *Behavioral Science,* II (July 1957). Also see George Von der Muhill, "Robert A. Dahl and the Study of Contemporary Democracy: A Review Essay," *American Political Science Review,* LXXI, No. 3 (1977).
57. Steven Lukes, *Power: A Radical View* (London: Macmillan, 1974), Chapter 5.
58. For illuminating accounts of this period in Congress see Lillian Hellman, *Scoundrel Time* (New York: Bantam, 1977); Victor Navasky, *Naming Names* (New York: Penguin, 1981); Robert W. Griffith, *The Politics of Fear: Joseph R. McCarthy and the Senate* (Rochelle Park, N.J.: Hayden, 1971); Walter Goodman, *The Committee* (New York: Farrar, Straus and Giroux, 1968).
59. This phenomenon is what Ira Katznelson and Kenneth Prewitt have called "low stateness." See their "Constitutionalism, Class and the Limits of Choice in U.S. Foreign Policy," in Richard R. Fagen, ed., *Capitalism and the State in U.S.-Latin American Relations* (Stanford: Stanford University Press, 1979), pp. 31–32.

2 Placing Congress in Context

Members of Congress, understandably, are not always conscious of the larger political economy within which they operate. They focus on immediate contexts: a particular bill on which they are working or on which they will have to vote; the next election—who their opponents will be and how much the campaign will cost; the most recent election; pressure from a district interest group or large campaign contributor; their troubles with the president, who does not listen to them or encourages them to take a tough stand and then changes his position; the length of the legislative session, the length of each day of the session, and the way in which the leadership schedules legislation; and how difficult it is to send two children to college, maintain two homes, contribute to forty charities, travel to the district three times a month, and still buy a new suit for an appearance on *Meet the Press,* all in the face of stringent restrictions on earning "outside" income now that "ethics" are in vogue.

This everyday world of Congress is the one with which most of us are familiar. It is the world that television, newspapers, and news magazines describe, because the journalists who cover the "Hill" see members of Congress in their immediate context. Also, journalists need to report immediate events. What contemporary journalists offer us is a major advance over the reporting of a generation or two ago. There is now more information than ever available about what Congress does: senators and representatives seem more human and less easy to stereotype. (Perhaps it is such familiarity that breeds contempt for Congress.) Despite the enormous growth of the federal government and the increasing complexity of Congress, the national legislature may be more comprehensible to the public today than it was in a less complicated era.

The public understands a world of personal insecurity about one's job, of pressures from a boss or client or customer, of cooperation and friction with colleagues, of making ends meet, of ambition, greed, and pride, and much of what legislators do is shaped by their personal characteristics and needs. Their behavior is also governed by the imperatives of the institution within which they work, by the limits that rules, traditions, and organizations-within-the-organization impose, and by the interaction between members of Congress.

As observed in Chapter 1, most political scientists who study Congress also examine these aspects of the legislature and the legislators. To the descriptions that journalists provide scholars add analyses of voting patterns, rates in congressional turnover, types of institutional pressures on members from interest groups, from the executive, from committees and subcommittees, and the characteristics of change in the organization of Congress and in its informal rules.

Scholars' systematic explanations of congressional behavior seem to support the journalists' descriptions. Although these analyses have much validity within the context of Congress, they provide only partial explanations because they situate behavior exclusively on Capitol Hill. The larger context of congressional behavior has been de-emphasized or ignored. This chapter offers one way of describing the larger context and uses this larger context as a useful starting place for the study of Congress. In doing so, it suggests some of the problems that confront the current approaches to the study of Congress.

A Changing Political and Economic Context

The forces that shape congressional behavior extend beyond Capitol Hill, beyond the institution and the personal needs and characteristics of the members of Congress. The larger context is the political economy of the United States, of which Congress is an influential part; Congress helps to shape the larger context and also responds to it. We can suggest the outlines of the larger context by considering its two aspects—the material base and the ideological base.

The Material Base

Domestic transformations. A useful approach to reviewing changes in the structure of production and distribution in the United States since 1900 is to divide the century into three periods—1900–1945, 1945–1970, and 1970 to the present. Of course, the end points of each period are not precise and do not necessarily relate to specific events. They are convenient dates that locate general changes.

From 1900 to 1945 the economy was characterized by the growing dominance of national corporations, whose profits came from nationwide operations in the United States.[1] These corporations arose quite dramatically between 1890 and 1910 as a result of mergers, heavy investments, and the takeover of failing companies, and they grew in influence and in the extent of wealth they controlled through the Depression years.[2] Until World War II their market was essentially private, despite the federal government's expenditures during the New Deal.

This period also saw great conflict between workers and companies, as when small armies were hired to prevent unionization in the coalfields[3] and when strikes in the steel and auto industries seemed to threaten "revolution."[4] In 1932 there were 841 strikes, and in 1934 there were 1,856 labor disputes that involved one and a half million workers.[5] In 1938 the Congress of Industrial Organizations—which threatened corporations more than the American Federation of Labor did, because it organized workers on an industry-wide basis—became a permanent organization. By 1939 nearly 8 million workers were union members, over twice as many as had been members in 1933.[6] The growth of large corporations was partly a response to labor strife, as growth afforded companies some geographic flexibility in their operations, provided a credible threat that a prolonged strike might force a company to move to a new location, and enabled them to accumulate sufficient capital to replace workers with machines.

The changes in the material base from 1900 to 1945 set the stage for the next two periods, as national elites came to focus on both national corporations and the potential for labor struggles. In the years 1945 to 1970, the second period, labor struggles diminished in intensity and frequency. Corporations successfully ousted militant union leaders from their posts through application of the Taft-Hartley Act and cold-war loyalty programs, and they raised the real wages of workers. Conflicts now occurred in a mediated form. Instead of direct struggles between workers and companies at the point of production—in factories—there were struggles over problems such as housing and schooling. Workers viewed themselves in these fights as members of particular groups and saw their opponents as other groups—school boards, zoning commissions, city hall, and the banks. These conflicts segmented the working class, though the roots of the conflicts lay in the class structure of the United States. Until the mid-1960s the expanding economy muted the intensity of the mediated conflicts. By 1970, however, even these conflicts had become intense, recalling the class-conscious strife of an earlier period.[7]

During the second period the private economy developed into two sectors, a pattern that persists today.[8] In the first sector, industries tend to be so highly concentrated that a few firms account for most of the output in any industry. Pricing tends to be administered; that is, supply and demand alone do not govern prices because companies are able to control their markets. Many of the industries in this oligopolistic sector are capital intensive—they have invested heavily in machinery. This has strengthened their positions vis-à-vis their workers, but it has made them less flexible. They are forced to keep prices high, and they must seek ways of cutting unit costs other than by increasing productivity. They look abroad for raw materials and turn to foreign manufacturing (which in many cases includes their own plants) for production of component parts.

Industries in the second sector tend to be smaller than in the first, and often their operations are only local or regional.[9] Because each industry is characterized by a large number of firms, pricing tends to be competitive. As a consequence, profit margins are lower in the competitive sector, and many companies fail each year. Companies here are usually labor intensive, but wages tend to be lower than in the oligopolistic sector because firms operate close to the margin and force workers to take less.[10]

The sectors are intimately related. Many of the products purchased in the competitive sector are produced by oligopolistic industries, so that costs are high for the small companies. More importantly, the oligopolistic sector employs a decreasing percentage of the labor force, and workers are thus forced to seek jobs in the competitive sector or in the government.[11] If they obtain jobs in the competitive sector, their wages will be lower, and they necessarily will seek assistance from governments (federal, state, and local) for services they can no longer provide for themselves, such as care for the elderly, day care for children, hospital and other health care, or assistance to send children to college. The dual burden, of absorbing these workers as government employees or of paying for their services, strains government budgets and has contributed to a fiscal crisis of the state.[12] Although the dynamics of the dual economy were evident by 1970, the crisis did not manifest itself until the mid-1970s, when New York City went into a state of emergency, other older cities seemed to be in similar circumstances, and the federal government annually ran a deficit of $60 billion.[13]

Cities began to experience a fiscal crisis, in part, because they were losing their tax base as middle-income people moved to the suburbs. This pattern was an aspect of the great internal migration that occurred from 1945 to 1970. Suburbs, which had begun to develop in the 1920s, mushroomed during this period.[14] Their growth was encouraged and supported by a $104 billion investment in the interstate highway system that surrounded cities with beltways.[15] In turn, the highway system was promoted by the auto and oil industries, on which many people came to depend for jobs. In effect, the stability of the economy depended on personal mobility, on movement to the suburbs, and on a "pro-growth" strategy. By 1973 these interrelated factors provided the conditions for instability, as "no-growth" coalitions developed in suburbs and high fuel prices stunned the auto industry.

The period since about 1970, the current period of transformation, is characterized by instability. High, unyielding levels of inflation, coupled with high levels of unemployment, persisted throughout the 1970s. For the black population, unemployment in the mid- and late 1970s continued at a rate of over 10 percent, despite a drop in the overall level; for black teenagers it was over 65 percent.[16] Private investment lagged, and the business community talked of a capital shortage.[17] But plants also were operating at an average of only 80 percent capacity.[18] Unionized workers responded to inflation with increasingly higher wage demands and with strikes. The steel, coal, and auto industries, for example, experienced long strikes in the 1970s. But real wages fell nonetheless.[19]

Perhaps the most noticed crisis of the 1970s was the "energy crisis." Long lines at the gas station in 1973 were followed by a steep rise in the price of fossil fuels and proclamations of an energy shortage. Whether the oil companies were to blame (and there was much evidence available to blame them[20]), or the Organization of Petroleum Exporting Countries (OPEC), or the auto manufacturers and their gas-guzzling cars, the crisis exposed the fragility of the American economy. It also indicated some of the many ways that the United States is linked to other countries in an international economic system.

International transformations. In the period after World War II, and especially after 1960, national corporations began to extend themselves overseas. The new transnational corporations differed from companies that merely engaged in international trade. Transnationals invested heavily in other countries, and they organized their internal operations on an international scale.[21] Their decisions affected development in other countries and contributed to an international economy characterized by dominant, capitalist, industrialized nations and dependent, resource-supplying former colonies.

The United States government provided important support to these corporations; significantly, much of it came in the form of defense expenditures. The postwar economy was very much a war economy.[22] Defense expenditures also went toward the emplacement of American bases abroad. By 1970 the United States had 155 bases in 46 countries.[23] American military assistance for "friendly regimes," covert operations against unfriendly states, and occasional direct military intervention to oust "undesirable" governments also provided some security for American investments in other countries.[24]

Banks are the most important institutions among transnational corporations. The names of most of these transnational banks are not household words,[25] but the banks themselves are the creations of well-known commercial bank holding companies, including those of the Chase Manhattan Bank, Bank of America, and Citibank (formerly the First National Bank of New York). In this light, a report by the Senate Government Affairs Committee in 1978, based on a survey of the ownership of stock in American corporations, takes on special significance:

> The leading banks in America are so closely tied together that they control the biggest blocks of stock in each other's parent holding company. . . . The survey disclosed that the power to vote stock in 122 of America's largest corporations . . . is held by just 21 institutional investors.[26]

International financial institutions contributed to a balance of payments deficit for the United States that helped to weaken the dollar vis-à-vis other currencies, driving up the price of imports, including the component parts of manufactured goods assembled here. Through their investment policies the transnational banks facilitated the export of jobs from the United States as they increased manufacturing investment in the Third World.

During this period, United States relations with Third World countries took on a new character. In Vietnam the United States lost its first war. Other countries began to feel strong enough to challenge American hegemony, by raising the prices of raw materials they sold to the United States. American influence was linked increasingly to repressive regimes—such as those in Chile, Argentina, South Africa, and the Philippines—and these regimes were not stable. American support for them also cost the United States a claim to moral leadership. Even in Western Europe, Communist parties grew in popularity. In France, Spain, and Italy, Euro-Communism flourished in the 1970s, and the left's influence threatened the close links between the American economy and the economies of other Western capitalist nations.

The Ideological Base

In 1969 political scientist Theodore Lowi announced the "end of liberalism" as we know it.[27] The next year, political analyst Garry Wills declared that President Nixon would be the "last liberal."[28] These writers had sensed something in the air: the American ideology of liberalism—the precepts that legitimated a widely uneven distribution of wealth and income and even the governing of 200 million people by a Congress of 535 legislators—was losing its hold.

The liberal faith had held that the United States was a classless society, a society without a feudal heritage in which any person could achieve success through hard work. There were no structural barriers to success.[29] Collaterally, the government was neutral; it favored no particular group and was supposed to provide an arena for the resolution of group conflict, or, at worst, finely tune the mechanism to restore a balance between groups.

Liberalism has always had a shaky foundation in the United States, because liberalism is based on the belief that private property ensures freedom. But the rights of citizenship in the United States have always been extended to people who do not own property. At first this group was small, but as it grew so did the contradictions between the rights of citizens and the rights of property. The collision of citizen rights and property rights lies at the heart of the two great controversies in this century—civil rights for blacks and women and workers' rights to form a union. Liberalism is the handmaiden of capitalism, because it justifies the unfettered use of private property and defines all values in terms of the market. Those who did not own property had accepted the justifications for two hundred years, in part because they believed that the possibility for everyone to own property existed and that the market had in fact benefited many people.

However, by 1970 the liberal vision was manifestly a distortion of reality. A War on Poverty had failed, and poverty in our midst appeared to be endemic.[30] Moreover, poverty was closely associated with race, as 25 million blacks experienced structural constraints in the competition to succeed.[31] The august and cautious Kerner Commission had found in 1968 that the United States was fast becoming two societies, one black and one white.[32] Even the white middle class was beginning to lose faith in the American Dream, as college graduates found fewer "good" jobs, engineers were laid off, and the number of university positions for those with doctorates rapidly decreased. By 1975 a Hart poll indicated that 34 percent of the American people no longer believed that capitalism worked.[33]

Associated with a decline in the legitimacy of the economic order was a decline in the legitimacy of the government. When 300,000 people came to Washington, D.C., in 1969 to demonstrate against the war, and nearly 500,000 came to protest the "incursion" into Cambodia in 1970, a turning point in the government's legitimacy was marked. The protesters in effect declared by their presence that they believed the government could be moved only by extraordinary measures, though they still believed in its legitimate authority. By 1972, however, rising apathy indicated a withdrawal of legitimacy. Fewer people voted in 1972 than in 1968, and by 1976 only 53 percent of the electorate went to the polls. In the mid-term congressional election of 1974 only 38 percent of the electorate voted. Meanwhile, Congress had reached a new low in public opinion ratings.[34] For many of the people who had participated in the urban and campus riots of the 1960s, major institutions had lost their legitimacy even earlier. Indeed, as Daniel Patrick Moynihan reports, this erosion of the ideological base had troubled several government leaders by 1970.[35] They saw the loss of legitimacy as a potentially prerevolutionary condition, one which could prove to be fundamentally destabilizing.

Interest Groups and the Political-Economic Context

While some might argue that political scientists consider the larger context within which Congress operates when they examine interest group demands, the larger context is more than merely the sum of such demands. This context is a web of structured relationships, relationships that involve struggles between sets of property owners and between owners and workers. These struggles may manifest themselves as interest-group demands, though not all group demands emanate from these struggles. An interest-group approach provides no guide to sorting out which demands are related to the transformation of the American political economy, because it offers no hierarchy of struggles. Indeed, implicit in an interest group analysis is the assumption that the interests occur randomly, that there is no structure to them.[36] If this were not the assumption, then scholars who take this approach would examine the structure that generates the demands, and they do not.[37] Instead they focus on Congress itself. Paradoxically, then, the interest-group model leads scholars to de-emphasize the larger political-economic context, even though the model rests on the importance of groups outside Congress.

One popular variant of the interest-group model focuses on the world outside Congress by referring to bribes or the control of congressional campaigns by rich contributors. Such analyses portray Congress as a tool, or instrument, in the hands of those who control wealth. This model echoes pluralism insofar as congressional behavior is explained in terms of the interaction between discrete actors, but it differs from pluralism on a key assumption, as Ralph Miliband argues: "What is wrong with pluralist-democratic theory is not its insistence on the fact of competition, but its claim . . . that the major organized 'interests' in these societies . . . compete on more or less equal terms."[38] Analysts who use this model point to congressional decisions on farm prices, subsidies, military spending, and tax exemptions that benefit large holders of wealth. They cite the campaign finances that flow to members of Congress and the lucrative jobs as lobbyists for corporations that former senators and representatives obtain when they retire from Congress.[39] They do not dispute the interest-group model; they argue in effect that there is a pattern to the success of groups—the wealthier ones win. This pattern, G. William Domhoff contends, is related to underlying structures in the economy, although its manifestation is experienced as an interest-group phenomenon.[40] In effect, this model portrays members of Congress as instruments, or tools, of the wealthy.

There are several difficulties with both the pluralist model and this variant—often called the "instrumentalist" view—that lead them to provide only partial explanations of behavior. First, both models attribute so much influence to groups that the groups would need to be omnipresent. Indeed, members of Congress may obtain many of their ideas from groups. As Chapter 5 demonstrates, the principal opposing sides in the conflict over the 1972 Higher Education Act relied on opposing interest groups for information and ideas. Instrumentalists claim that, among other strategies, groups can dominate Congress by setting the agenda through the control of information.[41] Little evidence, however, suggests that the groups control all information—Congress more likely uses the interest-group positions as rationales for behavior.

Furthermore, groups are often less powerful than muckrakers suggest because most groups narrow their scope of interest. A legislator who supports the position of a strong group in his or her district on an issue of primary importance to the group is likely to feel free of group pressure on most other issues.

In part, it was the observed lack of groups' influence that led scholars to focus on the internal dynamics of Congress to explain congressional decisions. Yet personal and institutional factors are too vague to explain patterns of decision making where the dynamics of the American political economy are concerned. They may help to explain particular decisions, but to focus only on these suggests either that decision making is idiosyncratic or that personal responses and organizational designs are unrelated to larger patterns in the United States—in other words, that Congress is isolated from its surroundings, a conclusion with which few could agree.

A further problem with the group model for explaining congressional behavior is that it assumes that the whole is no more than the sum of separate group interests. But Congress at times may assert a position that is in the common interest of all contending groups, though no individual group would claim it. Consider the situation of labor struggles during the early 1930s. Before 1934, labor unions had eschewed government involvement in labor-management disputes, because the government had so often entered such conflicts on the side of owners. In the 1930s the unions waged major battles in an effort to gain the right to bargain collectively, and corporations resisted fiercely. Each company in an industry believed that its competitive position against the other companies would be weakened if it alone recognized a union, because its workers could then force it to raise wages higher than competitors' wages. Yet low wages made corporations in general weak, because workers had insufficient buying power to stimulate the depressed economy. Enter the federal government—and specifically Congress—with legislation that gave workers the right to form a union.[42] It was legislation that neither side, for the most part, had advocated. Yet for workers it held the promise that the federal government would use its authority to establish unions permanently; for owners it held the promise that there would be industrial peace and that all companies in an industry would be affected similarly; for both it held the promise of economic recovery.

Congress may act similarly to serve the common interests of conflicting capitalists, whose antagonistic interests prevent them from realizing their shared objectives. The antagonisms may range from competition between two firms in the same industry to more fundamental differences such as those between labor-intensive and capital-intensive industries. Differences may involve foreign investment and policies that engender monopolization. Such "intraclass" conflicts can dominate the congressional agenda as they overwhelm the economy. This pattern may explain the inflation of the 1970s, when transnational corporations engaged in currency manipulations that strengthened their positions vis-à-vis wholly domestic corporations.[43] The congressional solutions to the problems this conflict caused were not necessarily on behalf of either side. Despite instances of Congress appearing to act as the dutiful servant of one set of interests, more often it fashions a unique solution to the problems.

The congressional solution may be a middle-ground compromise between the positions two sides advocate or, as with labor in the New Deal, a solution unique in itself. In such instances, Congress performs the task of coercion for the common good. That coercion must be imposed on a collectivity in order to provide common or collective benefits to the whole is generally recognized.[44] Without coercion, each party might try to maximize benefits by avoiding necessary payment while seeking its share of the common pot. If all parties acted only to maximize benefits—and there is no reason to assume that they would act otherwise—no common pot would exist. The pursuit of maximum self-interest by each party usually is not in the best interest of the whole and sometimes might not even be in the maximum self-interest of any member of the collectivity. There are collective interests in our society, and the society needs an agency to assert them.

Pluralists tend to deny the validity of such a formulation because it embraces the notion of the "public interest," which David Truman has argued correctly is inconsistent with a pluralist view.[45] Such a formulation is also indirectly linked to the concept of the "state," which David Easton has contended is inconsistent with behavioral investigations.[46] Yet the concept of the state is a useful for understanding how Congress relates to the larger context. The state offers a third level of analysis, beyond the personal and institutional worlds of a legislator. Without dismissing explanations based on those two worlds, an analysis that incorporates this third dimension enriches the other explanations. This theme is explored in Chapter 7, but the essential point here is that when they act on behalf of the whole, for the common interest, members of Congress act on behalf of the state.

But what is the common national interest? There is hardly an agreed-upon answer to the question, even within the government, and less agreement about serving whatever that interest might be. Many conflicts between Congress and the executive can arise over strategies for achieving the same goal or over the definition of that goal. The state is hardly omniscient: Congress and the executive often grapple in the dark and may make decisions that run counter to wealthy interests. The state is permeable and open to pressure from constituents and labor groups. Moreover, the state creates government organizations with lives of their own. Further, individuals make decisions that may be self-serving and may contradict the interests of other elites.

As the following chapters show, Congress often equates the common interest with the interests of those who own property. In cases where property owners are in conflict, it has increasingly equated the common interest with the interests of national and international corporations. One perspective from which to understand Congress's position is to appreciate that the members and the institution operate within a changing context. Their personal and institutional behavior is a response to the changes and an effort to shape the changes. In this effort, Congress is not a "tool" or a puppet of groups but an autonomous agency. An interest-group approach to Congress distorts both the meaning of the effort and the significance of the larger context, which is more than the sum of interest-group demands.

The Significance of the Larger Context

At the start of this chapter it was observed that members of Congress focus their attention on their immediate environment—on their personal interests and on their institutional lives. Both pluralist and instrumentalist approaches to the study of Congress follow this observation with an explanation of congressional behavior that centers on group pressures, arguing that legislators respond to group pressures in ways that enable them to enhance personal and institutional interests.

This explanation of congressional behavior appeals to the intuition and coincides with the everyday world of Congress defined by the five assumptions discussed in Chapter 1. Simply stated, the picture of Congress the pluralists and instrumentalists paint is of a helter-skelter institution where most members busily pursue a district-oriented measure, some notoriety that will help them get re-elected, a little bit of glory, and perhaps a taste of power. Interest groups can provide members with the means to achieve these ends, and at the same time they create the circumstances—in the district or through an association—that determine the direction in which a member must jump to realize them. There are also the members who seek good public policy, and interest groups affect their congressional lives by shaping the public policy agenda.

Two important problems undermine this explanation. First, the pluralist explanation assumes that group interests are random, that the larger context does not structure interests. By ignoring the structure of the larger context, pluralists effectively make it a constant in their explanations: they assume that it is a variable that does not change and whose effects do not change. Instrumentalists do not make such an assumption—they see the inequality among groups as derivative from a class structure in the society—but their explanation shares another problem with that of the pluralists. Both require that groups be the agents of behavior, that the behavior members of Congress display can be traced to group action, and that the views members articulate derive from some groups. They require a relation between members of Congress and some groups; they require a causal agent. But legislators may respond to a condition, and they may fashion unique solutions. They may even try to change conditions and initiate behavior.

As an alternative, consider that the larger political-economic context affects Congress and that the larger context is structured by class struggle. The same daily world of the members is relevant to this approach, but from this view members respond to the demands of the larger context— not groups—as they seek to enhance personal and institutional interests. Contradictions in the larger context provide members with opportunities to act in pursuit of their interests, including good public policy, while the conditions created by it shape the congressional agenda and limit what members can do.

This approach has two advantages over a group approach. First, it provides a focus for asking what members are trying to do when they relate to the "whole," when they try to go beyond the interests of particular groups. Recall that Richard Fenno and Roger Davidson found in separate studies that members articulate interests that are not subsumed under traditional categories of local, personal, group, or institutional interests. Some members articulate concern for making good public policy or hold Burkean trustee perspectives for a common national good, and an interpretation of the larger context helps the scholar appreciate their behavior.

Second, even where members who care principally about their immediate environment are concerned, an interpretation of the larger context includes the realistic assumption that the world outside Congress is changing. The changes shape interest groups' demands and alter personal pressures on members, whose responses are more than adjustments to mere groups. Legislators respond to the larger environment, even as it is mediated at times by groups and by the electorate. Their responses may lead them to fashion unique solutions for the whole, even though they perceive that they are dealing only with narrow interests. Consider how this might occur for members who focus only on their personal and institutional interests, that is, for members who would say in an interview that immediate interests are all that they care about.

Personal Interests and the Larger Context

As the political economy changes, the lives of a member's constituents change. They may bear the brunt of great dislocations. They may experience fears and anger that they take out on elected officials. Losses in struggles with employers may lead them to ask for new services from the government so that they can meet their families' needs. The demands on a member's time, the pressures he or she feels from constituents and groups, will change as the larger structure changes.

The increased frustrations that political scientists report the members of Congress now feel may be caused by the overwhelming responsibilities that confront members today and that they often feel they cannot meet. For example, in 1972 a senior member angrily remarked in an interview that his constituents had unreasonable expectations of Congress:

> People are looking more and more to Congress for the derelictions of the states and the cities. They're looking to Congress for relief. They want Congress to do everything now. They want me to fill potholes in the streets.

Earlier retirements from Congress may simply reflect the higher pensions members now receive, but the job itself is less attractive than it once was. The responsibilities that a changing political economy imposes on the legislator are extremely demanding.

Institutional Interests and the Larger Context

As contradictions in our system of production and distribution become more difficult to resolve, the members of Congress may even grow concerned about the government's legitimacy. This concern might lead to a search for institutional changes that would help members to relate to groups and constituents in new ways: possibilities include manipulation through the use of computer letters, novel media techniques, and other devices that enable them to shape the information constituents obtain; isolation through a congressional bureaucracy, fewer committees, or even less frequent elections; and the support of policies that can be used to repress dissent and discourage pressure.

When the Legislative Reorganization Act of 1946 reduced the number of committees in the House and the Senate by 75 percent, this institutional change may have been in part a response to the postwar national economy: members sought a means to weaken the influence of local interests that were institutionalized in the narrowly defined congressional committees. Notably, the Reorganization Act was merely one title of the Employment Act of 1946, which was an effort by the federal government to provide a national planning mechanism.[47] Of course, organizational structures create their own momentum. They may persist even when the context has changed and they no longer serve the purposes for which they were intended originally. Obsolete structures may contribute to struggles within Congress as some members try to equip the institution to respond to a new set of circumstances, while others emphasize a different set of concerns, such as power.

The case studies that follow will examine how the larger context seems to have affected Congress during the 1970s. As indicated in the general discussion here and in the following cases, some members sought to address the larger problems directly, while others focused on narrower concerns. Both responses are best understood when placed in the larger context that generated them.

NOTES

1. Alfred A. Chandler, Jr., *Strategy and Structure: Chapters in the History of the Industrial Enterprise* (Cambridge: MIT Press, 1966), Chapter 2; Edward S. Herman, *Corporate Control, Corporate Power* (New York: Cambridge University Press, 1981), Chapter 1; John Kenneth Galbraith, *Economics and the Public Purpose* (Boston: Houghton Mifflin, 1973), pp. 15–18.
2. Douglas F. Dowd, *The Twisted Dream*, 2nd ed. (Cambridge, Mass.: Winthrop, 1977), pp. 91–98.
3. George S. McGovern, *The Great Coalfield War* (Boston: Houghton Mifflin, 1972).
4. Frances Fox Piven and Richard A. Cloward, *Poor People's Movements: Why They Succeed, How They Fail* (New York: Vintage, 1979), pp. 104–113.
5. Ibid., p. 121.
6. Everett Johnson Burrt, *Labor in the American Economy* (New York: St. Martin's Press, 1979), p. 121.
7. For an illuminating discussion about the displacement of class conflict, see Ira Katznelson, *City Trenches* (New York: Pantheon Books, 1981).
8. James O'Connor, *The Fiscal Crisis of the State* (New York: St. Martin's Press, 1973), pp. 13–23; Manuel Castells, *The Economic Crisis and American Society* (Princeton: Princeton University Press, 1980), Chapter 3; Barry Bluestone, "Economic Crisis and the Law of Uneven Development," *Politics & Society*, 3, No. 2 (Fall 1972).
9. O'Connor, *Fiscal Crisis of the State*, p. 13.
10. Ibid., pp. 13–14.
11. Ibid., pp. 18–30.
12. Ibid., Chapter 2; Castells, *The Economic Crisis and American Society*, pp. 123–135.
13. On the New York City fiscal crisis see William K. Tabb, *The Long Default: New York City and the Urban Fiscal Crisis* (New York: Monthly Review Press, 1981). Also see Kenneth Fox, "Cities and City Governments in the Current Crisis," in Economics Education Project, *U.S. Capitalism in Crisis* (New York: Union for Radical Political Economics, 1977); Castells, *The Economic Crisis and American Society*, pp. 200–214.

14. John H. Mollenkopf, "The Post-War Politics of Urban Development," *Politics & Society*, 5, No. 3 (1975); Robert Wood, *Suburbia* (Boston: Houghton Mifflin, 1958). On black migration see Ira Katznelson, *Black Men, White Cities* (Chicago: University of Chicago Press, 1976), Chapter 7.
15. *Business Week*, 24 April 1978, p. 134. Also see Helen Leavitt, *Superhighway—Superhoax* (New York: Ballantine Books, 1970).
16. Roger Wilkins, "A New Approach to Job Problems of City Youths," *New York Times*, 16 January 1978, p. A23; U.S. Bureau of the Census, *Statistical Abstract of the United States: 1978* (Washington, D.C., 1978), p. 408; Michael Reich, *Racial Inequality: A Political-Economic Analysis* (Princeton: Princeton University Press, 1981), pp. 35–36.
17. *Business Week*, 13 September 1976, pp. 65–66.
18. Ibid., p. 67.
19. Castells, *The Economic Crisis and American Society*, pp. 95–98; Jerry Flint, "Big Labor Counting on Congress and Import Curbs," *New York Times*, 8 January 1978, sect. XII, p. 43.
20. Robert Engler, *The Brotherhood of Oil: Energy Policy and the Public Interest* (Chicago: University of Chicago Press, 1977); John M. Blair, *The Control of Oil* (New York: Pantheon Books, 1976); Richard J. Barnet, *The Lean Years: Politics in the Age of Scarcity* (New York: Simon and Schuster, 1980), Chapter 2.
21. Richard J. Barnet and Ronald E. Muller, *Global Reach: The Power of the Multinational Corporations* (New York: Simon and Schuster, 1974), Chapters 1, 2; Joan Edelman Spero, *The Politics of International Economic Relations*, 2nd ed. (New York: St. Martin's, 1981), Chapter 4; Stephen Hymer, "The Multinational Corporation and the Law of Uneven Development," in Jagdish Bhagwati, ed., *Economics and World Order: From the 1970s to the 1990s* (New York: Macmillan, 1972).
22. Seymour Melman, *The Permanent War Economy* (New York: Simon and Schuster, 1974); Richard J. Barnet, *The Economy of Death* (New York: Atheneum, 1969).
23. Congressional Quarterly, *Global Defense: U.S. Military Commitments Abroad* (Washington, D.C.: Congressional Quarterly, 1969), pp. 37–38.
24. Ira Katznelson and Mark Kesselman, *The Politics of Power*, 2nd ed. (New York: Harcourt Brace Jovanovich, 1979), pp. 234–242.
25. Barnet and Muller, *Global Reach*, p. 28; Howard M. Wachtel, *The New Gnomes: Multinational Banks in the Third World* (Washington, D.C.: Transnational Institute, 1977), pp. 3–10
26. *Washington Post*, 19 January 1978, p. A1. The report was: U.S. Senate, Subcommittee on Reports, Accounting and Management, Committee on Governmental Affairs, *Voting Rights in Major Corporations*, A Staff Study, 95th Cong., 1st Sess., January 1978.
27. Theodore Lowi, *The End of Liberalism* (New York: Norton, 1969).
28. Garry Wills, *Nixon Agonistes* (Boston: Houghton Mifflin, 1970). Also see Alan Wolfe, *The Limits of Legitimacy: Political Contradictions of Contemporary Capitalism* (New York: Free Press, 1977).
29. Louis Hartz, *The Liberal Tradition in America* (New York: Harcourt Brace and World, 1955).
30. Herman P. Miller, *Rich Man, Poor Man* (New York: Crowell, 1971); Howard Wachtel, "Capitalism and Poverty in America; Paradox or Contradiction?" *Monthly Review*, June 1972; Castells, *The Economic Crisis and American Society*, pp. 197–201; Michael Parenti, *Democracy for the Few*, 3rd ed. (New York: St. Martin's Press, 1980), pp. 22–30; Marvin Gettleman and David Mermelstein, eds., *The Great Society Reader: The Failure of American Liberalism* (New York: Vintage, 1967).
31. Reich, *Racial Inequality*, Chapter 1.
32. *Report of the National Advisory Commission on Civil Disorders* (New York: Bantam Books, 1968), p. 1.
33. Jeremy Rifkin, *Own Your Own Job* (New York: Bantam, 1977), p. 129. The question asked (p. 173): "How about when it comes to our capitalist system? Would you say in terms of performance: (1) that it . . . is still getting better; or (2) that it has reached its peak and now is on the decline. . . ." Only 22 percent responded that it is improving.
34. George H. Gallup, *The Gallup Poll: Public Opinion, 1972–1977*, I (Wilmington, Del.:

Scholarly Resources, 1978), p. 132. The poll was titled: "America's Confidence in Congress," and was taken in June 1973.

35. Daniel Patrick Moynihan, *The Politics of a Guaranteed Income* (New York: Random House, 1973), pp. 101–102. Also see Michael Lipsky and David Olson, "The Processing of Racial Crisis in America," *Politics & Society,* 6 (1976).

36. Isaac D. Balbus, "The Concept of Interest in Pluralist and Marxian Analysis," *Politics & Society,* 1, No. 2 (Feb. 1971), pp. 166–172. In his classic study, Bertram M. Gross does suggest briefly that groups are structured by the larger society. But he does not develop the point. See *The Legislative Struggle: A Study in Social Combat* (New York: McGraw-Hill, 1953), p. 147. This assumption of pluralists is a modern one; in the 1908 seminal work of the pluralist tradition, Arthur F. Bentley indicates the type of group formation in a particular society relates to the structure of the society. See *The Process of Government* (Cambridge, Mass.: Harvard University Press, 1967), Chapter 19.

37. A notable exception has been Barbara Sinclair. As an example of her work, see "Agenda and Alignment Change: The House of Representatives, 1925–1978," in Lawrence C. Dodd and Bruce I. Oppenheimer, eds. *Congress Reconsidered,* 2nd ed., (Washington, D.C.: CQ Press, 1981). Also see Lawrence C. Dodd, "Congress, the Constitution, and the Crisis of Legitimation," in the same volume.

38. Ralph Miliband, *The State in Capitalist Society* (New York: Basic Books, 1969), p. 146.

39. For example, see Mark Green, *Who Runs Congress?* 3rd ed. (New York: Bantam, 1979), Chapter 2.

40. G. William Domhoff, "I Am Not an 'Instrumentalist': A Reply to Kapitalistate Critics," *Kapitalistate,* Nos. 4–5 (1976).

41. G. William Domhoff, *The Higher Circles* (New York: Vintage, 1971), Chapters 5, 6.

42. Theda Skocpol, "Political Response to Capitalist Crisis: Neo-Marxist Theories of the State and the Case of the New Deal," *Politics & Society,* 10, No. 3 (1981); Piven and Cloward, *Poor People's Movements,* Chapter 3.

43. U.S. Tariff Commission, "Money Crisis and the Operation of Multinational Firms," in Philip Brenner, Robert Borosage, and Bethany Weidner, eds., *Exploring Contradictions: Political Economy in the Corporate State* (New York: David McKay, 1974).

44. Mancur Olson, Jr., *The Logic of Collective Action* (New York: Schocken Books, 1968), pp. 9–16.

45. David B. Truman, *The Governmental Process* (New York: Alfred A. Knopf, 1951), pp. 50–51.

46. David Easton, *The Political System* (New York: Alfred A. Knopf, 1953), pp. 106–115.

47. Otis L. Graham, Jr., *Toward a Planned Society: From Roosevelt to Nixon* (New York: Oxford University Press, 1976), pp. 79–90; Stephen K. Bailey, *Congress Makes a Law* (New York: Columbia University Press, 1950); Bertram Gross, *Friendly Fascism: The New Face of Power in America* (New York: M. Evans and Co., 1980), pp. 143–144.

PART II

Case Studies

3 Foreign Policy: Towards Normal Relations with Cuba—Congress's Role

Cuba has excited the imagination of more than its share of American "statesmen" in the last century. From the Grant administration, when the United States attempted to purchase the island, to Teddy Roosevelt's Rough Riders, to John Kennedy's missile crisis, Cuba has been a country of continuing importance to U.S. foreign policy. After President Richard Nixon traveled to China and declared a détente with the Soviet Union, many observers looked to the restoration of relations with Cuba as the last great foreign policy leap this former cold warrior would take during his term of office.

It came as something of a shock to many that Congress appeared to take the lead in opening relations with Cuba. From 1971 to 1975 several individuals and groups within Congress undertook a series of actions aimed at changing American economic and diplomatic policy toward Cuba. Between 1975 and 1978 congressional attitude ranged from ambivalence towards renewed relations with Cuba to hostility. But Congress continued to be involved in fashioning the American policy.

Here is a case, therefore, in which Congress helped to shape a major foreign policy and in which conventional explanations for its behavior do not suffice. Only in the larger context of congressional behavior, the world beyond Capitol Hill, does Congress's role in shaping Cuba policy begin to make sense. This chapter provides a review of the pre-1971 history of American policy towards Cuba, a chronology of congressional actions from 1971 to 1978 involving this policy, and a report on the motivations of the senators and representatives who were active in the case. In Chapter 4 their behavior and perceptions will be assessed in the context both of immediate events and of long-term changes that had an impact on the United States.

The Background of American Cuba Policy

To appreciate how important Cuba has been in American policy may be difficult. Many North Americans think of Cuba as a small Caribbean island that produces sugar, Havana cigars, and nightclub singers like Desi Arnaz. David Halberstam reports, for example, that in 1961, during planning for the Bay of Pigs invasion, a member of the Joint Chiefs of Staff proposed that United States troops invade Cuba and march the length of the island in a day. His perception that the country was the size of Long Island was shattered when another general superimposed a map of Cuba over a map of the United States, and Cuba stretched from New York City to Chicago.[1]

Cuba's size, its population of 10 million people, and its location 100 miles south of Florida, however, are only a small part of the reason it has been significant to the United States. Along with the Philippines and Hawaii, it was the first noncontinental territory the United States tried to gain. What we in the United States call the Spanish-American War is to the Cubans and Filipinos an episode in their respective wars of independence.

Following the Spanish-American War, the United States replaced Spain in many ways as the ruler of Cuba. Under the terms of the Platt Amendment of 1901—which the United States demanded Cuba add to its new constitution in return for the withdrawal of American troops—the United States was entitled to intervene in Cuba whenever it deemed necessary. Today the United States still has troops on the island, at Guantánamo Base. Cuba abrogated the Platt Amendment in 1934, but by then its economy was inextricably linked in a dependent relationship with that of the United States. Cuba sold its principal crop, sugar, largely to the United States.[2] In turn, Cuba imported machinery, processed goods, and even much of its food mainly from the United States.[3] American companies earned higher profits by selling Cuba goods from the mainland than by diversifying the property they owned to produce goods in Cuba. As late as 1958 this island could not even exploit its most basic natural resource, the sea, to provide food for its people. There were hardly any commercial fishing vessels in Cuba then, and even today Cubans do not favor fish in their diets owing to the earlier, structurally imposed tradition of not eating fish.[4] Until 1958 most Cuban land was controlled by a small oligarchy that was linked to American banks and corporations.[5] North American firms paid taxes that accounted for 20 percent of the Cuban government's budget, and in all, the United States had more than $1 billion of investment in Cuba when the revolution of 1959 took place.[6] This was the largest American investment in any Latin American country, and many American corporations used Cuba as a base for their Latin American operations.[7]

In terms of gross per capita statistics, Cuba was one of the richest Latin American countries in 1958. But beneath superficial calculations lay the fact that only 1 child in 20 had milk every day, 25 percent of the population was illiterate while 7,000 teachers were unemployed, 85 percent of the doctors were located in the urban centers (more than half in Havana alone), and slum shanties were the most typical form of housing.[8] Poverty and unemployment provided a ready source of cheap labor for American manufacturing, as Cuban workers would take any job that was available.[9]

During the 1950s the Cuban government was headed by General Fulgencio Batista, a dictator who had voided the 1940 Cuban constitution and seized power in 1952. Despite his willingness to protect American investments, in 1958 the United States government began to withdraw support from the Batista regime because his corruption and use of terror had made him so unpopular in Cuba. This worked to the advantage of the forces in Cuba opposing Batista, principally the 26th of July Movement led by Fidel Castro Ruz. This organization was broad-based, with guerrillas in the mountains and a well-developed underground network in the cities. Castro had captured the popular imagination in the United States following a series of on-the-scenes stories from the Sierra Maestra by *New York Times* reporter Herbert Matthews in February 1957.[10] Castro was described as a progressive fighter, from a middle-class background, who hoped to restore Cuban democracy. In Washington, Castro's background fostered expectations that he would lead a government that would protect American investments while it instituted some social reforms to ease the extremes of poverty in Cuba.[11]

Such dreaming ignored history. The problems in Cuba were not of Batista's making—they were rooted in the dependent relationship Cuba had with the United States. It soon became clear that the new government would be committed to major changes that threatened both the local domination of a few wealthy owners and the control by American corporations. Even before the reforms were instituted—the large sugar companies were permitted to own their land through 1960—the Cuban upper class had begun a civil war against the new government. In Washington, the Eisenhower administration felt betrayed by Castro's nationalization of several hundred million dollars' worth of American-owned property and began to supply arms to the counterrevolutionaries. United States public opinion, too, shifted against the new Cuban government, in part because of the show trials of former Batista soldiers and the prospect of a socialist Cuba. In late 1960 the United States cut back on the amount of sugar it permitted into the country in an effort to cripple the Cuban economy. Then, on January 3, 1961, in one of his last major acts in office, President Eisenhower broke diplomatic relations with Cuba. Meanwhile, he had authorized preparation of an invasion of the island by Cuban exiles who were trained and supplied by the CIA. The invasion became the ill-fated Bay of Pigs episode of April 17–19, 1961.[12]

Arguably, President John Kennedy ought to have been embarrassed by the flagrancy of this violation of a sovereign nation and chastened by its failure; in fact he reacted by authorizing increased expenditures for a covert war against Cuba. The covert war involved at least ten attempts to assassinate Premier Fidel Castro; weekly landings in Cuba of arms, supplies, and mercenary soldiers for the anti-government forces fighting in the civil war; the illegal creation and maintenance of a large CIA base in Miami to support the weekly attacks; and sabotage of Cuban production. This sabotage included the destruction of machinery, the burning of fields, and the poisoning of Cuban sugar for export.[13]

Cuba was no longer exporting its sugar to the United States. In April 1961 the United States banned the importation of goods from Cuba and in June banned the sale of goods to Cuba. For a country whose economy had been tied to the United States, these actions were a form of strangulation.[14] Cuba could sell sugar, cigars, and nickel elsewhere, but the replacement parts for its American-made machinery, its trucks, and its hospital equipment had to come from the United States. As with all dependent countries, it had to buy on credit with an internationally accepted currency, and American banks forced international lending agencies and the financial institutions of other capitalist countries to cut off Cuba's credit. In 1964 the United States succeeded in persuading two thirds of the members of the Organization of American States to institute a hemispheric embargo against Cuba. This meant that if Cuba did trade with a country such as Japan, a Japanese ship could carry cargo only to and from Cuba and could not dock elsewhere in the hemisphere. Thus these ships often travelled half full, which increased the cost of goods that Cuba imported.

An economic blockade is a highly hostile act, and Cuba alone was not enough of a threat to the United States to warrant such an action. "International Communism," however, was a credible threat, since the Cold War was still very much a part of the American outlook. In 1960 Senator John Kennedy had campaigned for the presidency on a promise to end the "missile gap" with the Soviet Union. Whether they knew or believed otherwise, officials in Washington all spoke of a monolithic Communist bloc. Cuba was a part of that bloc. It had turned to the Soviet Union, China, and other socialist countries for assistance when the United States cut off trade and aid. Now it was an archfoe. The placement of Soviet missiles in Cuba in 1962 confirmed fears of an armed advance line of Communists one hundred miles from Florida.

Debates about the missile crisis of October 1962 are likely to continue for years.[15] It has been described both as President Kennedy's (and the country's) finest hour and as treacherous irresponsibility that brought us to the brink of nuclear war. Most accounts focus on the relations between the United States and the Soviet Union. As with the Spanish-American War, the arguments tend to ignore Cuba. From the Cuban perspective, the missiles provided a deterrent to United States aggression; Cuba was attempting to stop the weekly landings, the sabotage, and the assassination attempts. Indeed, one element of the agreement between President Kennedy and Premier Nikita Khrushchev was that the United States would end the covert attacks in return for the removal of Soviet missiles.[16] This agreement was not public and could not be acknowledged by the White House, which had not told the public about the attacks against Cuba. The mythology of the missile crisis was that it had been a showdown between the United States and the Soviet Union, that the Soviet Union had created a situation of grave danger to world peace, and that Cuba was an agent of the Soviet Union. In short, Cuba was portrayed as a threat to world peace and most immediately to the United States. Under these circumstances, the congressional initiative seems quite remarkable.

Congressional Action on Cuba Policy

The official view of Cuba as an enemy prevailed into the early 1970s. There had been hardly any opposition to that view in the United States Congress. The Congress had participated in creating the embargo by passing amendments to existing laws such as the Foreign Assistance Act of 1961, the Export Control Act of 1949, the Agricultural Trade Development and Assistance Act of 1954, and the Mutual Defense Assistance Control Act of 1951. These were passed in the House and Senate by large majorities. In 1962, during the missile crisis, Congress passed a joint resolution (P.L. 87-733) that declared the intention of the United States to prevent the "subversive" activities of the "Marxist-Leninist regime in Cuba."[17] In contrast to the concurrent Tonkin Gulf Resolution that sanctioned military action in Vietnam two years later, the Cuban Resolution was signed by the president and had the force of law.

In 1971 several members of Congress began efforts to move the official American stance away from bellicosity to a position that might permit the eventual normalization of relations with Cuba—diplomatic and consular exchanges, regular travel and trade between the countries, and an end to hostile actions. No one in Congress believed such relations could be established quickly, but these members were staking out a role for Congress that was far more autonomous than the congressional role had been before. Congressional activity concerning Cuba between 1971 and 1978 can be divided into three periods: 1971–1975, 1976, and 1977–1978.

Congressional Activity, 1971–1975

In December 1970 the United States signed a treaty in The Hague on aircraft hijacking. Treaties require confirmation by two thirds of the Senate and are usually submitted first to the Senate Foreign Relations Committee for consideration before the full Senate debates the treaty. This process permits the committee to call witnesses and to gather relevant information. It also permits committee members to use the hearings as a forum for propaganda or public edification.[18] In this case, Senator J. William Fulbright, chairman of the Foreign Relations Committee, took the opportunity to raise the matter of United States relations with Cuba. As a leading analyst of United States–Cuban relations observes, Fulbright's argument was practical:

> Senator Fulbright . . . argued that since over 80 percent of the hijackings were to Cuba, the United States should attempt to strike an agreement with Cuba, especially since Cuba had rejected the multilateral approach as represented by the [Hague] Convention.[19]

Following the hearings on July 30, 1971, Senators Fulbright and Frank Church introduced a joint resolution to repeal the Cuban Resolution of 1962. The same day, Senator Edward Kennedy introduced a second resolution, co-sponsored by Fulbright and Church, to express the sense of the Senate that the president should review American policy towards Cuba with an eye to re-establishing normal relations. Kennedy accompanied his resolution with a major speech on the Senate floor that understandably gained wide attention. A week later, Senator Charles McC. Mathias introduced another resolution to repeal the 1962 resolution. The three resolutions themselves then became the subject of a Foreign Relations Committee hearing on September 16, at which several senators charged that the Nixon administration was putting up unnecessary resistance.[20]

In April 1972 ten senators and nineteen representatives sponsored a conference in the Capitol on United States–Cuba relations. Although the conference was conducted by the private Fund for New Priorities, its location and sponsorship added impetus to growing congressional interest in normalization. Perhaps of even greater significance was a report in January 1973 from an informal group of House Republicans—the Wednesday Group—recommending that the blockade against Cuba be lifted.[21]

Informal groups in the House have developed during the past twenty-five years to cope with problems of communication in the large body. Some groups have been only social, such as the Chowder and Marching Society. The newer groups tend to be legislatively oriented, to hire staff, and to restrict membership along party lines. Most prominent among them are the Democratic Study Group, the Wednesday Group, and the Congressional Black Caucus.[22] The Wednesday Group was formed in 1963 by moderate and liberal House Republicans, and it gained prominence in 1965 by supporting Representative Gerald Ford in his fight to unseat conservative House Minority Leader Charles Halleck.[23] By 1973 it had gained a reputation for moderation—several of its liberal members had left the House or the Republican Party and were replaced by more conservative colleagues. The Wednesday Group's report on Cuba was widely noticed on the Hill and, coming from this Republican group, it helped to defuse the emotionalism attached to proposals for normalizing relations with Cuba.

In March 1973 and again in April, a Senate Foreign Relations subcommittee held hearings on American policy towards Cuba. The subcommittee chairman, Gale McGee, was not ready to endorse a new Cuba policy. He was a committed anti-Communist who had been a hawk on the Vietnam War, and in this light his opening comments—on "the need for some rethinking about our relations"—set a positive tone for movement towards normalization.[24]

These activities were a prelude to a flurry of actions in 1974 and early 1975 that placed Congress in the forefront of efforts to change United States Cuba policy. At first, the Senate took the lead. Notably, even relatively conservative leaders such as Majority Whip Robert Byrd and the new chairman of the Foreign Relations Committee, John Sparkman, called for initiatives to re-establish normal relations, such as lifting the embargo against Cuba on food and medicine. In the House there were several representatives who were strongly opposed to a resumption of relations with Cuba. One in particular—Dante Fascell, who represented Miami Beach—was a senior and influential member of the House Foreign Affairs Committee. In October 1974, during a House-Senate conference-committee meeting on a bill to authorize funds for the State Department, he succeeded in deleting a provision of the Senate-passed bill that called for a new Cuba policy "based on current circumstances." Within a few days of the conference committee's action, a few House Foreign Affairs Committee members attempted to revive the issue indirectly, using as their vehicle an amendment to the foreign-aid bill up for consideration. Sponsored by Representative Michael Harrington, the proposed amendment would have removed the president's authority to impose an economic embargo against Cuba. Again Fascell rallied forces to defeat it in committee by a vote of 22 to 4.

Members of Congress who sought a change in policy had recognized by this time that the legislative route might not be the best. They therefore began a series of symbolic efforts intended to dramatize the issue and to encourage the president to act. In September 1974 Senators Claiborne Pell and Jacob Javits traveled to Cuba. They reported upon returning that they believed Premier Castro desired relations with the United States and that the United States should proceed towards that end promptly. They had brought with them on the trip seventeen American journalists anxious to file exclusive stories from Havana. Only a handful of North American reporters had been issued Cuban visas before and the trip received enormous publicity.[25] Within two weeks of their return and in response to appeals by the senators, Cuba announced that it would release four imprisoned United States citizens.

Meanwhile, in the House, an organizational change brought new opportunities for members who sought a change in American policy. Representative Fascell's influence on the Foreign Affairs Committee had come partly from his chairmanship of the Inter-American Affairs Subcommittee. In January 1975 the full committee renamed itself the Committee on International Relations ("Relations sound more serious than affairs," one member quipped) and reorganized its subcommittees along functional rather than regional lines. Fascell became chairman of the Subcommittee on Political and Military Affairs, with broad responsibilities, but the subcommittee authorized to oversee the United States embargo against Cuba was the International Trade and Commerce Subcommittee, chaired by Jonathan Bingham.

As a result of the "subcommittee bill of rights," which the House Democratic Caucus had instituted in 1973,[26] the Bingham subcommittee was granted a budget, a small staff, and a clear jurisdiction. The staff director, Roger Majak, had worked on the chairman's staff and enjoyed his confidence. Majak encouraged Bingham to seize the initiative on changing Cuba policy with his new subcommittee. In April 1975 the subcommittee—together with the International Organizations Subcommittee—opened extensive hearings on United States trade relations with Cuba, focusing on a bill (H.R. 6382) that Bingham had introduced revoking the president's authority to continue the embargo.

In the course of these hearings, which continued until September 1975, several members of Congress—including Senators George McGovern and James Abourezk, and Representatives Charles Whalen and Stephen Solarz—and their staffs traveled to Cuba. All returned with the same message: the Cubans are interested in negotiations, United States policy is outmoded, and the blockade stands in the way of progress towards normalization.[27] During his visit in May, Senator McGovern had sought as a sign of good faith from Cuba the return of $2 million in ransom money taken from the hijackers of a Southern Airways plane in 1972. In August the money was returned. (In addition, Cuba permitted star Boston Red Sox pitcher Luis Tiant's parents to visit the United

States, where they saw him whip the Cincinnati Reds in two games of the 1975 World Series.)

Throughout this period, opponents of normalization stepped up their efforts to counter the publicity that proponents were receiving. Bills and resolutions were introduced that called for the termination of the blockade only after Cuba had met extortionist demands, such as renouncing "its alliance with the Soviet Union." Numerous floor speeches and statements carried the same theme, peaking on November 13, 1975, when twelve senators took the floor in an organized colloquy to denounce Cuban foreign and domestic policies and to oppose any alteration of American policy.

At that point, however, the opponents had little to fear. Congressional efforts to change United States policy were waning. In October, Representative Bingham signaled this new phase by announcing that he had withdrawn his bill and would terminate efforts to gain House approval for such legislation in the "foreseeable future." None of the other major supporters of a changed American policy moved then to take the lead, and for more than a year Congress had little movement on the issue.

Congressional Activity, 1976

In contrast to the congressional ardor for normalization in 1974 and 1975, the issue palled in 1976. Not one resolution calling for steps toward normalization was introduced; no amendments were offered to lift the blockade, even partially for food and medicine, as some had proposed in 1975. In July 1976 the International Trade and Commerce Subcommittee held a hearing to investigate charges that some American businesses were violating the blockade by negotiating with Cuba for the sale and purchase of goods and services.[28] Little came of the investigation. Senator McGee introduced a resolution on April 19 (S. Res. 430) expressing the sense of the Senate that any action against Cuba be sanctioned by the Organization of American States—a resolution not so much supporting relations with Cuba as attempting to curb the president. There had been news reports that the National Security Council was developing contingency plans to attack Cuba militarily.[29]

Meanwhile, the opponents of normalization continued their efforts. The most prominent were those of Senator Richard Stone, who took any opportunity to speak out against Cuba. In March he introduced a resolution (S. Res. 405) that the Senate would welcome "proposals made to it by the president to counter further [Cuban] aggression." In June the Senate amended the International Security Assistance and Arms Control Act of 1976 with a section that condemned Cuban "intervention" in Africa.

Congress's posture clearly had altered. It had not reversed, but the momentum for a changed policy toward Cuba was gone. Interviews with nearly all of the key advocates of normalization, or their staffs, in June and July found that their positions had not changed. However, they explained that "the time was not appropriate," that they were waiting until after the presidential election before resuming their efforts. A few House Democrats attempted to include in the 1976 party platform a plank that mildly suggested support for a resumption of relations, but Maurice Ferre, the mayor of Miami, was on the drafting subcommittee of the Task Force on International Relations. He lobbied arduously to include a negative statement, declaring that "relations with Cuba can be normalized if Cuba refrains from interference in the internal affairs of other nations, and releases those United States citizens currently detained in Cuban prisons and labor camps for purely political reasons."

Congressional Activity, 1977–1978

The Ninety-fifth Congress convened on January 4, 1977. On February 10, Representative Bingham arrived in Havana for a five-day visit that included three meetings with Premier Fidel Castro.[30] Back in Washington, the congressman renewed his drive for a normalization of relations by calling for the partial lifting of the blockade to permit the shipment of food and medicine.[31] At first Congress appeared to be wasting little time after the election to seize the initiative and to move the United States towards resumed relations with Cuba. But Bingham's support was weaker than it had been in 1974 and 1975, and the opposition was stronger.

There had been several changes since 1975 that affected Congress's handling of the Cuba issue. At this point, to single out significant factors simplifies the case. The short- and long-term factors involved, all of varying weights, deserve separate consideration, and Chapter 4 evaluates the impact of each. Journalists, and the legislators themselves, naturally focused on the short-term factors, which required immediate consideration, but the less obvious factors played a part as well.

Congressional action in 1977 is best represented by the Senate's ambivalence towards an amendment sponsored by Senators McGovern and Sparkman. The amendment would have lifted the embargo on trade in food and medicine. McGovern had announced his intention to introduce such a measure when he returned in April from his second trip to Cuba. (On this trip he had traveled with Senator Abourezk, Representative Les Aspin, and the University of South Dakota basketball team.) A bill authorizing funds for the State Department and the United States Information Agency was the first available vehicle to which he could attach the proposed amendment.

In the International Operations Subcommittee, of which McGovern was chairman, the amendment sailed through without opposition, especially after he altered it to allow the president to regulate trade in a way that "did not result in undue hardship to sugar producers in the United States." But two weeks later, on May 10, the bill hit a snag during its mark-up by the full Senate Foreign Relations Committee.

Trade in food and medicine would have meant that Cuba could export both sugar and citrus products to the United States (and perhaps even cigars). This possibility aroused the concern of beet-sugar producers and Florida citrus growers, who, because their fruit matures about two weeks after Cuban fruit, would have lost their high-priced "first crop" position.[32] Because Idaho is a large beet-sugar state, Senator Church proposed that trade with Cuba be permitted in only one direction: from the United States to Cuba. Supporting one-way trade were Senators Hubert Humphrey and Javits. In the face of vociferous attacks on the McGovern amendment by Senator Stone, the Church-Humphrey-Javits position seemed to be a middle-ground compromise, and it passed the committee by a 10 to 7 margin. McGovern had little choice but to accept the changes: liberal support for his position had evaporated, and there had been rumors that administration lobbyists were pressuring senators to overturn the McGovern plan.[33]

When the State Department authorization bill reached the Senate floor in June, McGovern withdrew the compromise amendment, noting that it no longer served the purpose of heading the United States "in the direction of improved relations" with Cuba.[34] Moreover, the Cuban government saw the offer for one-way trade as an affront.[35]

Meanwhile, in the House, opponents of normalized relations with Cuba moved to prevent passage of even one-way trade. Two days after the Senate Foreign Relations Committee had reported the State Department authorization bill out, the House approved an amendment to the foreign-aid authorization bill that banned any trade between the United States and both Cuba and Vietnam. The House action did not have a direct bearing on the measure pending in the Senate, because the House had already passed its version of the State Department authorization. However, the vote was interpreted as an instruction to potential House conferees—when they met with Senate conferees following passage of the State Department bill—to push for deletion in the final bill of the one-way trade approval.[36] Had the House not spoken in this regard, the Senate conferees could have argued for retention of one-way trade in the final bill, since the Senate had indicated its position and the House would have indicated no position.

The Senate returned to symbolic measures again in August, as Senator Church visited Cuba for four days. Notably, he traveled with his twenty-person group on a presidential plane, and prior to his departure from Washington he conferred for several hours with National Security Council Director Zbigniew Brzezinski and NSC Latin American specialist Robert Pastor about the trip. Previous congressional visits to Havana had been undertaken with little executive branch concurrence, and the consultation underscored growing coordination during 1977 between the executive and members of Congress who supported normalization.

Church brought back a promise from President Castro (Cuba had changed its constitution in 1976, and Castro was elected President in 1977), to permit more than eighty Cuban families to emigrate to the United States. These were families in which one member was a United States citizen. The United States citizens had been permitted to leave earlier, but without their families. At an airport press conference in Havana, Church remarked that the families had been a "matter of much concern to the U.S. government and the American people."[37] In his post-trip report, he added himself to the list of those calling for an end to the embargo against Cuba.[38]

Still, during the 1977–1978 period, proponents of resumed relations with Cuba did not set the tone of congressional activity. They won some legislative battles, but their victories were defensive. For example, in May 1977 the House defeated an amendment that would have denied funds to the State Department for the purpose of merely negotiating with Cuba on the resumption of relations. In October the Senate barely succeeded in deleting House-passed provisions of the foreign-aid authorization bill that would have barred international financial institutions (IFIs) from using United States contributions for loans to Cuba and five other countries. (In August 1978 the Senate again beat back a similar House restriction.) The institutions included the World Bank and the International Monetary Fund. The restriction would have forced the institutions to deny any loans to these countries—and thereby to give the United States an effective veto—or to reject any contribution from the United States, which might have caused them bankruptcy. IFIs are not able to distinguish which country's funds are used for particular loans. The president strongly opposed the amendments in 1977 and 1978, but agreed in a letter to the conference committee in 1977 that he would instruct United States delegates to IFIs to vote against loans to the countries in question.[39] On this basis, House conferees acceded to the Senate position in 1977. However, in 1978 the compromise bill (H.R. 12931) included a symbolic provision that precluded any money being spent for "trade or aid . . . directly or indirectly to Cuba." Loans are not considered aid.

Clearly, a new mood of hostility toward normalization of relations with Cuba had developed in the Senate. This was underscored on June 28, 1978, when the Senate passed by a 53-29 vote an amendment to the

State Department authorization (S. 3076) that declared the sense of the Congress to be "That the President should recall the United States Interests Section from Cuba and expel the Cuban Interests Section from the United States, . . . [and] reverse any other action toward the normalization of relations with Cuba." Since the break in diplomatic relations on January 3, 1961, Cuban interests in the United States have been represented by a section of the Czechoslovakian Embassy, and the United States interests in Cuba have been represented by a section of the Swiss Embassy. In September 1977 these sections were staffed for the first time by Cuban and American personnel, respectively, and it was at these staffs that the resolution was aimed. The House did not pass the amendment and it was deleted in conference, but it marked a dramatic turnaround that brought the Congress back to 1971 in terms of its effort to shape United States policy towards Cuba.

Members' Perceptions

One important way to understand congressional actions regarding United States Cuba policy is to examine the members' perceptions of what they were doing and why they were doing it. Of course, members may have been only partially aware of their motives. Often legislators act on intuition rather than with a clearly defined rationale. What they sometimes refer to as their "sense of politics" provides the link between the environment and congressional policy. Congress is not a machine. The members translate impersonal interests and abstract forces into personal goals and tangible conflicts. Here, neat formulas fail, and personal foibles and institutional obstacles defy "rationality." Yet the members' sense of politics also embodies policy goals related to the environment.

Interviews with members can elicit only part of this mélange of motivations. Their perceptions can neither confirm nor deny that the environment is an important part of the explanation in this case. The environment existed as an objective factor, and the members' perceptions can merely suggest how it was linked to their behavior.

The issue of normalizing relations with Cuba did not occupy the attention of the whole Congress. In the period from 1971 to 1976, forty-three members of Congress were especially active in connection with the issue. They gave major speeches, wrote articles, organized and regularly attended hearings, sponsored legislation, and traveled to Cuba. (As might be expected, all of those who went to Cuba sought a new policy. Opponents said that travel there served to legitimate a government they did not believe should be recognized.)

Of the forty-three senators and representatives, twenty-three were

TABLE 3-1 **Committee Assignments of Members with Respect to American Cuba Policy**

	HOUSE INTERNATIONAL RELATIONS COMMITTEE	**OTHER HOUSE COMMITTEE**	**TOTAL**
Sample	11 (69%)	5 (31%)	16 (100%)
All Active Representatives	13 (68%)	6 (32%)	19 (100%)

	SENATE FOREIGN RELATIONS COMMITTEE	**OTHER SENATE COMMITTEE**	**TOTAL**
Sample	4 (57%)	3 (43%)	7 (100%)
All Active Senators	8 (33%)	16 (67%)	24 (100%)

	HOUSE OR SENATE FOREIGN RELATIONS COMMITTEES	**OTHER HOUSE OR SENATE COMMITTEE**	**TOTAL**
Sample	15 (65%)	8 (35%)	23 (100%)
All Active Members	21 (49%)	22 (51%)	43 (100%)

selected for interviews.[40] The sample tends to overrepresent members who were on either the Senate Foreign Relations or House International Relations committees (see Table 3–1). It also included a significantly greater proportion of members who undertook more than one kind of activity. Approximately half of the "active" members did no more than speak out on policy towards Cuba, but 70 percent of the sample engaged in more than one activity (see Table 3–2). The point of the interviews was to ascertain how the active legislators perceived the problem that a change in Cuba policy might address, and how they related what they did to the problem as they perceived it.

Notably, 68 percent of the active members in the House were on the International Relations Committee, while about the same percentage in the Senate were *not* on the Foreign Relations Committee. This distribution suggests greater specialization in the House than in the Senate. In both houses committee members are most likely to introduce legislation, and of the seven who traveled to Cuba, those not on the House or Senate foreign affairs committees did no more than give speeches.

Members described motivations that reflected personal, institutional,

TABLE 3-2 **Actions by House and Senate Members Active on American Cuba Policy**

	NUMBER OF MEMBERS			
ACTIVITY	Foreign Relations Committees	Other Committees	Sample Foreign Relations Committees	Sample Other Committees
Speeches	9	12	6	1
Legislation and speeches	7	8	4	5
Travel and speeches	0	2	0	2
Speeches, legislation and travel	5	0	5	0

or national interests. Personal interests are those that most people manifest in any work: concern for job security, ambition, pride, greed, sense of achievement, a feeling of power, and a desire for the respect of others and for self-respect, which often comes from carrying out responsibilities or from acting in a consistent manner. Institutional interests are those derived from the perceived needs of a member's committee, his or her particular chamber of Congress, or even the Congress as a whole. National interests are those that legislators see as needs of the United States. They include political needs vis-à-vis other countries and economic needs with respect to employment, profits, and production of goods and services.

Personal Interests

No member of Congress in this period had a district or state in which constituents actively petitioned for the normalization of relations between the United States and Cuba. In some cases, however, constituents were well disposed towards renewed links, and a member could gain favor by actively pursuing a changed United States policy. Three members of the sample fit this situation. John Breaux (D-La.), for example, claims to have traveled to Cuba principally in search of a market for his district's rice growers.

There were several districts—typically with large populations of Cuban-Americans—in which there was vociferous and sometimes violent opposition to renewed relations. Five members in the sample came from such districts. All but one actively opposed efforts towards normalization. These eight members with "high" constituency interest undoubtedly had many reasons for their policy positions, but in light of the importance of the issue to many of their constituents, their positions were likely influenced to a large degree by their personal interest in job security—that is, in re-election.

In almost every case, members tried to find some constituency interest that justified their position. For example, Charles Whalen (R-Ohio) took note on his trip to Cuba of the Trane air conditioners that he said needed replacement parts, parts that were manufactured in his home town of Dayton. In general, however, when members with "low" constituency interest in Cuba sought to serve personal interests, those interests appeared unrelated to re-election. Prestige was such an interest.

"Kissinger went to Moscow and Peking," one staff member said in an interview. "Havana was the only major place left to go, and Henry didn't seem ready to go there." Several staffers said that the pursuit of such prestige seemed to be important to Senator Pell. In September 1974 he was the first elected United States official since December 1960 to visit Cuba. (He was also the official who had made the trip fourteen years earlier.) For some members, being photographed with Fidel Castro would be anathema. But for others, a face-to-face discussion with Castro held the promise of increased stature that diplomatic ventures often bring to presidents. Senator McGovern seemed aware of this when he arranged to have Barbara Walters and the *Today* show accompany him.

The behavior of some legislators reflected a desire to be respected by their peers in Congress. When the issue came before the House Foreign Affairs and Senate Foreign Relations committees, it created a structure of opportunity for committee members with any inclination to be involved, though their concern may not have been intense. In such a circumstance they may have been guided by their previous behavior, in order to appear consistent and not be viewed by colleagues as rank opportunists. Though a legislator's rating by the liberal Americans for Democratic Action is an imprecise indicator of foreign policy outlook, it is notable that the ratings coincide precisely with behavior for members who did not have a "high" constituency interest.[41] Thus, the one member who was absolutely opposed to relations had a low liberal rating of 6. The other fourteen, who favored relations either conditionally or unconditionally, scored 89 or higher on their ADA ratings.[42]

The desire for respect by peers may also have influenced some members in 1976 to abandon their efforts to normalize relations. One member commented, for example, that he stopped espousing normalization because "Anyone who did that at this moment would be looked at as kind of a fool by his colleagues in Congress and by the press."

Institutional Interests

There is an often indistinguishable line between seeking power, glory, or prestige for one's organization and seeking it for oneself. For example, one senator's aide said, "Over the last few years there's been lots of feeling here that the Congress had to reassert itself. But, of course, the first guys to go to Cuba would be remembered most of all." Similarly, when the House Foreign Affairs Committee reorganized its subcommittees in 1975, the Cuba issue was seized by the new Subcommittee on International Trade and Commerce. Its chairman, Jonathan Bingham, apparently recognized that the issue could be a good vehicle for establishing the stature of his subcommittee and for contributing to his own stature as a "statesman."[43]

Organizational pride apparently played a hand in the Wednesday Group's early advocacy of normalized relations. Bill Richardson, the group's foreign policy specialist, reports that "the foreign policy task force was enthusiastic" about tackling the question of normalization. What gave them impetus for issuing a report was their suspicion—which was wrong—that the Nixon administration had been engaged in secret negotiations with Cuba aimed at normalization. Representative Whalen, the task force chairman, "also saw [Senator] Kennedy making moves in the direction of normalization, and he didn't want to be left out cold." According to Richardson, "Whalen told me to get a report out quickly, and I finished it in two weeks."

As a member of Congress, each legislator also has a stake in the power and glory of Congress. Recall that during this period the national legislature allegedly was reasserting its role in foreign policy.[44] Two presidents seemed to have ridden roughshod over Congress during the Vietnam War, and in part this led the new generation in Congress to abandon the traditional congressional deference to the executive branch. Undoubtedly the new mood gave comfort to those members who sought to change United States policy towards Cuba, because they could avoid many of the criticisms such a congressional effort might have encountered at an earlier time. But there was only a scant hint in interviews that the initiators were trying in this case to establish a new congressional role in foreign policy. For example, one representative on the House Foreign Affairs Committee argued against congressional design of foreign policy:

> I don't think Congress can be expected to initiate or conduct foreign policy . . . There's too little coordination and the process is slow. . . . So we must provide—by statute if necessary—opportunities for congressional review and modification of executive policies. That's our role.

This legislator was typical of the House and Senate foreign affairs committee members in the sample. Most favored a strong role for Congress, even when they did not see that role as initiation of policy. Of course, membership on one of these committees enhances opportunities as well as incentives for members to involve themselves in congressional efforts to change foreign policy, and members who choose to join these committees are likely to believe that Congress should play an active foreign policy role. The nature of the Cuban issue facilitated involvement: the major obstacle to renewed relations was the legislatively created embargo against Cuba, and Congress could attack the issue unambiguously by working on legislation to lift the embargo.

Political scientist Richard Fenno found in his interviews with House Foreign Affairs Committee members that these representatives tended to choose the committee because they were interested in developing foreign policies.[45] Similarly, in this case, members said that they were active in trying to shape policy towards Cuba because they wanted the United States to have sound policy. One Foreign Affairs Committee member, for example, explained his involvement in changing American policy by saying, "My interest runs into what I would have to say in a broad sense is the failure of American policy to deal with the emergence of what Castro essentially is." This sort of statement buttresses Fenno's finding that the legislators on this committee focus on "good public policy" as a personal goal.

National Interests

When discussing the national interests of the United States, members of Congress tended to relate normalizing relations with Cuba to one of six interests, ranging from general principles of conduct, such as the way in which the United States ought to relate to all Communist countries, to general goals, such as improving the position of the United States as a world power. Between these fell narrower goals involving American influence in Cuba and in the rest of Latin America.

General principles. Some members said that regardless of the nature of the regime in question, the United States should generally recognize an established government. These legislators argued that the United States should not use diplomatic recognition as a lever for negotiating matters of American interest. Said one proponent of normalization: "I believe we ought to seek to communicate; that's one reason why I believe in diplomatic relations."

In contrast, another liberal Democrat who had strongly supported the normalization of relations with Cuba until Cuba sent troops to Angola declared, "We have to make it very clear that we don't approve of that kind of activity." (As discussed in Chapter 4, Cuba sent approximately

20,000 troops to Angola in 1975 to support the Popular Movement for the Liberation of Angola.)

Interestingly, few members mentioned defense. No proponent of relations with Cuba saw the island as a real threat to the United States, "unless," as one member said, "they become a major military base of the Soviet Union." Opponents of recognition, however, considered Cuba a threat, though these members generally feared Communism more than they feared Cuba specifically.

American relations with Communist countries. While some members appreciated Cuba's stance in terms of the country's history and interests, others resorted to the Cold War argument that the United States should develop a single approach to the monolithic Communist world that Cuba had joined. One liberal Democrat articulated the latter attitude:

> We have to recognize the aggressive realities that are in international politics and that there are two competing forces in the world today. The two major forces are, of course, Russia and Communism, and the Western world. If I didn't feel there was a threat I couldn't support half of our budget going for the Department of Defense.

This legislator further indicated that he was not yet prepared to trust Cuba: "We were very much along that course [trusting Cuba] until Angola. And Angola just set it it back."

Some proponents of normalization said that consistency in relating to Communist countries would both promote stability in the world and make the United States seem more responsible. "We seem to be like a bully," said one member of American policy towards Cuba, "picking on the small guy, when we are still working on détente with the Soviet Union." Others, however, said that it was important to make distinctions between Communist countries because the threat to the United States was not "Communism" but "Russia." In contrast to China, one Democrat said, "the Soviets want to go out and proselytize around the world. They are pretty ruthless in the ways they'll do it." Cuba, he asserted, is linked to the Soviet Union, and he "didn't particularly appreciate the Cuban intervention in Angola." Nonetheless, he supported normalization so that the United States could influence Cuban behavior.

Influencing Cuba. Compared with the United States, Cuba is a small, poor country. To some members Cuba's size and poverty suggested susceptibility to influence by the United States were there relations between the two countries. Advocating normalized relations in place of the failed policy of hostility, a few legislators argued that if the United States had restored relations in 1973 or 1974, "when the time was ripe," Cuba might have been prevented from sending aid to the MPLA in Angola. A liberal Republican reasoned that Cuban efforts in Angola were "probably not inspired by Castro's own ambitions as much as [by] Soviet ambitions to use them as a client state there." Diplomatic relations, he claimed, would allow the United States to "communicate" with Cuba about such questions.

One question that concerned a few proponents of normalization was the matter of civil liberties in Cuba. Opponents of normalization criticized Cuba's lack of a "free press" and its internment of political prisoners, but often they did not link these factors to normalization—perhaps because these members also advocated aid to repressive dictatorships such as those in South Korea and Chile. Some proponents of normalized relations, however, pointed to conditions in Cuba and argued that only if there were good relations could the United States hope to "influence the way in which Cubans treat their people."

These three positions on restored relations with Cuba—stressing general foreign policy principles, improved relations with Communist countries, and influence on Cuba—had an idealistic ring to them. No doubt members were sincere in supporting these positions, but as serious policymakers they also knew that the "Washington community" often dismisses such idealism.[46] As statements of what members saw as the real national interests at stake in this case, the following three arguments were probably more cogent.

American relations with the rest of Latin America. In the mid-1970s, Latin America was receiving increased attention from corporations, the media, and other prominent shapers of opinion. Notably, members did not refer to specific corporate pressures or to policy papers such as the Linowitz Commission Report.[47] Many members spontaneously criticized Secretary of State Henry Kissinger's Latin American policy for its "ad hoc" quality. They charged that he had largely ignored Latin America, and when he did focus his attention on the region, he did it in such a way—as in Chile—that damaged United States relations with other countries there.

Some members of Congress saw United States–Cuba relations as a critical factor in the reform of Latin American policy. "Our Cuban policy," a proponent of normalization declared, "was not serving our own best interest in Latin America. It created great friction with our partners in the OAS." Another proponent voiced a similar observation:

A number of countries in Latin America have for some time wished to have more normal relations with Havana. And they felt they were placed in a position of choosing sides in doing so. By making any country uncomfortable in its choices it seems to me we disturb what ought to be the relationship we have with them. Nothing's worse for a neighborhood than a family fight or a neighborhood fight.

The idea of maintaining good relations with Latin America was not an abstraction to the members. Those interviewed said they were aware that several Latin American countries were angry about the embargo because it prevented the subsidiaries of United States–based multinationals in their countries from trading with Cuba.

Relations with Cuba and the American economy. When an American multinational corporation pressures or encourages a foreign country to make demands on the United States, it has involved itself in making foreign policy. Members of Congress expressed some concern about "threats" that large companies can pose to the interests of the United States. One member, for example, commented that "their very massed presence around the world tends to create an independent foreign policy parallel to the generalized American citizens' interest," advancing the companies' "own individual interest," which may be very different from the public's. Other "problems" that members said multinationals pose included:

1. loss of United States tax revenues by their overseas operations;
2. pressure on small, weak countries in pursuit of corporate interests, for ends that might be contrary to human-rights objectives;
3. loss of jobs in the United States;
4. damage to local economies in the United States;
5. destabilization of the dollar through international monetary manipulations.

However, most members cited "benefits" that accrue from the operations of multinational corporations and suggested that there is an equation between the profitability of the multinationals and the strength of the American economy. One supporter of normalization, noting that large companies and not small businesses engage in international trade, said, "This is a capitalistic society. We're interested in business and trade and making a buck. I'd like to stimulate the economy, to have a good flow, good trade, good business. Business counts a lot." Another member focused on the "tremendous benefits" of multinational corporations, even as he noted problems they create:

> The benefits are the acquisition of resources, the potential guarantees of a flow of resources efficiently gathered, and the development of market areas that wouldn't be available otherwise. There are market areas that we can only utilize through a multinational corporation in the region.

Such comments served to justify the members' advocacy of the multinationals' demands for unrestricted access to markets and resources in general. They also extended the argument to trade with Cuba in particular and pointed to its potential as a large market and resource base. One advocate of normalization advanced the public's potential benefits:

> The American people have naturally a very, very basic interest in international trade generally, and particularly in regard to Cuba, because sugar prices have been somewhat erratic. There is a lot to be said for resuming a relationship with Cuba. It represents a potential source of supply close to our country. It's a lot less expensive than importing from the Philippines.

Often critics of Congress will find simple explanations for congressional assistance to large corporations, contending that members of Congress are "bought" by large corporations or that corporations dictate congressional behavior through campaign financing. Corporate control may exist in some cases: one member remarked that he felt "helpless" in the face of the influence corporations exercised over tax legislation. But most of the legislators interviewed saw the situation with greater complexity than muckrakers usually describe. Legislators recognized that corporations dominate the economy because they own the productive wealth of the United States. Short of socializing this production, the legislators felt obliged to work with the corporations to ensure jobs, goods, and services. Some worried about the problems the large corporations created, but even these critics were unsure how to grapple with the problems. "I don't know exactly how to deal with them," one remarked. "I think codes of conduct may be helpful." Such a sense of impotence, along with sincere belief, may lead members to emphasize positive aspects of corporations and to take up the cause of multinationals. Wary of special pleading, though, some members argued that assisting multinationals would reduce budget deficits and thus help to fund social programs. "My big concern," one moderate declared with respect to multinationals, "is that they do a good job. They sell a lot of products and they pay taxes somewhat over here." Another member remarked, "It's to the advantage of the entire American economy, and therefore to the tax base, for the growth to take place that is occasioned in part by multinational corporations."

As these comments suggest, members of Congress do not view trade only in narrow terms of benefits to particular corporations. They see international trade as an aspect of a total foreign policy intended to maintain United States predominance in world politics.

The United States as a world power. Of course, the American embargo of trade with Cuba was one reason that the congressional initiative on United States–Cuba policy focused on trade. The United States had sought to undermine the Cuban government by preventing Cuban trade with the capitalist world. Members saw trade as a foreign policy lever. One representative explained this perception of trade in terms of Cuba:

> There was a period when I was trying to tighten up on trade with Cuba because of Cuba's relationship with Vietnam. This was a period in which I thought we were really trying to win the war. Well, circumstances have changed so radically that I have dropped that.

One circumstance that had changed was the prevailing attitude in Washington that the Cuban government could be toppled by strangling the island with an embargo. All of the members who had traveled to Cuba reported that the embargo had essentially failed, that Cuban production was growing, and that basic commodities were available and well distributed. Reiterating the conclusions of the Wednesday Group task force that he chaired, Congressman Whalen declared: "Our attempts to isolate Cuba have failed." Indeed, some noted that the embargo was having the undesirable effect of pushing Cuba ever more "into the Soviet orbit."

Some members said that an active effort to woo Cuba away from the Soviet Union should be an important goal for the United States. To allow natural trading partners to remain outside of the United States trade nexus—and to run risks of alienating other trading partners, as some claimed we were doing with the Cuba policy—would require fundamental changes in United States relations with the rest of the world. "I don't think we're in a position to rethink and restructure our entire global position," a proponent of normalization remarked. Opponents and proponents of normalization differed in their assessments of whether Cuba could be pulled into the United States orbit. The former argued that the Cuban economy was already so wedded to the Soviet trading network that only a small amount of trade with the United States would be possible. Those favoring normalization were likely to agree with the liberal Democrat who suggested, "One thing no [doctrinally isolated] country could withstand would be an onslaught of American tourists, and whenever markets open, a certain amount of mellowing takes place." Both points of view, however, shared the sense that the United States had a hegemonic position in the world that it should seek to preserve.

This sense came across clearly, for example, when one relatively junior supporter of normalization remarked, "Our global position is one of the vanguards, the protector of the Western world." For most members the notion of protecting the Western world meant two things. First, it meant maintaining the pattern of United States economic dominance over Third World countries: a senior member who favored normalization said that Cuba would be a threat to American interests "to the extent that Cuba . . . exports or seeks to export a revolution elsewhere in Latin America." Such an effort, he said, would be "a threat to stability and I think that our interests generally lie in stability." In another sense, protecting the Western world meant supporting those countries that hold open elections and that permit the operation of a privately owned press. One proponent, who had worked actively against American support of Third World dictatorships, felt that the United States should attempt to build "a more hospitable environment for the values we profess . . . a political system that we could identify with."

Taken together, the members' varied comments about United States Cuba policy indicate that during the period from 1971 to 1975 they perceived a problem that needed attention and an administration unwilling to act appropriately. After 1975, perceptions of the problem were less clear, as were perceptions of the appropriate solution. Interviews also indicate that members were motivated to act on the problem by three sets of interests—personal, institutional, and national—and that when the three coincided—for example, when a member gained prestige, fulfilled a committee responsibility, and contributed to the national interest by working toward resolution of the problem—a member's activity increased. Such a formula is highly speculative and necessarily imprecise because each component rests on its subjective evaluation by a member of Congress. Scholars have described quite sensitively how the first two components affect the motivations of members: the third is often missing.

A member's perception of a "problem" and of the national interest are linked, and both reflect the environment in which Congress operates. To understand how Congress behaves and how the members perceive their behavior, it is important to understand also the nature of the environment that generates the problems on which they act. In the case of relations with Cuba, the international environment was most relevant, and Chapter 4 explores this context.

NOTES

1. David Halberstam, *The Best and the Brightest* (New York: Random House, 1972), pp. 66–67.

2. According to a 1975 U.S. Commerce Department report, one half of the sugar industry was controlled by the United States in 1927. In the early 1930s, 22 percent of Cuban land and 90 percent of its electrical generating capacity were owned by American companies. See Arthur Downey, "United States Commercial Relations with Cuba: A Survey," reprinted as Appendix VI, U.S. Congress, House Committee on International Relations, "U.S. Trade Embargo of Cuba: Hearings on H.R. 6382," 94th Cong. 1st Sess., May, June, July, September, 1975, p. 586.

3. In 1958, 71 percent of Cuba's exports went to the United States and 64 percent of its

imports came from the United States. Fifty-eight percent of Cuba's sugar exports were sent to the United States. See "United States Commercial Relations with Cuba," pp. 588, 621–622. Also see Carmelo Mesa-Lago, *The Economy of Socialist Cuba: A Two-Decade Appraisal* (Albuquerque: University of New Mexico Press, 1981), p. 8.

4. Mesa-Lago, *The Economy of Socialist Cuba,* p. 70.
5. Martin Carnoy and Jorge Wertheim, "Cuba: Economic Change and Educational Reform: 1955–1974," World Bank Staff Working Paper No. 317, January 1979 (Washington, D.C.: The World Bank, 1979), p. 13.
6. Hugh Thomas, *The Cuban Revolution* (New York: Harper & Row, 1977), p. 390. Thomas also details that by 1953, 80 percent of Cuba's public railways were foreign-owned (p. 379), the Electric Bond and Share Company of New York "had a virtual electrical monopoly" (p. 385), and a handful of foreign banks held over 40 percent of the deposits in Cuban banks, though this was down from 80 percent in 1939 (pp. 402–403). One Cuban historian reports that American enterprises earned $700 million in profit between 1946 and 1956, of which only $100 million was re-invested: Julio Le Riverend, *Economic History of Cuba,* trans. Maria Juana Cazabon and Homero Leon (Havana: Ensayo Book Institute, 1967), pp. 250–251.
7. Thomas, *The Cuban Revolution,* p. 402. Direct American investment in 1958 controlled one third of Cuba's public utilities; in the Cuban mining and manufacturing sectors sales by American-owned firms exceeded one quarter of Cuba's GNP. See "United States Commercial Relations with Cuba," p. 588.
8. Thomas, *The Cuban Revolution,* pp. 311, 313–314, 323, 351. In 1958, Arthur MacEwan reports, "less than 10 percent of the rural homes were electrified, and less than 3 percent had any indoor plumbing." *Revolution and Economic Development in Cuba* (New York: St. Martin's, 1981), p. 19. Also see Mesa-Lago, *The Economy of Socialist Cuba,* pp. 9–10.
9. Thomas reports estimates of 11,500 prostitutes in Havana during the 1950s: "The prostitutes . . . were so numerous as to resemble a cattle market. The Prado . . . led up the centre of the old city, lined also with bootblacks, waiting taxis and beggars." *The Cuban Revolution,* p. 315. Also see Jorge I. Dominguez, *Cuba: Order and Revolution* (Cambridge, Mass.: Harvard University Press, 1978), pp. 91–93.
10. Herbert Matthews, *Revolution in Cuba* (New York: Scribner's, 1975) is an outstanding narrative about Cuba since 1900.
11. Theodore Draper, *Castro's Revolution: Myths and Realities* (New York: Praeger, 1963), Chapter 1.
12. Peter Wyden, *Bay of Pigs: The Untold Story* (New York: Simon and Schuster, 1979).
13. Christy Macy, "Terrorism: A Legacy of the CIA's Secret War Against Cuba," in Patricia Weiss Fagen, "Toward Détente With Cuba: Issues and Obstacles," *International Policy Report* (Washington, D.C.: Center for International Policy, November 1977), pp. 9–14. Also see U.S. Congress, Senate Select Committee to Study Governmental Operations with Respect to Intelligence Activities, "Alleged Assassination Plots Involving Foreign Leaders: An Interim Report," 94th Cong., 1st Sess., 20 November 1975, pp. 71–180. Also see Taylor Branch and George Crile III, "The Kennedy Vendetta," *Harper's,* August 1975, pp. 49–63.
14. Undersecretary of State George Ball spoke of denying Cuba "those categories of goods that are most vital to the operation of the Cuban economy." See "Principles of Our Policy Toward Cuba," *Department of State Bulletin,* 11 May 1964, p. 738, as quoted in Roger W. Fontaine, *On Negotiating With Cuba* (Washington, D.C.: American Enterprise Institute, 1975), p. 49. See also Bertram Gross, "Prepared Statement," in "U.S. Trade Embargo of Cuba," pp. 68–69.
15. Abraham Chayes, *The Cuban Missile Crisis* (New York: Oxford University Press, 1974); Graham Allison, *Essence of Decision: Explaining the Cuban Missile Crisis* (Boston: Little, Brown, 1971); Robert F. Kennedy, *Thirteen Days: A Memoir of the Cuban Missile Crisis* (New York: Norton, 1969); Matthews, *Revolution in Cuba,* Chapter 9.
16. Herbert S. Dinerstein, *The Making of a Missile Crisis: October 1962* (Baltimore: Johns Hopkins University Press, 1976), p. 229. Also see "Alleged Assassination Plots . . . ," pp. 134–35, 147–148.

17. Barry A. Sklar, "Cuba: Normalization of Relations," Congressional Research Service, Library of Congress, Issue Brief Number IB 75030 (1978).
18. David B. Truman, *The Governmental Process* (New York: Alfred A. Knopf, 1951), pp. 372–377.
19. Barry A. Sklar, "Congress and the Normalization of Relations with Cuba, 1971–1977," a paper presented before the Latin American Studies Association Annual Meeting, Houston, November 1977.
20. U.S. Congress, Senate Committee on Foreign Relations, "United States Policy Toward Cuba: Hearing," 92nd Cong., 1st Sess., 16 September 1971.
21. Charles Whalen, et al., "A Détente with Cuba," mimeo, 29 January 1973. The report was drafted by Bill Richardson, who was then on the staff of the Wednesday Group.
22. Burdette A. Loomis, "Congressional Caucuses and the Politics of Representation," in Lawrence C. Dodd and Bruce I. Oppenheimer, eds., *Congress Reconsidered*, 2nd ed. (Washington, D.C.: CQ Press, 1981). Also see Leonard Apcar, "House Scrutinizes 'Caucuses,' Often Run Like Lobbies," *Wall Street Journal*, 21 September 1981, p. 40.
23. Robert L. Peabody, *Leadership in Congress* (Boston: Little, Brown, 1976), Chapter 4. On the Wednesday Group, see John M. Elliott, "Communications and Small Groups in Congress: The Case of Republicans in the House of Representatives" (Ph.D. diss., Johns Hopkins University, 1974).
24. U.S. Congress, Senate Subcommittee on Western Hemisphere Affairs of the Foreign Relations Committee, "U.S. Policy Towards Cuba: Hearings," 93rd Cong., 1st Sess., 26 March, 18 April 1973, p. 1.
25. While they were there, CBS correspondent Dan Rather was in Havana to prepare a documentary on Cuba, and he covered their visit. The documentary was produced and filmed by Frank Mankiewicz, Kirby Jones, and Saul Landau. See Frank Mankiewicz and Kirby Jones, *With Fidel* (New York: Ballantine Books, 1975). The senators' visit was preceded by a trip that the Senate Foreign Relations Committee staff director, Pat Holt, made in June 1974. Holt had attempted to obtain State Department permission to visit Cuba since 1971 and received it only in 1974. In a staff report, he recommended lifting the blockade and initiating steps towards a resumption of relations. See U.S. Congress, Senate Committee on Foreign Relations, "Cuba: A Staff Report," 93rd Cong., 2nd Sess., 2 August 1974.
26. See Norman J. Ornstein, "Causes and Consequences of Congressional Change: Subcommittee Reforms in the House of Representatives," in Norman J. Ornstein, ed., *Congress in Change* (New York: Praeger, 1974), pp. 90–100. Also see David Rohde, "Committee Reform in the House of Representatives and the Subcommittee Bill of Rights," *The Annals*, 411 (January 1974).
27. "U.S. Trade Embargo of Cuba," pp. 51–62, 263–273, 376–384.
28. U.S. Congress, House Committee on International Relations, Subcommittee on International Trade and Commerce, "U.S.–Cuba Trade and Trade Promotion: Hearing," 94th Cong., 2nd Sess., 22 July 1976.
29. Fred Hoffman, "Pentagon Reviewing Plans for Action Against Cuba," *Miami Herald*, 26 March 1976.
30. This was not the first post-election congressional trip to Cuba. In November, Senators James Abourezk (D–S.D.) and Floyd Haskell (D–Colo.) traveled there. But in light of Bingham's withdrawal of support in late 1975, his visit took on greater significance. See his report, "Toward Improved United States–Cuba Relations," Report of a Special Study Mission to Cuba, 23 May 1977. Committee Print, House International Relations Committee, 95th Cong., 1st Sess.
31. In October, Bingham proposed "that the United States initiate discussions that might lead to a Helsinki type agreement" with Cuba. It would be, he said, "an approach [that] offers hope of progress within a reasonable time." *Congressional Record* (daily edition), 6 October 1977, p. H10731.
32. Sklar, "Congress and the Normalization of Relations with Cuba," p. 25.
33. Ibid., p. 26.
34. *Congressional Record*, 16 June 1977, p. S19438.
35. Personal interview with an official in the Cuban Ministry of Foreign Relations, July 1977.

36. This interpretation was encouraged by the amendment's sponsor, John Ashbrook (R–Ohio). He said: "There is within the Senate a very determined effort to remove prohibitions against trade and aid to Cuba and Vietnam. We should not sit back in the House and let the senior Senator from South Dakota [McGovern] be spokesman on foreign policy." *Washington Post,* 13 May 1977, p. A1.

37. Karen DeYoung, "Castro to Permit Americans' Kin to Leave Cuba," *Washington Post,* 12 August 1977, p. A16. Also see "Church's Cuban Visit Labeled a Significant Change in Relations," *Miami Herald,* 9 August 1977, p. A8.

38. However, in light of beet-sugar producer pressures, his recommendation was weaker than that of others. See "Delusions and Reality: The Future of United States–Cuba Relations," Report to the Senate Committee on Foreign Relations, Committee Print, October 1977, p. 10.

39. Congressional Quarterly *Weekly Report,* 1 July 1978, p. 1682. Also see Gail Reed, "The United States and Cuba: 'Normal Relations'?", *Cuba Update,* no. 2, February 1978 (New York: Center for Cuban Studies, 1978), p. 6.

40. From May to August 1976, nineteen of the twenty-three were interviewed directly, and the information about the other four members was obtained from interviews with key, long-term foreign policy aides to these members. In all, eighteen staff members were interviewed. The interviews were part of a study reported as: Philip Brenner and R. Roger Majak, "Congressmen as Statesmen: The Case of Cuba," delivered at the 1976 Annual Meeting of the American Political Science Association, Chicago, Illinois, 2–5 September 1976.

41. In a well-detailed and provocative study of congressional coalitions, Jerrold E. Schneider has argued that members rely on unidimensional ideological frameworks in addressing both domestic and foreign policy issues. While he suggests that ideology has a causal impact on the members' behavior, a less ambitious claim is made here that members see themselves in terms of ideological categories and might attempt to maintain consistency in their presentation of self. See *Ideological Coalitions in Congress* (Westport, Conn.: Greenwood Press, 1979), Chapters 3, 5.

42. Congressional Quarterly *Weekly Report,* 22 May 1976, pp. 1291–1293. The ratings were for 1975, the year of greatest congressional activity in favor of relations. John W. Kingdon has demonstrated that ADA and ACA scores "are nearly true reciprocals" when trichotomized, and thus only ADA scores are reported here. *Congressmen's Voting Decisions* (New York: Harper & Row, 1973), p. 292.

43. Brenner and Majak, "Congressmen as Statesmen," p. 9. From 1975 to 1977 the official name of the full committee was the House Committee on International Relations.

44. Thomas Franck and Edward Weisband, *Foreign Policy by Congress* (New York: Oxford University Press, 1979), introduction; Randall B. Ripley, *Congress: Process and Policy,* 2nd ed. (New York: Norton, 1978), pp. 380–381.

45. Fenno, *Congressmen in Committees,* p. 11.

46. The notion of "Washington community" is Richard Neustadt's shorthand for characterizing the Washington press corps and high-level government officials who dominate elite opinion in the capital. See *Presidential Power* (New York: Wiley, 1960), Chapter 4.

47. Commission on United States–Latin America Relations, *The Americas in a Changing World* (New York: Quadrangle, 1975).

4 Foreign Policy: Towards Normal Relations with Cuba—the International Context

Congressional policy towards Cuba did not develop in a vacuum: legislators make history "under the given and inherited circumstances with which they are directly confronted."[1] Their views, decisions, and behavior in connection with Cuba policy were shaped through the 1970s by the flow of events outside Congress, by resources and mechanisms that limited their options, and by preceding decisions or actions. Legislators also responded to vague pressures and attempted to anticipate events that produced such pressures. But Cuba policy and its seesaw quality were too complex to be explained simply in terms of mechanical responses to pressures. This chapter examines how the environment outside Congress affected congressional policy. Understanding the way in which the environment related to Congress's behavior enables consideration of how this case represented what some analysts have characterized as a new role for Congress in making foreign policy.

The Context of Congressional Policy

Many political scientists think of the environment as a variable, as something producing tangible and identifiable influences that sway Congress. In a discussion of the external environment, therefore, you might expect that a set of independent variables—labeled "environmental variables"—would be used to test the impact of the environment on Congress. This approach can yield insights, but it is not the only way to analyze the environment. One can also see the environment as a set of conditions to which Congress must relate in broad fashion if it chooses to act. In this indirect way, the environment affects what Congress does. There may be no direct input into Congress from interest groups or constituents. Congress may choose to act in response to its own concern with the environment. Such a situation is suggested by David Easton's notion of "withinputs"[2] and by Richard Fenno's report that some members of Congress shape their behavior as a result of having an interest in making "good public policy."[3] But neither Easton nor Fenno probed this phenomenon in terms of a particular policy. To do so, the peculiar nature of the congressional environment in each case must be examined, because the environment is not an ahistorical, unchanging variable distinct from Congress. Congress is part of the environment: it helps shape the environment to which it responds.

In reviewing the context of congressional Cuban policy from 1971 to 1978, the international environment is critical. As internal affairs in the United States increasingly come to revolve around international affairs, much that Congress does is related to events outside the United States. In the case of Cuba the imperative for change arose from changes in the international context. These changes fall roughly into three chronological periods that correspond with the congressional policy shifts covered in the last chapter.

The International Context, 1971–1975

The international economy. Prosperity in the United States after World War II derived from a combination of inexpensive energy, an unscathed industrial capacity that enabled the United States to export surplus goods and to keep prices relatively low at home, and the expansion of multinational corporations abroad that allowed them to earn high profits on foreign operations and to increase their domestic workers' wages. But it was a fragile prosperity.

As other countries regained their industrial capacity, they were able to compete successfully with American companies. American companies had not reinvested sufficiently in plant and equipment, and many had used their capital for wasteful diversification and for investment in other countries. Many had relied on military spending for domestic profit—on a single-source buyer who would pay cost plus profit, regardless of the price. The military budget also shifted production into areas that created too few jobs and generated inflation.[4] By the late 1940s, America's love affair with the automobile had become cruel dependence, as nearly one fifth of all jobs in the United States directly or indirectly involved automobile production. Dependence on the automobile was cushioned by inexpensive energy, which encouraged increased use. The daily life of millions changed as new highways opened up suburbs, and cars became necessities for daily commutation to work, for shopping, and even for visiting neighbors.

The first signs that postwar American prosperity may have been a fleeting phenomenon came in the mid-1960s. In the late 1950s the economy had stagnated, and the 1958 recession had been severe. But only in the 1960s did economists begin to appreciate that there were structural problems in the international economy that would fundamentally affect the United States. At this time the balance-of-payments deficit (the extent to which imports exceed exports) became chronic, and in 1964 the United States instituted a series of controls on capital flow out of the United States.[5] At the same time Britain was suffering a severe balance-of-payments problem that threatened the stability of the pound. As many banks and corporations held pounds, instability of the pound could undermine their economic health. The United States needed to bolster the British currency through purchases, which created a speculative run on the dollar.

By the early 1970s, speculation in the dollar by multinational corporations had become so great that it was no longer a stable currency. The weaker dollar disrupted international trade and had a profound inflationary impact on the domestic American economy.[6] In part the dollar had been weakened by massive spending on the Vietnam War ($80 million a day at its height) that inflated the economy through a budget deficit, sent money abroad, and encouraged speculators to increase their attack on the dollar.[7]

People experienced the monetary crisis as a recession that featured, for the first time, a combination of high unemployment and inflation. While the monetary crisis and the new form of recession troubled policymakers, what troubled them more was the banking crisis of the early 1970s. As a Senate staff study reported, worry about the international banking system "intensified in the wake of major bank failures in Europe and in the United States."[8] Difficult as it may be to imagine, a collapse of the international banking system in the 1970s threatened to plunge the world economy into a depression greater than that of the 1930s. The boundary between major banks and major corporations had become indistinguishable, as banks held essential control of much corporate wealth.[9] With Japan exerting enormous competitive pressure on American corporations, with multinational corporations wrecking the value of the dollar through speculation and foreign investments, and with inflation generating increased demands from labor at home for higher wages, the anarchy of the international capitalist economy had become intolerable. The dramatic increase in oil prices in 1973 twisted the knife in an already tottering beast and toppled the assumption of inexpensive energy on which the United States had based its earlier prosperity. This crisis would not go away with benign neglect and it required a serious response.[10] Development of the Third World held out the hope of solution.

Throughout the 1960s, United States–based multinational corporations expanded their activities in the Third World and began to take in large profits. For example, Fred Block reports that between 1965 and 1971 returns on investments in Latin America and the Middle East accounted for 75 percent of all balance-of-payments gains made in the period, including those made from investments in the industrialized countries, where 60 percent of U.S. investments had been made.[11] Returns on small foreign investments were large often because the companies used local sources of financing, for which they could unfairly compete against local companies.[12] The multinationals also tended to enhance their profit picture by buying up small companies and developing near-monopolies in some sectors. In Mexico and Brazil, for example, 80 percent of the sales of American multinationals were in markets that were controlled by four or fewer firms. In the chemicals, rubber, machinery, and transportation-equipment sectors, multinationals on the average accounted for a 70 percent share of the market.[13] They also tended to favor those countries where the labor force was unorganized or had weak unions in order to keep wages low and strikes to a minimum.[14]

A pliable labor force in developing countries was a concern of the corporations when they expanded operations during the early 1970s, in response to the international economic crisis. In the name of political stability, President Ferdinand Marcos of the Philippines declared martial law in 1972 and outlawed strikes. And most infamously, in 1973 a bloody coup in Chile—indirectly, if not directly, supported by the United States—overthrew the democratic government of Salvador Allende Gossens.[15] While murdering thousands of innocent civilians randomly,[15] the new government headed by Augusto Pinochet also focused on union members and leaders. Sustained repression in Chile became a part of an economic-development plan that brought in new investment from multinational corporations.[16]

The Third World became more important to multinational banks and corporations in the 1970s as they saw there part of the solution to the crisis. By 1975, economist Howard Wachtel reports, the twelve largest American banks derived 63 percent of their total income from the activities of foreign branches, in contrast to 23 percent in 1971.[17] Banks channeled some of their capital into developing countries, where they saw the promise of unloading excess funds that were undesired by developed countries and of reaping high profits from relatively short-term loans. However, Third World demand for the funds was neither fortuitous nor fortunate. The pattern of development that the multinational corporations had encouraged in the 1960s left the developing nations dependent on advanced capitalist countries for most of their basic goods.[18] They had to import these goods with scarce foreign exchange, at prices that rose steadily with inflation, while the price they received for the commodities they exported remained low.[19] They were thus forced to turn to Western banks for loans, and as a result, developing countries went so deeply into debt that they had to use large portions of their export earnings merely to pay off the interest on their new loans from multinational banks.[20]

Not all of the troubles for Third World countries could be attributed to multinational corporations. The oil price increase in 1973 also hurt these countries, especially in cases where agricultural production had been altered to make use of petroleum-based fertilizers. But many developing countries withheld criticism of the Organization of Petroleum Exporting Countries (OPEC), because they saw in OPEC an example of what they hoped to do themselves. Indeed, at the 1976 summit of nonaligned countries—attended by eighty-six countries, almost all of which were less developed—consensus was achieved on a declaration that called for "the strengthening and supporting of existing Producers' Associations and the application by them of effective methods of operation in order to secure just and remunerative prices for their export products."[21] They hoped that this would be the basis of the Third World response to an international economic order that favored advanced capitalist countries. In 1973, for example, the United States imported 96 percent of its cobalt, 100 percent of its natural rubber, 87 percent of its tin, and 72 percent of its nickel.[22] With producer cartels of these basic materials, Third World countries could gain a degree of commodity power that might allow them to challenge the hegemony of the more developed countries. They envisioned the creation of a new international economic order in which poorly endowed countries would be assisted through regional integration with nations that had abundant natural resources, developing nations would trade among themselves without unfair advantage, and the Third World would be able to achieve internal development by extracting high prices from the advanced countries.[23]

Talk of this new international economic order was taken quite seriously in the West, where it was seen as a threat—in part because Western leaders recognized that Third World countries were responding to pressures that the advanced capitalist countries had created.[24] Less developed countries appeared to have stopped cowering before the multinationals and to have begun to seek to manipulate them. Changes in Latin America signaled this shift for many Western leaders, who sensed an end of the "special relationship" American companies once enjoyed with countries there.

The healthy growth rate in Latin America was little affected by the worldwide recession and enabled countries there to increase their imports. Much of the new importation came from countries other than the United States: whereas Latin America took 40 percent of its imports from the United States in the 1960s, the rate declined to 30 percent in the early 1970s. Japan and Europe were quickly replacing the United States.[25] The growing independence of Latin America had a political dimension, too, that troubled many American policymakers, who saw it as part of a larger pattern. Though President Nixon had warned that the United States could not act as if it were a "pitiless, helpless giant," United States hegemony over many Third World countries seemed to be vanishing quickly.[26] Stalemate in Vietnam, and subsequent American withdrawal, indicated that troops would not be committed easily to such wars in the future. The Caribbean had once been considered firmly in the American sphere of influence, but in 1972 three West Indian countries—Jamaica, Barbados, and Trinidad and Tobago—joined Guyana to break the OAS embargo, establishing trade as well as diplomatic relations with Cuba. Perhaps more troublesome to Washington policymakers, one of the first actions in 1970 of the democratically elected Chilean administration of President Allende was to recognize Cuba. Using constitutional procedures, the Allende government subsequently nationalized the holdings of American corporations in Chile.[27]

The American response to events in Chile brought the United States more disrespect than appreciation in Latin America, even in countries unsympathetic to the Marxist Allende government. Evident American complicity in the military coup that overthrew Allende recalled the 1965 invasion of the Dominican Republic, when the United States sent 22,000 marines to the island to "restore order."[28] United States policy towards Latin America appeared to be little more than automatic, heavy-handed anti-Communism—a stance that insulted Latin Americans in general by continuing to treat them as dependents. Latin Americans had ceased to see Cuba as a threat to the hemisphere, and they considered American insistence on the embargo against Cuba as a symbol of what was wrong with United States policy. By 1975 eight OAS members had recognized Cuba, and three more had begun discussions about resuming relations. In November 1974, at a meeting called to discuss Cuba, a majority of the countries in the OAS voted to lift the embargo against Cuba. The United States abstained, and the resolution failed when it did not gain two-thirds of the vote, but in July 1975 the OAS finally voted to lift the embargo by permitting each nation to establish with Cuba whatever relations it deemed appropriate.

The domestic context vis à vis the international environment. Set against this international environment, several circumstances in the domestic context encouraged Congress to alter United States policy towards Cuba. These changes included the shift in attitude of the Nixon and Ford Administrations, pressures from the United States–based multinational corporations, and decreased hostility to Cuba measured in public-opinion polls.

Some members of Congress attributed the intransigence of the Nixon administration to the president's pique with Fidel Castro. At the United Nations in 1960, the Cuban leader allegedly had snubbed then–Vice President Nixon. Other legislators pointed to the close friendship between the president and Bebe Rebozo, a Cuban exile who shared with some of his compatriots in Florida a continuing commitment to rid Cuba of socialism. Whatever its source, policy towards Cuba during the Nixon years generally reflected the president's view that Castro had not moved "one inch from his determination" to export revolution and that relations with Cuba were not possible because "Cuba is engaged in a constant program of belligerence toward us."[29]

Despite this apparently firm stance, the administration took a few small steps in 1973 and 1974 to diminish official hostility towards Cuba. In February 1973 it signed a "Memorandum of Understanding" with Cuba, whereby both countries agreed to prosecute airline hijackers who sought refuge in either country and to prevent acts of terror against each other's airlines. Later in the year, the United States relaxed the blockade ever so slightly when it permitted the Big Three American auto-makers to export to Cuba cars that they manufactured in Argentina. And in the spring of 1974, Secretary of State Henry Kissinger granted approval for a trip to Cuba by Pat Holt, the staff director of the Senate Foreign Relations Committee. Holt's June visit became the forerunner for several trips by members of Congress. The Secretary of State had denied nearly all previous requests for approval of such trips to Cuba.

Though positive, these steps were limited and taken in response to immediate pressures. The hijacking agreement was initiated by Cuba and was in the interest of both countries in the wake of a series of hijacking incidents. In the case of General Motors, Ford, and Chrysler, Argentina had demanded in August 1973 that the companies be permitted to sell their Argentina output to Cuba in order to boost the economy of Argentina.[30] Argentina was a key ally in the "southern cone" of South America. Holt's request was approved at a point when the president's and Kissinger's support in the Senate was eroding, and it was seen as a modest effort to decrease tensions with Congress. Overall, the administration stood against normalization. In light of efforts to achieve détente with the Soviet Union, and inasmuch as Cuba was a close Soviet ally, the continuing hostility towards Cuba was all the more noticeable. The small steps were best characterized by Deputy Assistant Secretary of State for Inter-American Affairs Robert Hurwitch, when he remarked that such actions only "demonstrated our pragmatism. . . . There are no grounds for seeking accommodation. . . . Cuba has through its own policies and actions outlawed itself from the hemisphere."[31]

The assumption of the presidency by Gerald Ford changed this stance, and he signaled a new approach within a month of taking office. In September 1974—as Senators Pell and Javits were traveling to Cuba—the new president appointed William D. Rogers, a liberal lawyer from the prominent Washington firm of Arnold and Porter, to be Assistant Secretary of State for Inter-American Affairs. Prior to his appointment, Rogers had publicly advocated a normalization of relations with Cuba.

Senators Javits and Pell recommended, upon their return to Washington, that the United States relax the travel restrictions for Cuban diplomats at the United Nations. At the time, Cuban delegates to the UN were permitted to travel only within a 25-mile radius of UN headquarters. The new Assistant Secretary appeared to seize upon this proposal to provide a sign of goodwill, and in early 1975 the United States extended the travel limitation to a 250-mile radius. Beneath the surface of this gesture, moreover, was an even greater indication of willingness to change the course of United States policy. Secretly, Rogers had begun to meet with a small group of Cuban officials in the late fall of 1974 at airports and in a New York hotel. The travel extension was intended to facilitate these discussions.[32]

The talks covered narrow issues, such as the release of United States citizens being held on drug-related charges. But they also examined fundamental issues that stood in the way of a resumption of full relations, including the economic blockade. In part the talks paved the way for a decision, announced on August 21, 1975, to remove prohibitions on the sale of all goods to Cuba that were produced by American companies in "third" countries. This generalized the policy that had been established in the case of the auto companies in Argentina, and also in the case of United States-based Litton Industries, whose Canadian subsidiary had obtained permission to trade with Cuba in 1974. The August 21 announcement also brought the United States into concert with a protocol adopted by the OAS on July 25, lifting the embargo against Cuba. Notably, the United States voted with the two-thirds majority to lift the OAS embargo.

At the same time, a new set of lobbyists had entered the picture. Traditionally, there had been few interest groups devoted to the issue of United States–Cuban relations. In Miami and in a few other areas of Florida, organizations of Cuban exiles made quite clear their opposition to relations. But their influence had been concentrated in only a handful of congressional districts, and they further lost influence because of the dogmatism with which they usually presented their views.

In the early 1970s, representatives of large corporations and major financial institutions began to argue that trade and ultimately diplomatic relations with Cuba were desirable. For example, in the preface to a

major private commission report on Latin America, chairman Sol Linowitz called for a restructuring of American policy towards Latin America:

> Many of my colleagues . . . came to the same conclusion: that the fundamen-
> tal changes which have taken place in the world, within Latin America, and
> in the United States in recent years make timely—and indeed urgent—a
> reordering of relationships in this hemisphere.[33]

Linowitz was a former United States Ambassador to the OAS,
former chairman of the board of Xerox Corporation, and a partner in the
law firm of Coudert Brothers, which represented several multinational
corporations. His colleagues on the commission—which came to be
known as the Linowitz Commission—included W. Michael Blumenthal,
chairman of the Bendix Corporation (later Secretary of the Treasury);
G. A. Costanzo, vice chairman of the First National City Bank; Charles
Meyer, vice president of Sears, Roebuck and Company; Henry J. Heinz
II, chairman of the H. J. Heinz Company; and Peter Peterson, chairman
of the investment banking firm of Lehman Brothers. The Linowitz Commission report was released late in 1974 and urged that the United States
"should take the initiative in seeking a more normal relationship with
Cuba," and that it should "act now to end the trade embargo."[34]

Their voices were added to demands by officials of organized labor—
especially to that of United Auto Workers President Leonard Woodcock
in February 1974—that the economic blockade be lifted. Labor leaders
feared that trade with Cuba by Latin American and Canadian subsidiaries
of American companies might result in a loss of jobs in the United States.
They were also concerned about the loss of jobs to companies in Japan
and other capitalist countries.

Indeed, the 300 percent rise in sugar prices on the world market in
1973 and 1974 had permitted Cuba to increase its purchases from capitalist countries by 250 percent.[35] Though Cuba received no credits from IFIs
such as the International Monetary Fund, it did receive bilateral credits.
In 1976 it even received a $17 million loan from a consortium of Japanese
banks. As Professor Bertram Gross explained to a House subcommittee
in 1975, Cuba had been a potentially good market for American goods—
especially for replacement parts—because its infrastructure had been built
before 1959 with American equipment. But that market was eroding by
1975 because equipment from other countries was being used to develop
the island.[36]

Growing corporate and governmental interest in normalizing relations with Cuba undoubtedly had an impact on public opinion about
Cuba, and in turn the changed public opinion removed one obstacle in
the movement towards normalization. In contrast to broad United States

hostility towards Cuba in the 1960s, a February 1973 Gallup Poll found that 71 percent of those sampled would favor "sending Henry Kissinger to Cuba to try to improve our relations with that country." Only 19 percent opposed such an initiative.[37]

What impact such opinion had on Congress is of course difficult to assess. Public opinion on an issue is an imprecise factor that members of Congress may take into account in shaping their behavior. At times a member may use adverse public opinion as an excuse for inaction, when in fact the member had chosen inaction on other grounds. Foreign-policy issues are especially prone to such manipulation, because legislators sense that foreign policy does not preoccupy most citizens, although they recognize that in some cases there are particular segments of the public that monitor foreign policy closely and can retaliate at election time. Ethnic groups, for example, tend to be concerned about policies towards their "homelands." And during the post-Vietnam era, foreign policy in general has made a greater claim on the public's consciousness than it did during the 1950s and even much of the 1960s; more people than before recognize how international actions can affect their daily lives. Thus members approach foreign-policy issues with some ambivalence. They sense that there is some space for manipulation, but they also are wary about ignoring public opinion as they once did on foreign-policy issues.

Public opinion about Cuba was shaped by a variety of influences, and it is no more than speculation to attribute attitudes about normalization to particular sources. Some factors, however, are undeniably significant.

Until the early 1970s, revolutionary Cuba was shrouded in mystery for the public at large. There had been scholarly studies of the country, but rumors propagated by Cuban exiles—that the country had become a colorless, cold, police state—dominated the public's perceptions. Tourist travel began to alter that picture. The first tourists were Canadian and Western European, but by 1975 tours had been arranged for American medical and public-health professionals, lawyers, social scientists, and educators.

At the same time, Cuba began to permit large numbers of American journalists to visit and report from the island. Stories appeared in nearly every major weekly and monthly magazine, from *Newsweek* to *National Geographic*. They depicted the strides made in rural development, the extensive construction of new schools and health-care facilities, the equitable distribution of food and housing, and above all, the exuberant spirit of the Cuban people. The stories undermined the tales told by exiles, whose credibility was further eroded by reports of exile terrorist activity. The 1975 Senate study on American attempts to assassinate foreign leaders implicated Cuban expatriots.[38]

A failed policy. The failure of United States policy towards Cuba became clear during the early 1970s. The initial policy had been intended to generate internal pressure against the Cuban government by isolating the island and strangling it with an embargo that might have closed off markets for Cuba's sugar and prevented the country from importing necessary supplies.[39] Cuba had survived enormous hardhips in the 1960s. By 1975 it could provide a liter of milk for every child on the island; it had virtually eradicated all epidemic diseases and was training more doctors than were needed in the country; 98 percent of the population had achieved literacy and a third of the people were actively engaged in some form of schooling; paved rural roads, new housing, new towns, and light industries characterized its internal development.[40] In 1974 Cuba held elections in Matanzas province, and in 1975—after year-long, country-wide deliberations—the first Congress of the Communist Party proposed a new constitution (which was ratified in 1976) that provided for the institutionalization and decentralization of power into local elected assemblies.[41] To be sure, Cuba was still an underdeveloped country, as the 1980 exodus from Mariel later made evident. It still was sustained mainly by its production of sugar, and it continued to have problems in housing and food production. But Cuba had developed past the point where an American embargo could topple the regime.

Not only had the policy failed but it had the effect of isolating the United States from the rest of the hemisphere. In OAS meetings, member countries saw the United States as an irrational child with its finger in the dike, holding back the tide of Latin American sentiment in favor of normalization. The issue of normalized relations had become both symbolic of American imperialism and an unnecessary obstacle to harmonious relations between the United States and Latin American countries. As sovereign hemispheric countries sought trade with Cuba, they felt constrained by American regulations, which restricted even the Third World subsidiaries of American corporations from trading with Cuba. The United States, for example, had angered Argentina by preventing American-owned Argentine companies from exporting goods to Cuba when trade would have been beneficial to both countries and was legal according to Argentine law.

From the perspective of the companies, the symbolism of American imperialism hurt. It nurtured anti-American sentiment in Latin America, and the companies feared that in response to popular pressures, Latin American governments might attack them through controls. Moreover, the multinational corporations had grown so powerful that host countries were looking for excuses to curb their influence.[42]

These companies were also a growing concern to the United States government. Their independence and resources allowed them to act in ways that affected American foreign policy. In effect they had become states unto themselves, and as such were a threat to the sovereignty and power of the United States. To protect its own state interests, the United States government needed to relate to other sovereign states directly to control the multinationals, but the obstacle of American Cuba policy impeded such state-to-state relations.[43]

During this period, Cuba also initiated a series of measures designed to ease tensions with the United States. These measures were especially significant in light of the hostile embargo, which Cuba previously had said was an obstacle to the initiation of any talks on the normalization of relations. Included among the measures were invitations extended to a large number of legislators and congressional staff members to visit the island. In the year following the September 1974 trip by Senators Javits and Pell, two more senators, three representatives, and more than twenty staff members traveled to Cuba.[44] As noted, Cuba also responded positively to several executive branch invitations, such as the 1973 hijacking agreement.

Thus a combination of events led almost inexorably to a new American policy towards Cuba. The international economic crisis made Latin America more important to the United States, while the growing sense of American impotence encouraged the United States to readjust its relations with Latin America. Pressures from corporations combined with a new willingness by the public to open relations with socialist countries. In such a situation, where a broad array of national and international interests are involved, the executive typically initiates and supervises policy. But in this case, the executive seemed unwilling to confront the full dimensions of the problem and acted haltingly. This context did not *force* Congress to act. Circumstances in the 1971 to 1975 period, however, both *encouraged* Congress to act and *shaped* the way it behaved once it did act.

The International Context, 1976

Events in 1976 reversed the drive towards normalization. The circumstances that had encouraged Congress to pursue better relations with Cuba changed, and a new set of circumstances emerged that engendered new hostility. In terms of congressional policy towards Cuba, the year 1976 began in the summer of 1975.

Throughout the summer, Congress was still driving headlong towards lifting the embargo. As late as September, a conservative Louisiana representative, John Breaux, traveled to Havana to explore the possibility of selling his constituents' rice to Cuba. On the surface, it seemed as if normalization were a sure bet.

Beneath the surface the situation was altered, although this did not become clear until 1976. When the Organization of American States lifted its embargo against Cuba in July 1975 and the State Department announced in August that the United States would permit "third country" subsidiaries of large American corporations to trade with Cuba, it removed three spurs that were prodding the normalization movement. First, Latin American countries ceased to complain that the United States was dictating to them what their Cuba policies should be. Collaterally, it diminished slightly the image of the United States as the hemispheric Big Brother. Third, the demands of American corporations to be able to break into the Cuban market were partially satisfied as they saw the possibility of sales from their foreign subsidiaries.

At the same time, foreign troops began to enter the civil war in Angola, and the United States and Cuba supported opposite sides. Angola gained its independence from Portugal in 1975, after fourteen years of a struggle that had been waged by three forces in the colony: the Popular Movement for the Liberation of Angola (MPLA), the oldest and the leading group in the fight, the National Front for the Liberation of Angola (FNLA), and the National Union for the Total Liberation of Angola (UNITA). When Portugal agreed to leave Angola, the FNLA and UNITA turned on the MPLA and a new struggle ensued for control of the country.

The outcome of the civil war was of special interest to the United States. The United States had viewed the southern African region—extending from the Congo to South Africa and including Angola—as a whole. Rich in diamonds, strategic minerals, and oil, the region had been important to European economies and to American corporations. The United States thus had bolstered regimes that gave free access to European interests, had supplied covert aid to groups opposing regimes that might have been antagonistic to such interests, and had supported Portugal in its colonial wars.[45] In the case of Angola, American policymakers worried about the civil war not only in terms of Gulf Oil's $300 million investment there, but also in terms of the direct consequences for South Africa. American corporations had $6 billion invested in South Africa, with whom they carried on $2 billion in trade; the apartheid regime owed foreign banks $7.6 billion, of which $2.2 billion belonged to American banks.[46] Corporate interests feared that an unfriendly Angola might encourage anti-apartheid nationalist groups in South Africa to increase their fighting and might even provide a staging ground for armed forces.

The South African government was also worried about this possibility. In June 1975, when the MPLA was winning the civil war, South African troops crossed the border and began to fight inside Angola on the side of UNITA and the FNLA. The United States had already committed covert CIA aid to these two groups and was hiring mercenaries for action.[47] In response, the MPLA asked for Cuban troop assistance, and by late fall several thousand Cuban soldiers were fighting in Angola.[48]

Cuba had had "early special ties to anti-colonial liberation movements in the Portuguese- and Spanish-held territories of Africa," according to political scientist Jorge Dominguez. It had supported the MPLA for more than a decade.[49] Most analysts agree that in providing military advisors, teachers, technicians, and medical personnel to liberation forces and newly independent countries, Cuba was not acting as a pawn of the Soviet Union. Cuba had an independent and consistent foreign policy that reflected a commitment to revolutionary struggles and a desire to develop the nonaligned movement as a major force in world politics.[50]

However, Secretary of State Henry Kissinger chose to characterize Cuba as a puppet of Moscow, and Cuba's involvement in Angola as major intervention in Africa by the Soviet Union. The House and Senate appeared unwilling to accept his characterization and acted at first independently, and then in concert, to limit American involvement in the Angolan war. However, Kissinger's strong stance impeded the continued congressional initiatives towards normalization with Cuba.

By March 1976—after the FNLA, UNITA, and South African forces had been routed—Kissinger had halted all efforts to re-establish normal relations between Cuba and the United States. Indeed, he had renewed with a vengeance the theme that Cuba was the enemy. On March 4 he told the House International Relations Committee that Cuban assistance to the Angolan government held an "ominous precedent for intervention" in Latin America. He then laid down an implicit warning against Cuban involvment in the struggles of the Patriotic Front against the white minority government in Rhodesia.[51]

Less than three weeks later Kissinger escalated the warning. In a speech to the World Affairs Council of Dallas, he declared that the United States was ready to take "forthright and decisive action" against Cuba.[52] The same day reports circulated in Washington that the National Security Council had ordered contingency plans for a military blockade against Cuba, and perhaps even for an attack.[53] The stated reason for the threats was an alleged Cuban plan to enter the struggle in Rhodesia. Whether or not Cuba had made such plans—and later reports suggested Cuba had no intention of entering the Rhodesian conflict—the true reason for Kissinger's bellicosity remains unclear.[54] However, the episode clearly put a freeze on the efforts to renew Cuban-American relations.

The coolness between the two countries increased on October 3, 1976, when a Cuban commercial airliner was blown up over Barbados, killing all 73 people aboard. "The murder off Barbados," as Cuban newspapers described the act of terror, was soon identified as the handiwork of CORU, an international terrorist organization controlled by CIA-trained Cuban exiles. Two CORU members, Freddy Lugo and Hernan Ricardo Losano, were arrested by Venezuelan police within days of the bombing and were charged with the murders. In Washington, the White House lamely disputed charges of CIA complicity and refused to assist any investigation of the crime, even though the indicted exiles had been on the CIA payroll only two years before. In response, the Cuban government voided the 1973 hijacking agreement, on grounds that the United States had violated its terms by failing to prevent terrorists from sabotaging Cuban air traffic.

Another factor that sent some congressional sponsors of normalization ducking for cover was Cuba's sponsorship of a United Nations resolution, approved on November 12, 1975, declaring that Zionism was a form of genocide and racism. Although a legislator might support the existence of Israel without supporting Zionism, the distinction would need to be too finely drawn. Legislators feared that constituents would see Cuba as leading a fight against the existence of Israel and would in turn attack those members of Congress who supported normalization of relations with Cuba.

While the multinational corporations might have been satisfied with the removal of the embargo on their foreign subsidiaries, smaller companies still sought direct trade with Cuba. Many executives traveled to Cuba seeking to pave the way for future opportunity, and a Commerce Department study indicated that the Cuban market for American goods at the end of 1976 would have exceeded $750 million.[55] However, in 1976 a different group of businesspeople opposed to renewed relations gained strength. They represented domestic industries such as sugar and citrus-fruit growing that might have been adversely affected by American trade with Cuba.[56] While they advanced little more than narrow protectionist arguments, they came from states that had key representation on the Senate Foreign Relations Committee (Frank Church and Richard Stone), the House International Relations Committee (Dante Fascell and Andrew Ireland), the Senate Finance Committee (Chairman Russell Long and Spark Matsunaga), and the House Ways and Means Committee (Sam Gibbons, Joseph Waggoner, and L.A. Bafalis). The latter two committees would be involved in setting tariffs on Cuban products and in reviewing requests to give Cuba "most favored nation" trading status.

Opposition also came from businesspeople who had outstanding claims against Cuba for the alleged confiscation of their property. The United States Foreign Claims Settlement Commission had certified claims against the Cuban government totaling $1.85 billion.[57] But the issue was clouded by three problems. First, the commission's certifications were overly generous. Property evaluations were based on worth in 1958, although by 1961, when the United States severed relations, companies had let their properties deteriorate. Second, several of the claims had been sold to speculators, sometimes at the rate of $.02 on the dollar. For example, rights to a $1 million claim might have been sold for $20,000. The Claims Commission specified that claims could not be sold, but companies had in effect done so by selling their right to the money they would obtain under a claim while retaining a legal hold on the claim itself. Third, several companies had already written off their losses and received tax benefits from them. Whatever the merits of their claims, the voices of the claimants were an additional weapon that the executive used to discourage congressional initiatives.

Finally, in 1976 Cuba was not the only country in Latin America to occupy Congress's attention, or the public's. Panama was of more pressing interest because of the national debate over the pending Panama Canal treaties. Ronald Reagan had made the proposed treaties an issue in the Republican presidential primaries. Conservative opposition to any treaty that appeared to turn control of the canal over to the country through which it was cut effectively postponed negotiations with Panama. It also discouraged legislators who favored normalization with Cuba from pursuing that issue, which they saw as a double-edged sword. They reasoned that conservatives could transfer the mobilized anger against the treaties into antagonism against relations with Cuba; they could use the Cuba issue, in turn, against passage of the treaties.

Underlying this concern in 1976 was the fear of election retaliation. There was still a sufficient reserve of public sentiment that saw Cuba as the enemy, a reserve that, if brought to the surface in an election campaign, could hurt both efforts to restore relations with Cuba and the proponents of such a change. Public attitudes might change in the face of short-term events. But in an election year it would be too risky to assume that the effect of years of propaganda had been eradicated.

The International Context, 1977–1978

The situation in 1977 was more complicated for legislators who focused on Cuba than it had been from 1971 to 1975, when the initiative for normalization seemed to have a compelling logic. The locus of concern had moved beyond Latin America to include southern Africa. With the Cubans still in Angola, there was a new reason to establish a rapprochement with the island, but it required a delicate approach that buttressed a new Africa policy. Moreover, in the fall of 1976, the nonaligned movement designated Havana as the site of its 1979 summit, which meant that President Fidel Castro would become the new chairman of the movement and that Cuba's role in the development of United States relations with the Third World was potentially greater than before. Democratic members of Congress were also sensitive about usurping a foreign-policy initiative from the newly inaugurated Democratic president, who seemed receptive to altering the Nixon-Ford-Kissinger stance. The complexity of the situation encouraged a cautious approach by congressional leaders of the normalization movement, and in 1978 they quickly backed off when the issue again was transformed into an East-West confrontation.

Recall that in the 1971–1975 period American policymakers had been troubled by the emergence of a movement among Third World countries to develop a new international economic order. The industrial, capitalist countries had relied on inexpensive commodities from less-developed countries to sustain their own prosperity, and one factor that had contributed to the continuing low prices of commodities had been the raw competition between the commodity-exporting countries. The emergence of a cartel such as OPEC posed a threat to the West. Oil was seen as the first of many basic commodities whose prices might be regulated by the producers—not the buyers—and steadily increased. Even worse, from a boardroom perspective, a new international economic order might mean the development of trade patterns among Third World countries whereby they supplied each other's needs without buying from the industrial, capitalist countries. This could not only deny necessary supplies to the West but also diminish Western markets.

By 1977 the earlier fears had subsided. Despite the heady rhetoric of the 1976 nonaligned summit—in which the largest gathering ever of Third World nations had supported the OPEC price increases—these countries received little support from OPEC and were suffering themselves from the oil price rises. They needed increasing assistance from the West and were locking themselves into debtor relations that facilitated control of their economies by multinational banks. Their hope of opening a North-South dialogue over trade, under the auspices of the United Nations Conference on Trade and Development (UNCTAD), was also frustrated. Dubbed the Group of 77—although by the 1970s there were over 100—the Third World countries in the UN had hoped to extract concessions from the industrial, capitalist world, such as indexing and a common fund. Indexing would have regulated international trade by linking prices of the export commodities of Third World countries to the prices they paid for the finished products they had to import. A common fund—with a $6 billion kitty—could have provided price stability for commodities by buying up excess goods to keep market prices high and then selling stockpiles to keep prices from rising too rapidly.[58] But heavy pressure from the United States helped to divide the Group of 77, and the industrial, capitalist countries refused to make concessions on indexing or a common fund. The new international economic order seemed to be a fleeting dream—or nightmare—but Western leaders could still not be sure that the threat was eradicated. On the one hand, OPEC remained very much a reality that could be imitated by Third World countries. And on the other, the more than forty nations of Africa were growing united in their opposition to South Africa. Unity on this issue, it was feared, might not only cost the West easy access to a strategic area but might provide the basis for a common African front on other issues.

The Carter strategy for handling OPEC in 1977 seems to have been to divide and conquer: the United States wooed major OPEC countries through separate deals. Thus Iran was permitted to buy seven Airborne Warning and Control Systems (AWACS) planes and sixteen F–16 fighters, and discussions began with Saudi Arabia in 1977 that ultimately led to the sale of sophisticated F–15 warplanes.[59] Relations between the United States and Nigeria, another major OPEC country, had been strained. The Carter administration moved quickly to open a dialogue with Nigeria, and by 1979 it became the second-largest supplier of foreign oil to the United States.[60] The focus on Nigeria—the most populous African nation—had the added advantage of giving the United States a new opening to Africa.

During the Nixon-Ford years, Africa had been accorded a low priority. African countries resented this neglect and objected to American assistance to Portugal in its African colonial wars and to continued American support of South Africa. Early in the Carter administration, Andrew Young moved Africa up on the foreign-policy agenda and undertook a series of meetings with African leaders. He forcefully articulated President Carter's human-rights policy, which was interpreted as a diplomatic denunciation of South African apartheid, and his opposition to Ian Smith in Rhodesia carried the day in shaping American policy against the white regime. Notably, in contrast to the Kissinger rhetoric, Young described Cuban support of the MPLA in Angola as a "stabilizing influence."

American hostility to Cuba in 1976 was seen in Africa as support of South Africa, because the Cubans and South Africans were on opposite sides in the Angola struggle. Cuba had won plaudits from the Organization of African Unity for its efforts and enjoyed high esteem throughout Africa.[61] At the same time, several other Caribbean nations had begun to develop closer ties to Africa and had supported the liberation movements with food, clothing, and symbolic encouragement. They had also supported Cuban involvement in Angola.[62] Clearly they did not view Cuba as a threat, and some openly spoke of the Cuban model as the one they sought to emulate for their own internal development.[63]

The Caribbean had been North America's lake, firmly in the American sphere of influence. One strategy for dealing with the region's new "independence" was to muscle Caribbean regimes. (The United States allegedly tried in 1976 to damage the Jamaican economy just before the December parliamentary elections in an effort to oust the Peoples' National Party, headed by Prime Minister Michael Manley, from power.) An equally sound strategy was to re-establish relations with Cuba and suggest to Caribbean nations American receptivity to change, to remove an irritant that had irked several Caribbean countries, and to diminish the image of the United States as the "colossus of the north"—as one representative put it—which set small countries apart from the United States and encouraged them to act as a bloc, with Cuba as the leader.

In the light of these alternative policies, reducing hostility to Cuba, and perhaps even moving towards normalization of relations, took on a new logic in 1977. Better relations with Cuba would smooth the way for a complex interplay of American initiatives designed to secure stable relations with the Third World. Better relations with Cuba would send signals to Africa about American intentions towards southern Africa; it might reduce friction between Caribbean countries and the United States, which in turn would benefit American policy towards Africa, owing to the new links between Caribbean countries and Africa; and it would indicate to the Caribbean states that the United States was intent on making an overture to the region for its own sake. Notably, in the spring of 1977 Ambassador Young and Rosalynn Carter met with Caribbean leaders on separate trips through the region.

Certainly the imperative for normalization was different from that of 1971–1975, when legislators could clearly see that American policy towards Cuba had prevented good relations with Latin America. Now the case for normalization was more subtle. Moreover, the need for Congress to act was less compelling, because the executive had seized the initiative early. Ten days after taking office, Secretary of State Cyrus Vance declared that the administration welcomed discussions with Cuba, without any of the preconditions that President Ford had articulated. And on March 24, 1977, in New York City, the United States and Cuba opened high-level talks on fishing rights and coastal boundaries.[64]

Then in April, in a surprise move, Assistant Secretary of State for Inter-American Affairs Terence Todman traveled to Havana to conclude the talks and sign a fishing and maritime-boundary agreement. It was the first time in sixteen years that an American diplomat had gone to Cuba. In addition to signing the agreement, Todman proposed that the United States and Cuban Interests Sections in the Swiss and Czechoslovakian Embassies be staffed by American and Cuban diplomats respectively. In September 1977 the plan was put into effect. In August, in a further conciliatory gesture, the State Department announced that Cuba and the United States would share information about terrorist activity that affected each country.

The administration's initiatives undoubtedly had a hand in shaping public opinion about normalization. In the early months of 1977 the press buttressed the new policy by returning to its earlier emphasis on the positive aspects of the Cuban revolution. In April 1977 a Gallup Poll (conducted in conjunction with a study by Potomac Associates) found that 60 percent of those interviewed favored the United States entering into negotiations with Cuba to re-establish relations.[65] For members of Congress who wanted to pick up their pro-normalization efforts where they had left them in 1975, the Carter policy and the favorable polls gave them a comfortable atmosphere in which to operate.

However, the Carter efforts were limited. The president refused to take the greatest step necessary for relations to move forward—lifting the embargo. The statutory basis for the embargo gave the president authority to impose and to lift trade restrictions, and Carter would have had only to detail his reasons to Congress for lifting the sanctions. Indication of the president's unwillingness to lift the embargo came in May 1977 during Senate Foreign Relations Committee deliberations on an amendment to permit two-way trade with Cuba in food and medicine. Officially the administration was neutral. Culver Gleysteen, the director of Cuban Affairs in the State Department, "told the committee he had instructions to say the administration neither supported nor opposed McGovern's original proposal."[66] But unofficially senators were told of the administration's displeasure with two-way trade.

Meanwhile, Cuban activities in Ethiopia confirmed for some members of Congress earlier fears that Cuban troops would be used in Africa as a roving force throughout the continent. After initial statements by the Cuban government that its soldiers were leaving Angola, some returned home, but most were sent to East Africa. In late 1977 and early 1978, 16,000 to 17,000 Cuban troops joined Ethiopian forces that were fighting Somalia in the Ogaden region.[67] There was no question that Cuba had been called in by the legitimate government in Ethiopia and that it was supporting a defensive action against the Somalian invasion. The Organization of African Unity, despite American urging, refused to criticize Cuba's involvement in the Ogaden war. Under pressure from Congress, the executive provided no military assistance to Somalia in the war. But again, as in the case of Angola, Cuba and the United States took different sides in a regional war.[68]

By November 1977 the glow created by the early, limited efforts had vanished as the White House opened a propaganda offensive against Cuba. On November 17 the *New York Times* carried a front-page story, accompanied by a large map, headlined: "U.S. Sees Cuba's African Buildup Blocking Efforts to Improve Ties." The story took officials in the State Department by surprise, and they noted in interviews that there was little new information in it. They attributed its release to Zbigniew Brzezinski, national security advisor to the president.

Over the next six months the Cuban presence in Africa came to dominate executive branch statements about Cuba. Cuba was regularly described as a pawn of the Soviet Union. Some analysts contended that this reflected a power struggle in Washington, in which Brzezinski was attempting to take responsibility for African policy away from both the State Department and UN Ambassador Andrew Young by depicting African events as major elements in an East-West struggle. Others argued that the focus on Cuba and the Soviet Union reflected administration fears that revolutionary struggles in Rhodesia and South Africa were gaining headway so quickly that American interests in southern Africa were endangered. The anti-Communist rhetoric, these observers reasoned, served as a cover to justify American activity in southern Africa.

This tension peaked in May 1978, when a large contingent of Katangese exiles entered Zaire's Shaba province from Angola in an effort to capture land on which they had once lived. Shaba (formerly Katanga) province is a mineral-rich area that had been in dispute since Congolese independence from Belgium in 1960. In response to the May 13 and 14 attacks in Shaba, the United States airlifted more than 1,000 French and Belgian troops into Zaïre to fight the Katangans. White House sources simultaneously charged that Cuban advisors in Angola had trained and directed the Katangese fighters.[69]

President Carter himself declared on May 25 that Cuba had acted irresponsibly in not preventing the attack in Shaba. His contentions came one week after President Castro had informed the United States government—through Lyle Lane, head of the United States Interests Section in Havana—that Cuba had learned of the planned attack in April and had tried, but failed, to prevent it. In an interview with the *Washington Post* on June 12, the Cuban leader "emphatically denied United States charges of Cuban complicity" in the Shaba raid.[70] Carter responded on June 14 by releasing a summary of intelligence information that he said refuted Castro's claims. But by then the information had already lost credibility. Several senators who had seen the full intelligence reports said that the administration had "apparently overreacted."[71]

Subsequently, bellicosity towards Cuba subsided. In September 1978 Cuba responded to the relaxation of tension by agreeing to release hundreds of prisoners to the United States, and to permit several hundred "dual nationals" to emigrate to the United States with their families. However, the fracas over Shaba had transformed the Cuban issue from a Third World context into an East-West context. Once again, key administration officials and most of the press described Cuba as a Soviet puppet or surrogate. These descriptions became the effective reality for Congress in 1978. For advocates of normalization, Cuba took on an enormity that it did not have in 1977, and the new reality affected the way in which the issue could be handled.

Congress and Foreign Policy

The Limits of Initiative

Recall from Chapter 3 that the members of Congress had only a dim appreciation of the stakes involved in the Cuba issue. What they understood in general terms was that the old Cuba policy did not serve either the economic interests of large corporations or the political interests of the United States as a world power.

The context for this congressional initiative was the disorder of the international economy and the emergence of Third World countries as important entities to which the United States had to relate in a new, less cavalier way. In the first half of the 1970s, the economic disorder seemed to contribute to inflation, unemployment, and a growing fiscal crisis at home. With a failed policy in Vietnam, the United States also seemed to be the object of scorn by Third World countries just when these countries might have figured into a strategy for overcoming the economic disorder. Such scorn was especially evident in Latin America and Africa, where Cuba was respected if not revered. By 1974 a majority of the members of the Organization of American States had called on the United States to cease its recalcitrant stand on the OAS embargo against Cuba. American policy towards Cuba appeared to provide few benefits and to interfere with other objectives.

The international context did not dictate what action Congress would take; it did not even ensure that Congress would do anything, but it created the conditions that placed the Cuba issue on the congressional agenda. The members started from the operating logic of "our global position," and during the 1971–1975 period normalization of relations with Cuba was within the bounds of that logic.

Congress will not necessarily act, however, merely because an issue is on its agenda. There are an enormous number of issues for the members to confront, and their time is limited. Especially in the case of a non-crisis issue, when there is no imperative to act immediately, legislators tend to act only to serve personal and institutional as well as national interests.

For some members, the Cuba issue served all these interests. With the administration pursuing a United States–Soviet détente and the normalization of relations with China, the Nixon-Ford Cuba policy had an air of irrationality about it. This appearance made it a likely candidate for attack, while the diminution of anti-Communist rhetoric that accompanied détente made the Cuba issue less difficult for legislators to approach. It was also relatively safe because the executive seemed divided on the question of normalization. Some senior officials sent signals to Congress that they actually supported a change in policy. If executive criticism came, it was likely to have emanated from the president himself, who was in a weakened, Watergate-shocked condition in 1973–1974.

It is not surprising, then, that Congress dropped the issue in late 1975 when the executive took a more resolute, unified position against normalization. This raised the personal costs for members to pursue a new Cuba policy. Notably, the international context also had changed by November 1975. As one member remarked, referring to the July 1975 OAS vote on lifting the embargo against Cuba, "Our problem with Latin America has been resolved. That was our principal concern." Whether legislators would have continued their efforts if the context had not changed and whether the pursuit of national interests would have outweighed the pursuit of personal safety are difficult questions to answer, but by 1976 Congress did not perceive these two sets of interests to be in conflict. Similarly, in 1978, when the Carter administration attacked Cuba and made support of normalization a potentially difficult stance for members of Congress, American objectives in Africa, which a new Cuba policy was intended to serve, were partially realized.

From 1973 to 1975 there was general public support for normalized relations with Cuba, but this opinion was easily susceptible to manipulation. In contrast to the small though extremely attentive public that opposed a resumption of relations, the public that supported relations was diffuse. Noting this lack of cohesion, one Democrat said in July 1976, "The basic obstacle to a resumption of relations now is the lack of a constituency to turn around" the executive's position. The administration's hard line was buttressed by the media, as newspapers throughout the country wrote editorials condemning Cuba's assistance to the MPLA. Whereas before November 1975 a legislator might have felt safe pursuing the Cuba initiative because he or she had an inattentive or generally supportive constituency, that assumption could no longer be made.[72]

E. E. Schattschneider has described the mobilization of bias in a conflict,[73] and his model applies here to the administration's ability to rally public opinion against congressional action. "Congressmen don't want to expose themselves to criticism," one legislator observed. "Why are they so hot to normalize relations, a constituent might ask, after what Cuba just did?" A Senate Foreign Relations Committee staffer summarized the situation by saying: "The president can make you look like a dope."

As a volatile issue without a natural constituency, a resolution to lift the embargo could hardly muster support in Congress. A legislator who pursued the issue might be judged a poor strategist by his or her colleagues. Fear of such judgment added to the reluctance of the leaders of the initiative to continue their efforts. "If you make a fight and lose," one supporter explained, "you're worse off than if you never fought at all."

The executive thus sharply limits Congress's ability to initiate foreign policy. The executive can create constituency pressure when little existed before. Besides the aura of their offices, the president or secretary of state can claim exclusive knowledge of critical information. They can also create conditions that favor their positions, as when President Ford "rescued" the *Mayaguez*: one representative said that he had envisioned Cuba becoming another *Mayaguez* when Secretary Kissinger, in March 1976, threatened Cuba with retaliation if Cuba supported the liberation forces in Rhodesia.

New Patterns of Policy Initiation

A rule of thumb about Congress's role in foreign policy was, until recently, that the president proposed and the Congress disposed.[74] Regarding policy initiation, political scientists generally supported James Robinson's finding that, before World War II, Congress had been first ascendant and then equal in influence to the executive, but that after the war the president was supreme. Robinson further observed that the policies Congress did initiate tended "to be on marginal and relatively less important matters."[75]

Robinson's formulation no longer applies. Since 1968, Congressman Lee Hamilton asserts, Congress has thrust itself "more to the fore" and has involved "itself even more deeply in the actual execution of policy."[76] Similarly, political scientists Thomas Franck and Edward Weisband conclude that "an entire system of power has been overturned. The presidency itself . . . has been the subject of a revolution that radically redistributed the power of government."[77] Although this description exaggerates the change, its characterization of Congress's new role summarizes the prevailing view among many analysts, who point to the 1973 War Powers Resolution, the 1975 cutoff of funding for the CIA's covert war in Angola, and several amendments to foreign-aid bills that forced the executive to withhold assistance to some governments that violated basic human rights. Congress's new power has not, however, found universal acclaim: critics have noted that congressional independence has made foreign observers uneasy about American resolve and ability to act decisively.[78]

The charge that Congress has weakened the United States by violating the old dictum that politics should stop at the water's edge adds fuel to an equally old debate about Congress's proper role in making foreign policy. Traditionally, critics of heavy congressional involvement argued that Congress lacked sufficient information to make rational policy.[79] They also said that Congress was unable to act quickly enough in a crisis to protect the nation.[80] In general they asserted—and contemporary critics agree—that the organization of Congress makes it ill-suited to deal with foreign affairs. They point to the lack of strong congressional leadership and to the dispersion of responsibility among several committees, which fragments policies and produces inconsistency.[81] Even Congressman Hamilton and Michael Van Dusen, staff director of the subcommittee Hamilton chairs, assert that Congress is best suited to formulate foreign policy equally with the executive and should remove itself from independent execution of policy. In what amounts to the restatement of an old prescription, they call for increased consultation between the executive branch and Congress during the process of formulating policy.[82]

The most interesting aspect of this debate is the critics' fear that the legislature can be "captured" by domestic constituencies, which they claim would make Congress unable to shape foreign policy in terms of national interests.[83] For example, in 1974 when the national interest seemed to be best served by easing tensions with the Soviet Union and by extending trade concessions to it, the Jackson amendment to the Trade Reform Act attempted to pressure the Soviet Union into permitting more Jewish emigration by withholding trade concessions. As Paula Stern describes the case, domestic considerations figured heavily in the fight over the legislation, and the issue attracted the attention of numerous domestic interest groups.[84] The critics would prefer Congress to be insulated from particular interests so that it could serve a generalized national interest that might run counter to the interest of any narrowly focused domestic group. Such insulation facilitates planning and coordination. It would in effect confer more power on the group of decision makers that Richard Barnet has called the "national security managers."[85]

However, the national security managers appear to be drawn from a narrow spectrum. While they claim to represent the national interest, they often define that interest in terms of the needs of multinational corporations and of the United States as an aggressive world power. Notably, in the case of normalizing relations with Cuba, the members of Congress who led the effort were those without significant constituency interest. They felt free to take the broad view of the national interest that is usually associated with the president.

Taking the broad view has been characteristic of Congress in its post-Vietnam foreign-policy resurgence. The Cuba case in this respect supports recent observations about Congress's new role in making foreign policy. Four factors in the case correspond to what analysts have said accounts in general for the resurgence.[86]

Increased staff.   Since 1971, the House International Relations Committee staff has more than tripled in size. This increase has not only allowed the staffers to become more specialized and knowledgeable, but has also encouraged activity as each highly paid assistant seeks a rationale for his or her salary. Most relevant to this case, the so-called "subcommittee bill of rights" designated that each subcommittee should have a staff of its own. This gave the Bingham subcommittee (House International Relations Subcommittee on International Trade and Commerce) the capacity to hold hearings and develop legislation on lifting the embargo against Cuba.

Breakdown of congressional norms.   With an unusually large turnover of members during the 1970s, neither the House nor the Senate had the opportunity to socialize newcomers to the old ways of Congress. First-term senators and representatives spoke up more often and ignored the aphorism that to get along they had to go along. Increasingly, members introduced key amendments from the floor, bypassing the relevant committees. Committee circumvention helped to weaken the norm of specialization, although often an amendment's sponsor was both informed and knowledgeable about the amendment's substance. Thus Tom Harkin (D-Iowa), a first-term member who was not on the House Foreign Affairs Committee, made a major impact on American policy with an amendment to a 1975 foreign-aid bill that restricted aid to countries where there were gross violations of human rights.[87] In the case of Cuba, members of the House and Senate foreign relations committees took the lead on normalizing relations. But several non-committee members were heavily involved as well, especially by way of travel to Cuba. For example, freshman senators James Abourezk (D-S.D.) and Floyd Haskell (D.-Colo.) went there in November 1976; Representative John Breaux (D-La.) went to Cuba in 1975 when the civil war in Angola was heating up, and Representatives Les Aspin (D-Wisc.), Frederick Richmond (D-N.Y.), and Richard Nolan (D.-Minn.) visited the island in 1977. Senator Edward Kennedy (D-Mass.) had actively proposed normalization-oriented legislation since the early 1970s, and in late 1974 he sent two key staffers to Havana for discussions with high officials.

Increased availability of information.   Traditionally the executive had supplied Congress with almost all of its foreign-policy information, but during the 1970s, as members believed less and less of what the president was telling them about the Vietnam War, American involvement in the overthrow of the Chilean democracy, and the Watergate cover-up, they developed independent sources of information and analysis and relied less on official embassy briefings when they traveled abroad. Notably, the travelers to Cuba seemed to have more accurate information than the executive, because the United States did not have diplomats in Havana until September 1977. The first-hand impressions of how Cuba had overcome the obstacles of the American embargo diminished for several legislators what John Manley has described as an "inferiority complex" in making foreign policy.[88]

Lack of a foreign-policy consensus. Consensus in the foreign-policy establishment over the objectives and means of American foreign policy was a casualty of the Vietnam War. For at least twenty years after World War II, policymakers—convinced that this was the "American century"—had sustained their arrogance with bellicose anti-Communism that became the totem of American policy.[89] With the collapse of the dream, the shaping of the new consensus was up for grabs, and legislators believed that they could and should have a strong hand in the task. Members were trying to establish a new foreign-policy consensus, rooted in principles of human rights and respect for each country's sovereignty, when they restricted the executive's freedom to intervene in Angola, to support repressive regimes in the Third World, and to be an arms merchant to the world.[90] The initiative on normalizing relations with Cuba was an aspect of this effort to define a new consensus, as members attempted to foster a less bellicose posture towards socialist countries. Of course, the executive branch also sought to establish its version of the new consensus. Under President Carter the executive position became a reversion to dogmatic anti-Sovietism.[91] The congressional coalition that had been pieced together for aid restrictions and arms cutoffs—as well as for a new Cuba policy—was both fragile and badly organized. In the face of concerted executive bellicosity, the coalition was an unworthy advocate.[92]

Lessons of the Cuba Case Study

Despite the ultimate submergence of the congressional effort to establish a new Cuba policy, the efforts from 1971 to 1975 and in 1977 stand out for the distance they went and for the variety of techniques senators and representatives used. These efforts included speeches, the introduction of "sense of the Congress" resolutions, congressional hearings, trips to Cuba, and sponsorship of legislation to end the embargo against Cuba. Notably, the legislation was only a small part of Congress's effort here; Congress can play a significant role in making foreign policy in several other ways. As Franck and Weisband correctly explain, legislation can have significant unintended side effects because, by its very nature, it is public, comprehensive, and universal in application.[93] In many circumstances, these characteristics might serve the

United States well, but at other times quiet negotiation towards limited, specific ends might be more beneficial; legislation might preclude such negotiation.

What Congress did when confronted with an outmoded United States Cuba policy was put pressure on the executive for change; legitimate a new policy by espousing it in several forums; test the water for those in the executive branch who were arguing internally that circumstances made a new Cuba policy appropriate; and send signals to Cuba and other countries that the United States might alter its course. As political scientist Alton Frye has indicated, sending messages to foreign governments about American intentions is one important way in which Congress involves itself in policy development. While observers in the United States may disregard what legislators say, foreign governments often scrutinize congressional statements with great care.[94] Scholars, journalists, and American officials who have traveled to Havana report that the Cuban government combs the *Congressional Record* and has paid close attention to the public statements of members of Congress. The failure of these efforts to initiate a new Cuba policy does not diminish their significance. They even may have contributed to President Carter's halting moves towards normalization in 1977 by legitimating a new course.

In reviewing this case, three lessons stand out. First, traditional descriptions seem valid when applied to the way in which members of Congress view the world in their daily lives. They care immediately about personal and institutional interests and understand the world most clearly in these terms.

Second, members act on what they perceive to be national interests and they attempt to fashion policy in accordance with national interests. They support national interests most easily when free from constituency pressure, and in doing so see the national interest ideologically. The ideology that dominates their view is that profit maximization for large corporations and power aggrandizement for the United States best serve all Americans.

Third, legislators do not act in a vacuum where they might choose whatever issues strike their fancy. They act within the context of a changing international economy that generates problems for giant corporations seeking a steady accumulation of wealth. The issues Congress addresses, and the range of its solutions to the problems with which it chooses to deal, fall within this context.

To appreciate the nature of congressional involvement in foreign policy, the nature of the international context must be included in such analyses. And to appreciate the nature of the international context, it is important to recognize that problems there do not arise randomly. They arise out of the structure of the international economy. Ultimately, the key to understanding Congress and foreign policy is to comprehend the international context systematically.

NOTES

1. The phrase, by Karl Marx, obviously pertains to a different set of circumstances but can serve as an apt guide here. See "The Eighteenth Brumaire Of Louis Bonaparte," in Karl Marx, *Surveys from Exile,* ed. David Fernbach (New York: Vintage, 1974), p. 146.
2. David Easton, *A Framework for Political Analysis* (Englewood Cliffs, N.J.: Prentice-Hall, 1965), Chapter 7.
3. Richard F. Fenno, Jr., *Congressmen in Committees* (Boston: Little, Brown, 1973), pp. 9–13.
4. Seymour Melman, *The Permanent War Economy* (New York: Simon & Schuster, 1974), Chapters 1, 4.
5. Fred L. Block, *The Origins of International Economic Disorder* (Berkeley: University of California Press, 1978), pp. 152–158, 181–193.
6. U.S. Tariff Commission, "Money Crises and the Operation of Multinational Firms," in Philip Brenner, Robert Borosage, and Bethany Weidner, eds., *Exploring Contradictions* (New York: David McKay, 1974).
7. Block, *Origins of International Economic Disorder,* p. 153.
8. U.S. Congress, Senate Committee on Foreign Relations, "International Debt, The Banks, and U.S. Foreign Policy," a staff report prepared for use of the Subcommittee on Foreign Economic Policy. Committee Print, 95th Cong., 1st Sess., August 1977, p. 23. Also see "Banks: Skating on Thin Ice," *Monthly Review,* February 1975.
9. David M. Kotz, *Bank Control of Large Corporations in the United States* (Berkeley: University of California Press, 1978). Also see U.S. Congress, Senate Committee on Governmental Affairs, "Voting Rights in Major Corporations," a staff study. Committee Print, 95th Cong., 2nd Sess., January 1978.
10. Manuel Castells, *The Economic Crisis and American Society* (Princeton: Princeton University Press, 1980), pp. 87–103. Also see Arthur MacEwen, "World Capitalism and the Crisis of the 1970s," in *The Capitalist System,* 2nd edition, eds. Richard Edwards et al. (Englewood Cliffs, N.J.: Prentice-Hall, 1978), pp. 459–461. Also see Carlos F. Diaz-Alejandro, "Delinking North and South: Unshackled or Unhinged?" in Albert Fishlow et al., *Rich and Poor Nations in the World Economy* (New York: McGraw-Hill, 1978), p. 131.
11. Block, *Origins of International Economic Disorder,* p. 153. Also see Castells, *The Economic Crisis and American Society,* pp. 107–109.
12. Richard J. Barnet and Ronald Muller, *Global Reach* (New York: Simon & Schuster, 1974), p. 153.
13. John Connor and Willard Mueller, "Market Power and Profitability of Multinational Corporations in Brazil and Mexico," a report to the U.S. Senate Subcommittee on Foreign Economic Policy of the Committee on Foreign Relations. Committee Print, 95th Cong., 1st Sess., April 1977, p. 6. Also see Richard Newfarmer and Willard Mueller, "Multinational Corporations in Brazil and Mexico: Structural Sources of Economic and Noneconomic Power," a report to the U.S. Senate Subcommittee on Multinational Corporations of the Committee on Foreign Relations. Committee Print, 94th Cong., 1st Sess., August 1975, p. 93.
14. Barnet and Muller, *Global Reach,* p. 138 and Chapter 11. It is not clear if multinational corporations caused a net loss of jobs in the United States, but it appears that they may have altered the composition of the labor market in directions away from unionized sectors.
15. U.S. Congress, Senate Select Committee to Study Governmental Operations with Respect to Intelligence Activities, "Covert Action in Chile, 1963–1973," a staff report. Reprinted in "Intelligence Activities: Hearings Before the Committee," Vol. 7, Appen-

dix A, 94th Cong., 1st Sess., 4 and 5 December 1975. Also see James Petras and Morris Morley, *The United States and Chile: Imperialism and the Overthrow of the Allende Government* (New York: Monthly Review Press, 1975).

16. Orlando Letelier, *Chile: Economic Freedom and Political Repression*, Transnational Institute Pamphlet No. 1 (Washington, D.C.: Institute for Policy Studies, 1976). Also see Barnet and Muller, *Global Reach*, pp. 191–192.

17. Howard M. Wachtel, *The New Gnomes: Multinational Banks in the Third World*, Transnational Institute Pamphlet No. 4 (Washington, D.C.: Institute for Policy Studies, 1977), p. 9.

18. Connor and Mueller, "Market Power and the Profitability of Multinational Corporations in Brazil and Mexico," p. 12.

19. Albert Fishlow, "A New International Economic Order: What Kind?" in Fishlow, *Rich and Poor Nations in the World Economy*, pp. 21–22. Also see Wachtel, *The New Gnomes*, pp. 12–13.

20. Subcommittee on Foreign Economic Policy, "International Debt, The Banks, and U.S. Foreign Policy," pp. 49–55; Wachtel, *The New Gnomes*, pp. 18–19; Orlando Letelier and Michael Moffitt, *The International Economic Order, Part I*, Transnational Institute Pamphlet No. 2 (Washington, D.C.: Institute for Policy Studies, 1977), p. 7. Also see Cheryl Payer, *The Debt Trap* (New York: Monthly Review Press, 1974).

21. Jorge Ovieda Rueda, *The Five Summit Conferences of the Non-Aligned Countries: Documents* (Havana: Editorial de Ciencias Sociales, 1979), p. 290. Also see Letelier and Moffitt, *The International Economic Order*, pp. 25–28.

22. Wachtel, *The New Gnomes*, p. 40; Letelier and Moffitt, *The International Economic Order*, pp. 8, 34–35.

23. A.W. Singham, *The Non-Aligned Movement in World Politics* (New York: Lawrence Hill, 1978); Geoffrey Barraclough, "The Haves and the Have Nots," *New York Review of Books*, 13 May 1976; Letelier and Moffitt, *The International Economic Order*, pp. 5–7.

24. Geoffrey Barraclough, "Waiting for the New Order," *New York Review of Books*, 26 October 1978, pp. 45–53.

25. Albert Fishlow, "The Mature Neighbor Policy: A New United States Economic Policy for Latin America," Institute of International Studies Policy Papers in International Affairs (Berkeley: Institute of International Studies, 1977), pp. 15–16, 30.

26. Bertram Gross, *Friendly Fascism: The New Face of Power in America* (New York: M. Evans, 1980), Chapter 5.

27. Richard E. Feinberg, *The Triumph of Allende's Chile: Chile's Legal Revolution* (New York: New American Library, 1972).

28. Abraham F. Lowenthal, *The Dominican Intervention* (Cambridge: Harvard University Press, 1972); Tad Szulc, *Dominican Diary* (New York: Delacorte, 1965); Piero Gleijeses, *The Dominican Crisis* (Baltimore: Johns Hopkins University Press, 1978).

29. The statement was made in an interview with Dan Rather, January 2, 1972, as quoted in Roger Fontaine, *On Negotiating With Cuba* (Washington, D.C.: American Enterprise Institute, 1975), p. 61.

30. Barry Sklar, "Congress and the Normalization of Relations with Cuba, 1971–1977," a paper presented before the Latin American Studies Association Annual Meeting, Houston, November 1977, p. 61.

31. U.S. Congress, Senate Subcommittee on Western Hemisphere Affairs of the Foreign Relations Committee, "U.S. Policy Towards Cuba: Hearings," 93rd Cong., 1st Sess., 26 March and 18 April 1973, pp. 4–5.

32. Phil Gailey; "U.S. and Cuba Had Direct Secret Talks in 1975," *Miami Herald*, 15 February 1977, p. 14-A.

33. Commission on United States–Latin American Relations, *The Americas in a Changing World* (New York: Quadrangle, 1975), p. 6.

34. Ibid., p. 29. In a related development in 1974, former Undersecretary of State George Ball—then a well-respected international investment banker—called for a resumption of relations with Cuba.

35. Patricia Weiss Fagen, "Toward Deténte with Cuba: Issues and Obstacles," *International Policy Report* (Washington, D.C.: Center for International Policy, November,

1977), p. 7. Imports from capitalist countries amounted to $300 million in 1972 and $1.06 billion in 1974. The Treasury Department reported in 1976 that it had authorized the sale of $300 million worth of goods to Cuba by foreign subsidiaries of American companies; Phil ·Gailey, "Trade With Cuba Up Despite U.S. Ban," *Miami Herald,* 27 July 1976, p. 1.

36. U.S. Congress, House Committee on International Relations, "U.S. Trade Embargo of Cuba: Hearings on H.R. 6382," 94th Cong., 1st Sess., May, June, July, September 1975, p. 65.

37. Reported in "U.S. Policy Towards Cuba: Hearings," pp. 56–57.

38. U.S. Congress, Senate Select Committee to Study Governmental Operations with Respect to Intelligence Activities, "Alleged Assassination Plots Involving Foreign Leaders: An Interim Report," 94th Cong., 1st Sess., 20 November 1975, pp. 124–125.

39. "The U.S. Blockade: A Documentary History," *Cuba In Focus* (New York: Center for Cuban Studies, December 1979).

40. Jorge I. Dominguez, *Cuba: Order and Revolution* (Cambridge: Harvard University Press, 1978), pp. 165–173; Carmelo Mesa-Lago, *The Economy of Socialist Cuba: A Two-Decade Appraisal* (Albuquerque: University of New Mexico Press, 1981), pp. 158, 166–168; Arthur MacEwan, *Revolution and Economic Development in Cuba* (New York: St. Martin's, 1981), pp. 165–168; Herbert Matthews, *Revolution in Cuba* (New York: Scribner's, 1975), Chapters 13–16.

41. William M. LeoGrande, "Party Development in Revolutionary Cuba," *Journal of Interamerican Studies and World Affairs,* November 1979; Dominguez, *Cuba: Order and Revolution,* pp. 286–298.

42. Newfarmer and Mueller, "Multinational Corporations in Brazil and Mexico," p. 156.

43. Ibid., p. 155. Also see Block, *The Origins of International Economic Disorder,* pp. 152–153; Barnet and Muller, *Global Reach,* Chapter 4.

44. The senators were James Abourezk (D–S.D.) and George McGovern (D–S.D.). The representatives were John Breaux (D–La.), Stephen Solarz (D–N.Y.), and Charles Whalen (R–Ohio).

45. Philip Brenner, "Marching to Pretoria: Roundtable Discussion," *Cuba Review,* October 1978, pp. 26–27. Also see George Houser, "Carter's Africa Policy," *Cuba Review,* October 1978, pp. 12–13.

46. Corporate Data Exchange, *U.S. Bank Loans to South Africa,* CDE Handbook (New York: Corporate Data Exchange, 1978), p. 6; Houser, "Carter's Africa Policy," p. 11; Lawrence Litvak, Robert DeGrasse, and Kathleen McTigue, *South Africa: Foreign Investment and Apartheid* (Washington, D.C.: Institute for Policy Studies, 1978), pp. 43–57; U.S. Congress, Senate Committee on Foreign Relations, "U.S. Corporate Interests in South Africa," a report by Senator Dick Clark. Committee Print, 95th Cong., 1st Sess., January 1978.

47. John Stockwell, *In Search of Enémies* (New York: W.W. Norton, 1978). Also see Nathaniel Davis, "The Angola Decision of 1975: A Personal Memoir," *Foreign Affairs,* 57, No. 1 (Fall 1978).

48. William M. LeoGrande, *Cuba's Policy in Africa, 1959–1980,* Institute of International Studies Policy Papers in International Affairs, No. 13 (Berkeley: Institute of International Studies, 1980), pp. 17–18. He reports that 230 Cuban military instructors arrived in June, but that combat troops went to Angola only after increased South African intervention in August. Also see Jorge I. Dominguez, "Cuban Foreign Policy," *Foreign Affairs,* 57, No. 1 (Fall 1978), 97.

49. Dominguez, "Cuban Foreign Policy," pp. 94–95; LeoGrande, *Cuba's Policy in Africa,* p. 21.

50. For example, see Gordon Adams, "Cuba and Africa: The International Politics of the Liberation Struggle," *Latin American Perspectives,* VIII, No. 1 (Winter 1981), pp. 114–116; Abraham F. Lowenthal, "Cuba's African Adventure," *International Security* (1977), pp. 6, 9; Dominguez, "Cuban Foreign Policy," pp. 83–84; LeoGrande, *Cuba's Policy in Africa,* pp. 21–22.

51. "Kissinger: Castro Adventure Ominous to Latins," *Miami Herald,* 5 March 1976, p. 22-A. He re-issued the warning more sharply two days later at a press conference in

Atlanta: "Kissinger Warns Cuba and Soviet Union Again," *Washington Post,* 7 March 1976, p. A16.

52. Phil Gailey, "U.S. to Cuba: Lay Off Africa," *Miami Herald,* 23 March 1976, p. 1.
53. Fred S. Hoffman, "Pentagon Reviewing Plans for Action Against Cuba," *Miami Herald,* 26 March 1976.
54. Murray Marder, "Cuban Bars Sending Troops to Rhodesia," *Washington Post,* 21 May 1976, p. 1; Phil Gailey, "Castro Snub Behind Rift With Cuba?" *Miami Herald,* 28 March 1976, p. 1; Martin Schram, "Ford Is Floating Cuba as a New *Mayaguez,*" *Miami Herald,* 6 April 1976, p. 7-A.
55. "U.S. Firms See Cuba as a $750-Million Market," *Miami Herald,* 12 January 1977, p. 5-A; Don Bohning, "Minnesota Firms Set Trip: Talks Planned on Cuba Trade," *Miami Herald,* 23 March 1977. One consulting firm—Alamar Associates—was established in Washington, D.C., in 1975 to assist companies in planning future trade with Cuba.
56. "Cuban Citrus Crop Has Top Potential, State Expert Warns," *Miami Herald,* 16 June 1977, p. 15-D.
57. Robert Dallos, "Firms Press Cuba for Reparations," *Los Angeles Times,* 5 June 1977, Part VI, p. 1. Also see Foreign Claims Settlement Commission of the United States, *Annual Report to the Congress for January 1–December 31, 1972* (Washington, D.C.: 1973), Section II.
58. Letelier and Moffitt, *The International Economic Order,* pp. 36–39, 43–44. Also, Joan Edelman Spero, *The Politics of International Economic Relations,* 2nd ed. (New York: St. Martin's, 1981), pp. 208–214.
59. Michael T. Klare, "Arms and the Shah," *The Progressive,* August 1979. Notably, Iran channeled some of the arms to other Mideast countries. By becoming a regional arms merchant, it gained influence that was translated into support at OPEC meetings.
60. Litvak et al., *South Africa,* pp. 71–72.
61. Adams, "Cuba and Africa," pp. 115–116.
62. Linus A. Hoskins, "The Caribbean and Africa: A Geo-Political Analysis," in Vincent P. McDonald, ed., *The Caribbean Issues of Emergence: Socio-Economic and Political Perspectives* (Washington, D.C.: University Press of America, 1979), pp. 162–165.
63. "Small Countries in the Caribbean Are Starting to Follow Cuba's Example," *New York Times,* 16 July 1976, p. 3.
64. William Montalbano, "U.S. and Cuba Open Talks," *Miami Herald,* 25 March 1977, p. 1. In addition, President Carter lifted restrictions on tourist travel to Cuba on March 18.
65. William Watts and Jorge I. Dominguez, *The United States and Cuba: Old Issues and New Directions* (Washington, D.C.: Potomac Associates, 1977).
66. Lee Lescaze, "Senate Panel Votes to Relax Embargo Against Cuba," *Washington Post,* 11 May 1977, p. 1.
67. LeoGrande, *Cuba's Policy in Africa,* pp. 39–40; also see Joseph Kraft, "Letter from Addis Ababa," *New Yorker,* July 31, 1978.
68. LeoGrande, *Cuba's Policy in Africa,* pp. 46–48.
69. Brenner, "Marching to Pretoria," pp. 18–19.
70. Karen DeYoung, "Castro Again Denies U.S. Charges of Cuban Complicity in Zaïre Raid," *Washington Post,* 13 June 1978, p. 1.
71. Bernard Gwertzman, "Carter's Case on Cuba Not Proved, Foreign Relations Chairman Says," *New York Times,* 10 June 1978, p. 1.
72. In April 1976 a nationwide poll by Opinion Research Corporation found 58 percent opposed to relations with Cuba, with only 29 percent in favor. *Miami Herald,* 20 May 1976, p. 1.
73. E. E. Schattschneider, *The Semi-Sovereign People* (New York: Holt, Rinehart and Winston, 1960), Chapter 2.
74. Robert Dahl, *Congress and Foreign Policy* (New York: Harcourt Brace, 1950); James A. Robinson, *Congress and Foreign Policy-Making,* revised ed. (Homewood, Ill.: Dorsey Press, 1967); Marcus Raskin, *Notes on the Old System* (New York: David McKay, 1974), Chapter 3, especially pp. 87–92.
75. Robinson, *Congress and Foreign Policy-Making,* p. 15. For a cogent analysis of the way

in which Congress has been limited in the key foreign-policy processes of budgetary control, intelligence oversight, and war powers, see James A. Nathan and James K. Oliver, *United States Foreign Policy and World Order* (Boston: Little, Brown, 1976), Chapter 13.

76. Lee H. Hamilton and Michael H. Van Dusen, "Making the Separation of Powers Work," *Foreign Affairs*, 57, No. 1 (Fall 1978), 17. However, they argue that "even at its peak, the enlarged congressional role" left Congress in a "secondary" position (pp. 21–22).

77. Thomas M. Franck and Edward Weisband, *Foreign Policy by Congress* (New York: Oxford University Press, 1979), p. 3. Also see Douglas J. Bennett, Jr., "Congress in Foreign Policy: Who Needs It?" *Foreign Affairs*, 57, No. 1 (Fall 1978), 40–43; Robert A. Pastor, *Congress and the Politics of U.S. Foreign Economic Policy 1929–1976* (Berkeley: University of California Press, 1980). However, John T. Rourke argues that the new role is likely to be short-lived if Congress "is reluctant to act during times of crisis." Rourke, "The Future is History: Congress and Foreign Policy," *Presidential Studies Quarterly*, IX, No. 3 (Summer 1979), 276.

78. Franck and Weisband, *Foreign Policy by Congress*, pp. 35, 55.

79. For example, see Edward A. Koledziej, "Congress and Foreign Policy: Through the Looking Glass," *Virginia Quarterly Review*, 42, No. 1 (1966).

80. Rourke, "The Future is History," pp. 276–277.

81. Bennett, "Congress in Foreign Policy," pp. 47–48; Franck and Weisband, *Foreign Policy by Congress*, Chapter 9, pp. 256–257.

82. Hamilton and Van Dusen, "Making the Separation of Powers Work," pp. 27, 32–33.

83. For example, see Bennett, "Congress in Foreign Policy," pp. 47–48; Bayless Manning, "The Congress, the Executive and Intermestic Affairs: Three Proposals," *Foreign Affairs*, 55, No. 3 (January 1977).

84. Paula Stern, *Water's Edge: Domestic Politics and the Making of American Foreign Policy* (Westport, Conn.: Greenwood Press, 1979), Chapter 6.

85. Richard J. Barnet, *The Roots of War* (New York: Atheneum, 1972), Chapter 3; William Minter and Laurence H. Shoup, *Imperial Brain Trust: The Council on Foreign Relations and United States Foreign Policy* (New York: Monthly Review Press, 1977).

86. Hamilton and Van Dusen, "Making the Separation of Powers Work," p. 23; Franck and Weisband, *Foreign Policy by Congress*, pp. 7, 34, 211–214, 227–234; James Chace, "Is a Foreign Policy Consensus Possible?" *Foreign Affairs*, 57, No. 1 (Fall 1978). Also see Richard J. Barnet and Richard A. Falk, "Cracking the Consensus: America's New Role in the World," *Working Papers*, March/April 1978.

87. Franck and Weisband, *Foreign Policy by Congress*, pp. 86–89. Also see Patricia Weiss Fagen, "U.S. Foreign Policy and Human Rights: The Role of Congress," in Antonio Cassese, ed., *National Control Over Foreign Policy-Making* (Leyden, Netherlands: Sijthoff and Nordhoff, 1980).

88. John F. Manley, "The Rise of Congress in Foreign Policy-Making," *The Annals*, 398 (1971), 69.

89. Chace, "Is a Foreign Policy Consensus Possible?" pp. 3–4. Also see Marcus Raskin, "The Kennedy Hawks Assume Power from the Eisenhower Vultures," in Leonard Rodberg and Derek Shearer, eds., *The Pentagon Watchers* (Garden City, N.Y.: Doubleday, 1971); Alan Wolfe, *The Rise and Fall of the "Soviet Threat"* (Washington, D.C.: Institute for Policy Studies, 1979), Chapter 1 and pp. 7–22.

90. For an account of these restrictions, see Franck and Weisband, *Foreign Policy by Congress*, pp. 46–57, 86–89, 98–103.

91. Marcus Raskin, *The Politics of National Security* (New Brunswick, N.J.: Transaction Books, 1979), Chapter 1. Also see Wolfe, *The Rise and Fall of the "Soviet Threat"*, pp. 25–32.

92. Philip Brenner, "Congress Watch: The Shifting Coalitions," *The Nation*, 4 November 1978. Also see Weiss-Fagen, "U.S. Foreign Policy and Human Rights."

93. Franck and Weisband, *Foreign Policy by Congress*, pp. 159–162.

94. Alton Frye, *A Responsible Congress: The Politics of National Security* (New York: McGraw-Hill, 1975), Chapter 7.

5 Domestic Policy: Restructuring Higher Education

In 1972 the picture for higher education in the United States was anything but rosy. Many of the post-World War II baby-boom children had graduated from college, leaving unused facilities and expanded faculties with too few students to justify their size. Five years of demonstrations on college campuses had created a backlash among the rich donors who funded private institutions and state legislators who funded public ones; both groups had become miserly. Federal funds channeled through research agencies, such as the National Institutes of Health and the National Science Foundation, or through the Department of Defense, the Atomic Energy Commission, and similar units had been cut back or were maintained only at past levels. The institutions of higher education were increasingly unable to meet their rising costs, and some small, weak colleges had folded. To make ends meet, private colleges began to raise their tuitions dramatically, which pushed more students towards the public institutions.

At the same time, students and their families began to question the value of obtaining a college degree. The baccalaureate once seemed a sure route to a job that would pay a comfortable middle-class salary and provide good working conditions, but by the early 1970s that was no longer the case. And what was true for the B.A. was increasingly true for graduate degrees as well, including the Ph.D.

Thus when one member of Congress explained his support for the far-reaching Higher Education Act of 1972 by exclaiming that "education is like motherhood," he was being simplistic in the extreme. Support for education was not an easy position for a legislator because the problems of education had become complex. The education system mirrored many of the underlying problems in the organization of society—from basic values to work. In attempting to deal with this complexity, Congress took on a domestic-policy problem that touched many other issues, the resolution of which promised to affect society as a whole.

Congress could have handled the problem of higher education in several ways. However, members both narrowed the full range of possibilities Congress would consider and went beyond the limited scope that major interest groups advocated. They circumscribed the possibilities because of ideological factors and their assessment of the "problem." On the other hand, Congress indicated that it can in some cases try to resolve fundamental national problems and transcend the limits imposed by interest groups. This chapter examines the details of the Higher Education Act of 1972, reviews what members perceived they were doing in passing the act, and relates their behavior and perceptions to the larger context.

The Higher Education Act of 1972

On June 8, 1972, the House passed the conference report on the Education Amendments Act of 1972, the so-called Higher Education Act. Much of the controversy surrounding the bill concerned provisions on busing school children for the purpose of desegregation.[1] However, key provisions pertaining to higher education also had their share of notoriety and conflict. The legislation was nearly four years in the making: Representative Edith Green (D-Ore.), who chaired the House higher-education subcommittee, first held hearings in 1969 on legislation that she had proposed. Subsequently, President Nixon proposed a higher-education bill, as did Senator Claiborne Pell (D–R.I.), chairman of the Senate higher-education subcommittee.

This section briefly reviews significant aspects of the legislation, describes the legislative struggle between the interest groups and the legislators involved in shaping the act, and examines how factors such as personality and personal interests affected the outcome. Isolated from the larger political-economic context, this description of the Higher Education Act might provide a flawed analysis of why the act took the shape it did. It implies that the act reflected the demands of the interest groups. What such an analysis ignores is the way in which the larger system generates interest-group demands and shapes the congressional agenda.

In some ways the Higher Education Act was a typical congressional "Christmas-tree" bill, under which legislators place all their pet projects. The act contained twenty titles, covering such topics as youth-camp safety, Indian education, the University of Guam, and the College of the Virgin Islands.[2] However, the titles on federal aid to college students and to institutions of higher education were significant. The act authorized a new program of Basic Educational Opportunity Grants (BEOGs) that would entitle students to receive up to $1,400 each, depending on their tuition (no more than half could be paid by a BEOG entitlement) and family income. Determination of the family-income level that would constitute ineligibility for the program was left to the United States Commissioner of Education. But Congress made clear that BEOGs were meant for students from relatively poor families, and it declared in the conference report that the program "is viewed as the foundation upon which all other federal student-assistance programs are based."[3] The other programs—Supplemental Educational Opportunity Grants, College Work-Study, and National Direct Student Loans—were re-authorized by the 1972 act.

Institutions were to receive money according to a tripartite formula, but 90 percent of the institutional allocation was to be linked to the presence of subsidized students at an institution. The first 45 percent of institutional aid was to be distributed at schools on the basis of the amount of money that students at a school received from federal student-aid programs. The second 45 percent was to be distributed on the basis of the number of students receiving BEOGs at a school. Only the last 10 percent was to be based on school size, measured by graduate-school enrollment, with a school receiving $200 for each enrolled graduate student. Congress further emphasized that the act was intended to shape higher education to federal purposes, by focusing on students rather than institutions, when it declared that money for the first 45 percent of institutional aid could be spent only after the executive had spent at least 50 percent of the money authorized for BEOG entitlements.

The act also authorized the expenditure by fiscal year 1975 of $150 million to assist states in the development and expansion of community colleges, and of $500 million to encourage the development of occupational-education programs that emphasize "manpower needs in sub-professional occupations."

The act was generally described as landmark legislation, not only because it authorized the spending of nearly $25 billion in three years on higher education, but also because it appeared to involve the federal government in shaping higher education more than before.[4] Previous higher-education legislation of comparable impact had come at key points in the country's history. The Morrill Land Grant Act of 1862 gave public land to each state for the purpose of endowing colleges of agricultural and mechanical arts, and the 1944 Servicemen's Readjustment Act, the so-called G.I. Bill of Rights, provided money for over two million veterans to study at colleges and universities.[5] But the 1972 act was more complex and addressed less tangible problems, such as equal opportunity.

Interest Groups, Policy Elites, and the Executive Branch

With so much at stake, one would have expected a large number of interest groups to be involved in the development of the Higher Education Act. In fact, there were only a few, and notably the voice of students was hardly heard at all. "It is ironic," one legislator remarked during an interview in 1972, "that we heard so little from the group which would be affected the most."

College administrators and their national associations in Washington were the most intensely interested in the legislation, undoubtedly because of their circumstances. In the early 1970s most colleges and universities were experiencing what Earl Cheit characterized as the "new depression in higher education."[6] Higher-education institutions had expanded in the 1960s and were faced with slower-than-anticipated increases in enrollment, or losses of students, while their costs continued to rise. The large, research-oriented universities that had depended on federal contracts to pay for their normal operating expenses suffered when the federal government began to retrench on its support for research.[7]

Several members of Congress reported in interviews that university administrators from their districts had come to them and had appealed for federal assistance. But the greatest activity came on the part of six major national higher-education associations: American Council on Education (ACE), National Association of State Universities and Land-Grant Colleges (NASULGC), American Association of State Colleges and Universities, Association of American Universities, Association of American Colleges, and the American Association of Junior Colleges. As political scientists Lawrence Gladieux and Thomas Wolanin note, the groups taken together "could claim to represent virtually every accredited, nonprofit postsecondary institution in the country."[8] The ACE is the largest of these associations, all of whose members are institutions of higher education, regional associations, or affiliated institutions. Often called higher education's "umbrella organization," its pre-eminence also stems from the fact that 80 percent of its more than 1,300 members also "hold membership in at least one of the other five organizations."[9]

Befitting its status, the ACE was the leader of the higher-education associations' lobbying effort, but it shared much of this work with the NASULGC. Though this group had only 130 members, approximately 30 percent of all college and university students attend the institutions that the NASULGC claims to represent. Its Washington office, opened in 1947, had a staff of fewer than fifteen people in 1972.[10] But its influence in part came from the access to Congress of its executive director, Ralph Huitt, who had been Assistant Secretary of HEW for Legislation under President Lyndon Johnson.

The major higher-education groups differed over what they wanted from the federal government, and the differences reflected the varying characteristics of their members. Some advocated a formula of allocation based on absolute enrollments; others stressed "degree production." Some argued that the level of instruction should be considered; others emphasized the type of instruction involved. But on the nature of federal aid, there was unanimous agreement among them: they all favored broad institutional grants and some form of allocation on a per student basis, and they advocated an increase in federal responsibility for funding their schools.[11] Their position established one pole of the federal-aid debate carried on in Congress.

The other pole was established by an amorphous group of people who constituted a higher-education policy elite. They rarely congregated in a formal way, although they would meet at conferences and work together occasionally on studies of higher education. They were people who knew and respected each other, and over a short period of time in the late 1960s they came to view the federal government's role in higher education similarly. The process of creating such consensus among policy elites occurred in a "cloudy way," according to Chester Finn, an education advisor in the Nixon White House. Finn described the situation as it appeared in 1969:

> One could detect agreement that the federal government had a proper role in ensuring that access to a college education was not denied people on account of poverty, that the existing *pot pourri* of programs did not adequately discharge that responsibility, and that the time had come to consider necessary changes.[12]

At the center of the group was the Carnegie Commission on Higher Education, which was often called the Kerr Commission after its chairman, Clark Kerr, former Chancellor of the University of California at Berkeley. The commission had been created by the Carnegie Foundation for the Advancement of Teaching in 1967, and its fifteen members included several college and university presidents, a former governor, and executives from three major corporations. But its importance emerged from the respect that policy elites accorded its numerous studies and reports issued between 1967 and 1973.

While the Kerr Commission was gearing up, Secretary of Health, Education and Welfare John Gardner created an Advisory Task Force on Higher Education within HEW to develop a coherent higher-education policy in place of the seeming patchwork that characterized the numerous programs in operation. Gardner had been president of the Carnegie Foundation before joining the Johnson administration. Notably, as political scientist Norman C. Thomas reports, his approach to the development of educational policies "resembled the operational pattern of a large philanthropic foundation,"[13] and he was inclined to attach great weight to recommendations of his several task forces.

The first Kerr Commission report, *Quality and Equality: New Levels of Federal Responsibility for Higher Education,* came out in December 1968. One month later the HEW task force issued its report, *Toward a Long Range Plan for Federal Financial Support for Higher Education.*[14] Though the two reports differed, they both argued that the federal government should increase aid to higher education and that aid should go primarily to the students themselves, in order to secure the goal of equal opportunity to attend an institution of higher education. Both rejected the higher-education associations' call for institutional aid based on enrollment. They asserted instead that institutional aid should be allocated on a "cost of instruction" basis.

Alice Rivlin, Assistant Secretary of HEW for Planning and Evaluation, had headed the HEW task force. With the arrival of a new administration, she took a position at the Brookings Institution, a research organization in Washington. From that post she continued to be an active member of the higher-education policy elite, and some members of Congress reported in interviews that they regularly called on her to articulate what came to be known as the Carnegie-Rivlin perspective.

The convergence of the two reports, Gladieux and Wolanin contend, was not the result of consultation between the Kerr and Rivlin groups, but an instance of the general phenomenon that "commission reports tend to codify thinking and opinions that [have] already gained at least some currency."[15] Undoubtedly the formation of a consensus was facilitated by the links that the Carnegie Foundation helped to forge.

The Carnegie link was forged initially into the Nixon administration by Alan Pifer, head of the Carnegie Foundation, who served as chief of the Nixon "transition task force" on education. This group emphasized that "existing student-aid programs failed to provide equal opportunity."[16] The link was maintained by Daniel Patrick Moynihan, who had served briefly on the Kerr Commission and became counselor to the president for domestic affairs in 1969.

In most cases, the hub of public-policy making is the executive branch, with interest groups and interested elites focusing their attention there. In this case attention was focused on Congress, and the executive seemed to act as merely another interest group, and not the strongest or most concerned of the lot. In the first month of the new administration, there were reports the president would issue a message to Congress on kindergarten through graduate-school education. But by early November 1969 higher education had been dropped from the proposed message. President Nixon decided to develop a policy on higher education only when the White House staff realized late in November that the 1968 Education Amendments required the president to report by the end of 1969 on the "feasibility of providing universal higher education."[17] The vehicle for generating the policy was the high-level Working Group on

Higher Education, chaired by Edward Morgan, an assistant to the president for domestic affairs. Moynihan was the most senior administration official in the Working Group.

Moynihan had been an Assistant Secretary of Labor in the Kennedy and Johnson administrations and was a professor at Harvard University when Nixon invited him to join the Cabinet. Today, as a Democratic senator from New York, he is a leading "neo-conservative," and these ideas were evident in his social outlook during the late 1960s. At that time Moynihan's ideas were predicated on a simple concept: American society was basically sound and that what ailed the poor was only their lack of money. Moynihan's solution was equally simple—give them money. The solution coincided with his expressed belief that the government could not devise programs to reform society or to change the poor.[18] Similarly, with respect to education, he believed that the government should give money directly to students to create a "floor" of support and should not attempt to help poor people obtain a higher education by controlling what colleges and universities did.

His intention to limit government involvement also seemed to reflect his concern about academic freedom. He recognized that any program of assistance to institutions of higher education would necessarily impose a set of constraints on the institutions, because the program would embody a set of purposes that the government was trying to achieve.[19] It is unclear whether Moynihan's association with the Kerr Commission influenced his ideas or merely encouraged him to rely on the commission for proposals that he recognized were consistent with his ideas.[20] Whatever their ultimate source, providing direct student assistance became a dominant theme in the Working Group.

The Carnegie emphasis on student aid had found ready support in the White House Working Group. To be sure, there were disagreements among the group members, which reflected the diverse concerns of the agencies the group members represented, but there were also common interests. The group included Assistant Secretary of HEW Lewis Butler, Richard Nathan of the Office of Management and Budget, Lee Du-Bridge, former president of the California Institute of Technology and President Nixon's Science Advisor, and James Allen, the Commissioner of Education. Allen was vociferous in advocating grants to students, according to Chester Finn, because he "championed the idea that the first responsibility of the federal government was to break down the . . . barriers that kept the poor and black" from going to college.[21] Nathan, too, favored providing aid directly to students, but he focused less on equal opportunity than on the way direct aid would reduce the Washington bureaucracy and remove some of its operational influence.[22] The group considered several forms of student aid and mechanisms for distributing it. Ultimately, it agreed on recommending a basic grant to which all students with family incomes under $10,000 would be entitled.

Late in March 1970 President Nixon took the recommendations and with little alteration delivered a message to Congress on higher education. In it he emphasized equal educational opportunity for the poor, and he proposed a program of guaranteed loans and a $1,400 stipend to poor students to achieve this goal. But the message, and its accompanying bill, were not accorded much attention on Capitol Hill. The president was little interested in domestic policies other than welfare reform, and there was a sense that he lacked enthusiasm for his proposals.[23] Members of Congress did not expect that he would pressure them to support his higher-education bill. They were aware of the rumor that the president had gone beyond the mandate of the 1968 Education Amendments and had requested in November 1969 that the Working Group develop major higher-education legislation mainly because the White House had learned that Congresswoman Green was organizing December hearings on her own major bill. Indeed, when much of the active lobbying occurred on the higher-education act in 1971 and 1972, members of Congress heard little from the executive branch. By that time Moynihan and Allen had departed from the administration, and no senior officials were left who had an intense interest in the legislation. Pride, not commitment, fostered the Nixon bill.

Pride is an intangible, unpredictable factor that complicates any easy explanation of congressional behavior. The members of Congress act from many motives and respond to diverse pressures that can be catalogued objectively. But they also respond to subjective personal needs. This case was no different from many others in that regard.

Personal Interests of the Members

In addition to pride, two other subjective factors were especially evident among the members in interviews: time constraints and interpersonal hostility. Interviews about the 1972 Higher Education Act were conducted with sixty-one members of the House from June to October 1972. The interviews were semi-structured and ranged from twenty-five minutes to three and one-half hours, with most lasting forty-five minutes. As Tables 5–1 and 5–2 indicate, the sample approximated the House as a whole in terms of party and seniority.[24] From the interviews it appears that the three subjective factors seem to have influenced the way in which members acted in shaping the higher-education legislation.

Pride. Edith Green was considered one of the most knowledgeable members in Congress about higher education. She saw herself as a na-

TABLE 5-1   **Party and Seniority of the Sample**

PARTY	SENIORITY				
	0-2 years	3-9 years	10-21 years	22+ years	Total
Democratic	7	11	11	5	34 (56%)
Percent	*21*	*32*	*32*	*15*	*100*
Republican	9	10	7	1	27 (44%)
Percent	*33*	*37*	*26*	*4*	*100*
Total	16	21	18	6	61 (100%)
Percent	*26*	*34*	*30*	*10*	*100*

tional spokeswoman for the higher-education community, and she was known to have taken great pride in developing her version of the higher-education act. Passage of the act became a personal quest, especially when other members of the committee and key senators opposed her version of the bill. Her intense personal identification with the bill she introduced in 1971—which emphasized aid to institutions and loans—undoubtedly contributed to her 1972 vote against the final conference report, which altered her bill in fundamental ways. She explained that in her view the conference report was worse than no bill at all.

Like Green, John Brademas (D–Ind.) was described by other members as seeing himself as a spokesman for higher education. A supporter of the Carnegie/Rivlin/Moynihan approaches, he prided himself on his close association with presidents of major universities and foundations. For example, at the annual meeting of the American Political Science Association in 1968, he shared a panel with Cornell University President James Perkins and Ford Foundation head McGeorge Bundy. Brademas began his talk by noting that he thought each of the three could readily switch jobs and fill the others' shoes. (In 1981, after losing an election, Brademas became the president of New York University.)

Pride took other forms as well. One member indicated that his sense of self-importance was so great that he was responsible for the well-being of all young people. Lamenting about the tendency of some bright students to forgo college, he spoke about his own children: "One child is toying with the idea of not going to college. I fear for him, though, that he will be crippled in 20 years. Likewise, I feel like a parent for all children." Some members may have been especially sensitive to the beseeching appeals from universities because of their own particular histories. "Most of these members," a Republican explained, "have been to college, so they naturally think college is a good thing, without reflecting on it." A Democrat remarked that several members who grew up in

TABLE 5-2   **Party and Seniority of the Complete House, June 1972**

PARTY	SENIORITY				
	0-2 years	3-9 years	10-21 years	22+ years	Total
Democratic	54	79	78	43	254 (59%)
Percent	*21*	*31*	*31*	*17*	*100*
Republican	41	76	55	7	179 (41%)
Percent	*23*	*42*	*31*	*4*	*100*
Total	95	155	133	50	433(100%)
Percent	*22*	*36*	*31*	*12*	*100*

near-poverty attributed the status they had attained to a college education and supported aid to colleges without question.

Time.   There are far more demands made on a member than he or she can reasonably meet, and members must therefore budget their time.[25] One time-consuming activity that concerns all members is campaigning for re-election. Several members focused on campaigning to explain why the bill was crafted as omnibus legislation. (An omnibus bill—the word *bus* derives from *omnibus*—carries with it miscellaneous legislation. In this case the legislation included such topics as student aid, community colleges, and occupational education.) These members said that Senator Pell was worried about his re-election in 1972. He had wanted to complete all pending education legislation by the end of 1971 so that he would be free in 1972 to wage a vigorous campaign in what he anticipated would be a difficult race. The only way to complete the legislation in his view was to lump it all together. In a similar vein, one member of the House subcommittee said that he did not have the time to consider all points of view on the issue and did not attempt to go beyond the interest groups with which he was allied because he was chairman of another subcommittee and needed to devote time to it as a first priority.

Interpersonal hostility.   The personal antagonism between Representative Green and other members of the Education and Labor Committee was well known in Congress. Some of those interviewed attributed the tension to Green's personality and called her "irascible" or "strong-willed." Others betrayed in their comments—such as "she's a bitch," or "what she needs is a good lay"—blatant sexism which suggested that for them to accept a strong woman leader would be difficult. In an interview, she acknowledged the apparent sexism of her detractors and said that she had felt excluded from some decision making in the House because she is a woman. But, she remarked, "I try not to think about that. I get very angry when I do."[26] Other members said that they opposed her because of her strong anti-busing stands and her efforts to penalize students involved in campus demonstrations.[27] Indeed, in 1969 and 1970 a block of liberals on the subcommittee she chaired boycotted the higher-education hearings in an attempt to deny her a quorum and thus block the legislation she had sponsored. A few members reported that Carl Perkins (D–Ky.), chairman of the full committee, was antagonistic towards Representative Green because she had asked the House formally to instruct the conferees on the higher-education bill to maintain the House position (which embodied much of her original bill). Perkins was said to have taken this as a vote of no confidence in his committee members who made up the House side of the conference. This apparently led him to approve of a meeting between Senator Pell and Representatives Brademas, Albert Quie (R–Minn.), and John Dellenback (R–Ore.) during the conference that resulted in a victory for the side that supported the Carnegie approach to federal aid.[28]

These three subjective factors reflect the personal interests that most people attempt to satisfy in a variety of situations. However, the personal interests of the members in this case are too vague to explain the particular nature of the Higher Education Act. Personal interests may have influenced the dynamics of the process in this case, but to argue that Representatives Brademas and Green, for example, pursued different bills merely because they disliked each other or each was too proud to acquiesce to the other's bill would strain credibility.

Not all personal factors can be dismissed so readily. The quest for job security, that is, the concern with re-election and so with the desires of constituents, can have a powerful influence on the content of legislation. In this case, however, constituent interests seemed to have played a minor role. Some members said that their support for federal aid to higher education was responsive to constituent demands, because tuition was rising to a point higher than many people could afford to pay. But most admitted that they had received very little mail from their districts about the higher education act. They said that they heard principally from college administrators. Indeed, when members were asked how the final bill would affect people in their districts, 79 percent (n=46) of those who responded said that they did not know, 5 percent (n=3) said the effect would be unclear, and 16 percent (n=9) said it would benefit their districts.

In theory, the legislators should have known how the bill might have affected their constituents because opposing sides in the two-year struggle over this act had made vociferous claims about who would benefit. The Green version was said to be a "middle-class" bill because it would have funneled two thirds of the institutional aid to colleges and universities on the basis of per capita enrollments. As a result, the large state institutions, to which the bulk of the middle class sent its children, were expected to benefit more than relatively smaller private institutions, according to the bill's supporters. Student aid would have been continued principally in the form of loans and work-study. In contrast, the final bill (embodying the Brademas approach) was said to favor the rich and poor. The equal opportunity grants, its supporters said, would enable poor students to attend private institutions. The institutional aid formula— under which aid would be linked to the amount of federal student aid and the number of poor students at an institution—was thus expected to go mainly to black colleges and to the schools of the rich.[29]

The reality of these apparent differences, however, was less dramatic. A $1,400 grant to a needy student would still have left the student far short of being able to afford the $2,000 to $3,000 tuitions at private universities in 1972. Such a student was likely to have attended a state university, which then would have received institutional aid because of the student's presence.[30] This reality may have made legislators unsure about the material consequences of supporting one version or the other, but it does not diminish the evidence that they were not responding to their constituents when they were dealing with the bill.

Members of Congress may even have acted against their constituents' wishes. While the legislators received few letters from their districts, they could not readily take this absence of articulation as tacit support for federal aid to colleges and universities. A Gallup Poll as early as 1969 had indicated public disapproval of major federal support for higher education. When asked if the federal government should pay for all of the costs of a college education or whether the cost principally should be "paid, as now, by parents and students," 70 percent of the Gallup sample said that parents and students should pay; only 16 percent favored the federal government paying all costs.[31] The poll may have tapped the public's general discontent with colleges and universities, one aspect of which educators were beginning to recognize. Higher-education officials in the early 1970s were citing diminishing enrollments with alarm."[32]

An Instrumentalist Explanation Rejected

The absence of constituent support for the higher-education bill, and the weakness of an explanation that would rely too heavily on the personal interests of the legislators, focuses attention once again on the groups who encouraged Congress to pass the legislation. The interest groups' demands raise intriguing questions as to what the groups' interests were and why legislators listened to these groups. The apparent ability of the groups to influence the congressional decision-making process in this case also suggests that key members of Congress may have been "captured" by the groups and may have been no more than the pawns—or instruments—of powerful forces outside Congress.

Such an explanation of congressional behavior has been called an instrumentalist analysis.[33] An analyst who uses this approach would likely explain action of the government by pointing to close links between government decision makers and those who control productive wealth. The links might be forged by personal ties of friendship, by graft, or by campaign contributions. The "real" interests of legislators—in contrast to personal interests—are assumed to reside with forces outside Congress. The method of investigation from this perspective is to locate the links between Congress and a particular set of groups, ascertain what the groups wanted and what Congress produced, and conclude that, if the results approximate what the groups wanted, Congress acted on behalf of the groups as their instrument. Consider how the details of this case seem to support an instrumentalist analysis.

First, all of the principal House actors were part of the higher-education subgovernment in Washington. A subgovernment consists of the members and staff of a subcommittee that handles policy in a particular area, the people in an executive-branch agency who also work with that policy, and relevant interest groups. The American Council on Education and its allied associations had worked with Representatives Brademas, Green, Quie, Dellenback and Frank Thompson (D–N.J.) for several years on previous bills. Indeed, when Representative Green held hearings on higher-education legislation in 1969 and 1970, the associations at first did not support her efforts and were close to Representative Brademas because they opposed the federal involvement in campus turmoil that her bill proposed.[34] That bill died in the full Education and Labor Committee in the summer of 1970. Shortly thereafter, the associations approached Representative Brademas, according to one source in Congress, and proposed that he sponsor a new bill. He rejected this plan, arguing that it was too late in the session to bring up new legislation. They then turned to Representative Green, and in February 1971 she announced hearings on a new bill. The associations never went back to Representative Brademas, nor did they make an effort to work closely with the ranking Republican on the committee, Representative Quie. One spokesman for the associations contended that they ignored these two powerful legislators because their positions were antithetical to that of the associations.[35]

While both representatives said that they were not fixed in their positions and would have been open to suggestions from the associations, they had already begun a close association with Carnegie-Rivlin-Moynihan policy elites. Representative Brademas had sponsored legislation in

1969 that embodied the Carnegie cost-of-instruction approach to institutional aid. He was a Harvard overseer and was one of those who made up the consensus on equal opportunity that Chester Finn claimed to have discovered among elites in 1969. Understandably, Representative Green was thought to distrust Representative Brademas during the nine-week conflict in conference that tried to resolve House-Senate differences on the legislation. She believed that he was in a covert alliance with the Senate conferees who espoused the Carnegie approach.[36] The belief was borne out when Senator Pell and Representatives Brademas, Quie, and Dellenback broke the conference deadlock with a compromise they had worked out secretly.[37]

The links between the groups and the members of Congress reflected the structures of the House and Senate. Members of the House Education and Labor subcommittee on higher education tended to be closer to the lobbyists from the higher-education associations than were the senators on the Labor and Public Welfare education subcommittee.[38] By specializing in higher education, the representatives formed a natural part of the higher-education subgovernment. In contrast, the Senate subcommittee handled all levels of education, and its members moved in and out of the subgovernment. They tended to take a broader view and such a perspective meshed neatly with the sort of proposals that the Kerr Commission advocated.

Perhaps because it was not part of a subgovernment, the Kerr Commission saw the whole Congress as its audience, not merely the members of the subcommittees. Its reports and recommendations were distributed to every office, and members who were not on the Education and Labor Committee explained their support of the higher-education bill in terms that closely paraphrased the Carnegie volumes. For example, a conservative Democrat said, "We need enlightened equal opportunity. We have too many chiefs and not enough Indians." In another interview, a moderate Democrat remarked, "We got the idea that everyone had to have a college degree. We had lowered our standards too far." And a moderate Republican commented, "Many people shouldn't be going to an academic course—it should be a kind of technical or vocational training for which there is a requirement."

These comments echo the Carnegie Commission recommendations:

The Commission believes that access to higher education should be expanded so that there will be an opportunity within the total system . . . for each high school graduate or otherwise qualified person. This does not mean that every young person should of necessity attend college—many will not want to attend, and there will be others who will not benefit sufficiently from attendance to justify their time and the expense involved. . . . Within the system

of higher education, the community colleges should follow an open enrollment policy, whereas access to four-year institutions should generally be
more selective.[39]

Of course, from an instrumentalist perspective, the best evidence that
a group has been able to exert control over Congress is the final outcome.
In this case the Carnegie Commission seemed to get almost everything it
called for in 1970:

> . . . financial aid to students, with a substantial component of grants for
> low-income students and a moderately expanded loan program primarily for
> middle-income students; cost-of-education supplements to institutions; and
> creation of new places to accommodate all qualified students.[40]

It then proposed that the existing program of educational opportunity
grants be expanded and that up to $1,000 be given directly to each stu-
dent "in the lowest income quartile." Further it recommended that institutional aid go "to colleges and universities based on the numbers and
levels of students holding federal grants enrolled in the institutions."[41]

As noted earlier, the final bill closely matched these recommendations. It authorized a new program of basic educational opportunity
grants and the expansion of the student-loan program, cost-of-education
payments to colleges and universities based on the number of students
receiving BEOG funds and on the number of students receiving all federal assistance, and $275 million "in order to encourage and assist those
states and localities which so desire in establishing or expanding community colleges."

The instrumentalist case would seem to be on solid ground from this
evidence. Further, analysts who take this approach—such as G. William
Domhoff—have emphasized the way in which corporations control government behavior by setting the limits on debate through the use of
supposedly objective studies by research organizations. The Carnegie
Commission and the Brookings Institution, which figured prominently
here, are the sorts of organizations to which he has pointed.[42] As economists Samuel Bowles and Herbert Gintis note, the Carnegie Foundation
has worked closely with corporations to reform education in ways that
serve the needs of corporations and it appeared to be following this
course though the Kerr Commission.[43]

From an instrumentalist perspective this case appears to have been a
lovely little conspiracy. This conclusion identifies precisely a weakness of
the perspective: little conspiracies do not construct major policy changes
such as the Higher Education Act. The links between the legislators and
higher-education policy elites were real, and the links between the elites

and major corporations were probably real as well. But the fact of inter-action is not simultaneously a fact about influence. Knowing that one group influenced the other cannot logically derive from knowing that links existed. What we would need to know first is the dynamics of policy formation to appreciate why the links might be important.

The dynamics are critical, as Professor Domhoff has argued in de-fending his approach.[44] The focus on individuals and their connections is no more than a research strategy for learning about the process of domi-nation by an owning class. This evidence, he elaborates, can indicate the nature of class formation and class struggle, which are correctly under-stood as dynamic processes, not as the static aggregates that an emphasis on powerful people might suggest. Thus an instrumentalist might say that when we see the Carnegie Foundation—which surely reflects the interests of the owning class—propose certain policies, we should understand that this is an aspect of their strategy in a class struggle. An emphasis on the Carnegie Foundation therefore facilitates an appreciation of the struggle manifested in the policies.

Such a claim might be valid, but it does not explain why Congress adopted the policy. An instrumentalist analysis would assume that Con-gress is influenced in particular cases by the particular powerful people with whom members have contact. As a corollary, it would assume that Congress is passive, merely responding to such influence.[45] These assump-tions in effect deny the significance of other interests a legislator might have, interests that are unrelated to the connections with powerful people on a particular policy.

A representative, for example, might be concerned about the very legitimacy of Congress. He or she might worry about this for several re-asons, including a patriotic concern about representative democracy and a selfish concern about re-election if voters think the whole Congress is a bunch of incompetent scoundrels. Congress's loss of legitimacy may reflect the dynamics of class struggle, because Congress makes decisions that affect the struggle. In turn, its efforts to regain legitimacy may affect the struggle, because Congress may attack "big business" or wealthy interests in order to seem evenhanded. In this way, owning-class domination of the society may affect what Congress does. But the effect would be indirect, and, significantly, the fact that members have multiple interests to try to satisfy leads them to be active, not passive. By starting with their links to powerful people, a researcher would tend to de-emphasize the class bias embedded in their other interests, and the degree to which they act inten-tionally. Especially in the case of the Higher Education Act, such de-emphasis would distort a picture of the dynamics that were taking place.

The deeper dynamics of class domination are not clear from the personal connections between the Kerr Commission and Congress. The commission had no resources with which it could "threaten" legislators, and did not try to operate as a lobby. Although higher-education associations might have tried to influence the House, these groups had few resources to be used as "threats," and the evidence suggests that Representative Green actually pressured them to work solely with her rather than vice versa.[46] Friendship with Daniel Moynihan and Clark Kerr conceivably may have influenced Representative Brademas, but such an argument gives the congressman too little credit and does not explain the behavior of the rest of Congress. The bill was, after all, "landmark" legislation and not a dam project. In producing a major act, Congress does not usually operate according to a simple notion of reciprocity or defer totally to specialization.[47] What seems most likely in this case is that there was a meeting of like minds, that Congress relied on the Carnegie-Rivlin-Moynihan arguments because they were a well-articulated rationale for an approach that Congress wanted to take.

The Carnegie Commission may have acted as a reference group for Congress, indicating to the members the "acceptable" outer limits of behavior. But a reference group is an organization that acts on behalf of an identifiable set of interests, such as the producers or consumers of particular products, the companies in a sector of the economy, or even corporations that are identified as predominantly local or national by their markets. Such interests are not evident here. The Carnegie Commission was funded by national corporations, but it espoused the same ideas that local education officials were advocating. In a study of eighty-six legislators and fourteen executive-branch officials in nine states who were responsible for making education policy in their states, Heinz Eulau and Harold Quigley found that these people emphasized the goal of equal educational opportunity, as did the Carnegie reports. And like the Carnegie Commission, the state officials also focused on benefits to community colleges.[48]

Even if the Carnegie Commission served to establish the lines of debate for Congress—and that proposition now seems dubious—its link to Congress does not explain why the members felt compelled to act, to take the occasion of renewing existing higher-education programs as an opportunity for restructuring higher education. Personal pride might explain why Representatives Green or Brademas seized the opportunity, but not why the whole Congress did. Direct external pressure is not a plausible explanation, because there was little observable pressure, especially from White House. The development of this legislation appears to have emanated from Congress itself, as the members sought to address a problem they recognized. In effect, if there were a meeting of minds between the Carnegie Commission and Congress, it is important to discern what was in the legislators' minds and to appreciate the nature of the problem they addressed.

TABLE 5-3 **Class and Ideology of the Sample**

IDEOLOGY *	CLASS AND PERCENT IDENTIFYING WITH PARTICULAR IDEOLOGY			
	Middle (%)	Upper Middle (%)	Upper (%)	Total
Liberal	1 (13)	3 (15)	12 (67)	16
Percent	*6*	*19*	*75*	*100*
Moderate	6 (75)	11 (55)	4 (22)	21
Percent	*29*	*52*	*19*	*100*
Conservative	1 (13)	6 (30)	2 (11)	9
Percent	*11*	*67*	*22*	*100*
Total	8 (100)	20 (100)	18 (100)	46**

* Ideology percentages indicate the class identification of those subscribing to a particular ideology; i.e., 6 percent of those who considered themselves liberal also thought of themselves as belonging to the middle class.

**The number of representatives in the sample who identified themselves in terms of both class and ideology:

Members' Perceptions

As the legislative history indicates, the members were not of one mind about the solution to the problem they faced. What is interesting, however, is the view they expressed of the problem itself. Interviews with active members show that Congress had a common sense of the larger crisis and an intuitive grasp of how to handle the crisis. The members' general approach was to restore the legitimating function of higher education.

The reasons members gave for their support of the higher-education act are summarized in Table 5–4. (Members classified themselves according to ideology and class. The totals for responses under class and ideology are different because not every member identified himself or herself according to both ideology and class.) The largest number of responses can be categorized as relating to equal opportunity, with 37 percent of the total falling into this category. Many members said that they tried to increase the possibility of opportunity by providing guaranteed loans, aid to institutions, and/or basic educational opportunity grants to students. In this regard, divisions between those who supported aid to institutions based on the number of poor students enrolled and those who favored institutional aid on a per capita basis were not significant. Both claimed that their approaches provided for equal opportunity, with the former emphasizing opportunity for the poor and the latter for the middle class.

TABLE 5–4 **Members' Views on the Purposes of Higher Education**

PURPOSE	CLASS			IDEOLOGY		
	Middle	Upper Middle	Upper	Liberal	Moderate	Conservative
Equality of opportunity—remove barriers	3	10	10	7	12	3
Way to get ahead	3	1	5	7	5	1
Vocational education provides country with needed skilled labor	2	4	4	1	10	2
Vocational education is place for those unsuited to academic education	0	5	5	2	6	5
Broadening experience—improves quality of life	2	4	2	3	5	1
Tones down divisions—gives a stake in the system	1	3	3	3	5	2
Makes people more responsible, better citizens	2	1	2	4	3	0
Other	4	8	3	4	11	5
Total responses	17	36	34	31	57	19
n =	9	19	18	18	26	11

For example, members said that higher education was a "way to get ahead," to get a good job. A first-term conservative Republican said the bill would give people "the opportunity to develop their potential as far as they can take it." A moderate Republican freshman spoke of removing the "financial barriers from those who ought to be going" to college. A senior Democrat said that Congress's intention was "to make it possible for anybody who is motivated to have post-secondary education, regardless of the status of the father's pocketbook." A liberal freshman Democrat laid out his perspective in detail:

> Education is considered a good thing. It's a means of getting ahead. Blue-collar workers like it because it's a chance for their kids to have a better life than they had. It's the opportunity for a kid with initiative and drive and intelligence to rise.

When asked if an emphasis on higher education might not create the problem of a new group of losers in the society—those without a B.A.—he responded:

Only if the distinction is made on something other than ability. When all the barriers are knocked down, and the guys who are running things are there because they're better than someone else, how do you argue then? But we're far from that. The barriers to people getting an education are not just ability. The higher-education act is a way of doing away with *artificial* barriers.

But legislators were not ready to send everyone to a four-year college. A moderate Democrat, for example, commented that when people get a "college degree, and can't get a job, they're disillusioned. And here we are with fine jobs going begging in the service industries." Of course, were such a member to suggest that students be directed into service-sector jobs without a post-secondary education, he would have seemed to violate the promise of equal opportunity. Thus members focused on post-secondary vocational education as a way to resolve the potential contradiction. As one Republican said:

I think you'd find that additional money for vocational education would have pretty broad appeal throughout the Congress. We kind of recognize that we've put the emphasis for too many people on trying to get them through college. A lot of people just shouldn't be in college.

A senior liberal Democrat commented on the merits of public junior colleges:

Community colleges are the most exciting thing that's happened in higher education. They're accessible. And they're inexpensive, and they're near-by. If it doesn't provide them with a way to succeed, it provides them with an opportunity to say "I was able to try it, I was financially able to do it, and I either cut it or I didn't cut it."

A moderate Democrat described the community college in his district:

[It has] a new program called "building maintenance." Now what is building maintenance—it's being a janitor. But if these kids can be useful that way, they shouldn't be ignored. They're going to get out [of high school] at 16, and they are the ones who cause us trouble. But if we can find a place for them, so that everyone has a role, that's what we should do.

Community colleges also function to break up the college community, by placing large numbers of students in isolating circumstances. Gladieux and Wolanin indicate that legislators had perceived on the college campuses "a growing and self-conscious youth culture standing in many ways counter to the style and values of the larger society."[49] Members saw community colleges as a corrective to this situation, but at the same time community colleges would develop in students the desirable values higher education is thought to impart. Thus one moderate Democrat said, "Through vocational education you keep him in school. Good students aren't troublemakers. We can keep them in an atmosphere that's conducive to learning." This attitude was echoed by another moderate Democrat:

> I'm not for shoving people out into the job market with a quickie-training program in voc. ed. [sic], because that develops the blue-collar kind of political syndrome which I detest, where they have absolutely no sophistication with issues, with concepts, with the importance of history.

Thus students in community colleges could develop their capacities as workers without acquiring the "alien" values found in college communities, because community colleges are, as one member said, "commuter schools."

The two-year schools also appeared to be addressing another aspect of the higher-education crisis: they were oriented to training students for skilled jobs that companies were seeking to fill. This was related to the emphasis that both educators and the United States Office of Education had placed on "career education." (Members also sought to meet this goal through the occupational-education provisions of the Higher Education Act.) Career education, W. Norton Grubb and Marvin Lazerson write, calls for all phases of the curriculum to be job-oriented so that "students possess immediately marketable skills."[50] The emphasis on career education, they contend, stems from the same concerns that have historically dominated vocational education; like vocational programs, career education is intended "to teach the skills necessary for success in the new industrial order."[51]

In a similar vein, members spoke about the need to provide trained workers for the new "knowledge industries." Two members said that they were concerned about minorities being left behind unless they could develop the necessary skills. But others focused on "society's need" for skilled workers. For example, a liberal Democrat commented:

> You need people who come in at a certain time, and who are in a certain reasonable number of days a week. . . . All the office and service skills are highly sophisticated skills which require certain basic understanding of middle-class values, of dress and manners and controlling your temper and things like that.

Remarked a conservative Republican:

We have a need for certain kinds of technical people in fields of medicine. Not doctors and nurses, but other categories. We could take a trained person out of high school, give them two or three years of training in the so-called paramedical field, and do a far more effective job of utilization of education resources. . . . We have a surplus of teachers. . . . I'm sure many of them are frustrated. . . . It's the ability of the system at all levels to deal more responsibly, for channeling, or encouraging, people in the direction of where there is need.

In emphasizing career education, legislators did not perceive that they were manipulating their constituents. In this instance they perceived that they were responding to constituent demands for education that would help the constituents' children obtain jobs. In contrast to the Gallup Poll that found most people opposing federal payment of all college costs, 90 percent of the respondents in a 1972 poll said that schools should give more emphasis to the study of business, trades, and professions.[52] Thus, unlike the enactment of basic student grants, passage of the career-education titles was in accord with constituents' views. At the same time, legislators attempted to realize other interests as well—such as social control of the work force through stratification—by channeling career education through community colleges.

The Larger Context: A Legitimacy Crisis

Several analysts have observed that Congress passed the Higher Education Act at a time when colleges and universities were experiencing a "depression" resulting from rising costs and falling enrollments. Small institutions, and even some major ones, were in such serious trouble that a federal bailout seemed to be the only solution for them. Had institutions' financial problems been the principal issue that Congress addressed in the Higher Education Act, the bill would have taken Green's route and provided institutional aid on a per capita enrollment basis. Instead Congress linked institutional aid to student aid for the poor. Gladieux and Wolanin suggest that Congress took this approach because in the 1960s there was both a "national reawakening" to the existence of poverty in our midst and a common agreement among leaders to break down barriers to equal opportunity. Unequal access to higher education seemed to be one of those barriers. Thus it was "the vision of equal education opportunity, a legacy of the 60s," they contend, that "remained a driving force" to which Congress responded in 1972.[53]

In that analysis, the authors focus helpfully on the larger problem of equal opportunity rather than on the immediate financial problems of colleges. But equal opportunity was not merely an altruistic concern. And the way in which Congress sought to address the problem of equal opportunity indicates the complexity of the link between education and equal opportunity and also suggests that Congress was attempting to handle an even larger problem. To appreciate the complexity, and what Congress may have been doing, consider first some important functions of the higher-education system in the United States and how poorly the system was fulfilling these functions by 1970.

The leaders of any complex social system generally search for ways to maintain and reproduce the system they lead. They will not attempt to re-create the society with each new generation as a carbon copy of the last, nor will they try to obviate all changes. Change is inevitable because there is a tendency for people to struggle for better conditions of life. Leaders attempt to reproduce the dominant patterns in which people organize their lives and to maintain the society this way. Ours is a pluralist society and people organize their lives in relation to different ethnic groups, in a variety of spatial patterns, and in ways that enhance a multitude of values. But the dominant characteristic revolves around the way in which we produce the goods and services we need. A very small percentage of the population owns and controls the factories, offices, land and other means of producing goods and services. The vast proportion of people obtain these goods and services by purchasing them with wages they earn in return for the work they do. This pattern is neither natural nor inevitable; it is maintained and re-created through several mechanisms in the society. One of the most important of these is the higher-education system. The higher-education system serves other purposes as well, but there are at least two ways in which it functions as a mechanism for re-creating the system we have for producing goods and services.[54]

In the first instance, colleges and universities teach future workers the skills necessary to perform their jobs. A trained employee saves a company the money it would otherwise spend to train the worker, and the skill is used ultimately to generate the goods that provide a worker with his or her salary and the company with its profits. Notably, colleges and universities have altered their curricula significantly in the twentieth century to accommodate the skill requirements of corporations.[55] Workers trained in colleges seem to acquire the additional quality of being adaptable to changing circumstances, according to V. Lane Rawlins and Lloyd Ulman. They found in a survey of employers that firms hire college graduates with the belief that such employees will be "more versatile because they have more education."[56]

Rawlins and Ulman found that firms desire college-trained workers perhaps even more for a non-specific skill they seem to acquire with more education. Employers said that a college degree indicated to them that a potential employee had not only intelligence and motivation, but also a "certain ability to get along with peers and superiors."[57] This skill may be the consequence of four more years of schooling, during which time troublemakers are weeded out and the socialization process continues to reinforce the earlier pressure to work and play well with others. But it is also likely that employers' impressions of college students were shaped at a time when there was a decided class bias to the college population. Even as late as the 1960s there was a significant difference between high-school seniors of working-class parents and those of professional parents, and similarly between poor and rich students, with respect to their decision to attend college.[58] For example, 40 percent of the college freshmen in 1961 came from the top socioeconomic quartile, and only 12 percent came from the bottom quartile.

Dominated as they were by the upper class, colleges bred a sense of elitism among their students, a sense that they would be the leaders, innovators, and major beneficiaries of the productive wealth in each succeeding generation. They also encouraged students to think independently and creatively, in short, to develop an ability to be "versatile." While they provided students with a respect for authority, rules, and the social order, colleges also endowed students with a belief that they would be the ones in authority and be able to make the rules.

College socialization contrasts sharply with the process in elementary and high schools, where the effort is one "of integrating young people into adult work roles" that are expected to be for most of them the role of subservient worker.[59] Schools tend to emphasize obedience to authority; they reward punctuality and regular attendance and punish lateness and absence. A student works for a tangible external reward—a grade, which is similar to a wage—not for any purpose intrinsic to the work itself. Ultimately, students are taught to think of themselves as machines—as human capital—that they must sell on a labor market where they compete against other workers.[60]

While their education may be dissimilar, the difference between college-trained and non-college-trained workers may be more myth than real. It provides a convenient rationale by which employers can segment workers and differentially reward them. As Margaret Gordon reports, "Employers tend to raise their selection standards when there is a surplus of job seekers and to lower them when there is a shortage."[61] That is, it appears employers need a standard for differentiation, not for particular skills. This conclusion is buttressed by the findings of Ivar Berg and Sherry Gorelick that educational requirements for many jobs bear little relation to the skills necessary to perform the jobs.[62]

Until the 1960s, the claim that college-educated workers were worth more because of what they had learned was hardly challenged. Those who graduated from college generally earned more or had the opportunity to earn more than high-school graduates.[63] As a mechanism for conferring elite status on only a small portion of the population, a college education had clear advantages over inheritance because it seemed to apportion rewards on the basis of individual merit. In this way higher education served an important ideological function. It reinforced the prevailing ideology of individualism and meritocracy, and it provided a justification for inequality in a society where many people held egalitarianism as a high value.

The justification for inequality is that those who have more deserve more because they have earned it. From this perspective, those without wealth have only themselves to blame, because an individual's fate is a consequence of his or her own merit. The educational system provides the instrument for measuring merit. As Bowles and Gintis argue, it thus

> fosters and reinforces the belief that economic success depends essentially on the possession of technical and cognitive skills—skills which it is organized to provide in an efficient, equitable and unbiased manner on the basis of meritocratic principle.[64]

The educational system became part of an ideological arsenal that has been used to convince working people to accept the system of inequality. Indeed, it had such widespread acceptance that advocates of societal change turned to it as a mechanism for reform. As David Cohen and Marvin Lazerson explain, reformers have seen "education as a vehicle for promoting social reform through individual mobility":

> The notion that education was a means for deferring direct (redistributive) social change by displacing it onto individual achievement has been a central element in modern American liberalism. It rests on a desire to promote social justice without attacking the distribution or ownership of property.[65]

Several factors in the 1960s combined to undermine the higher-education system as a mechanism for fulfilling the two functions of training skilled workers and legitimating the social order. College enrollments had soared in the late 1950s and 1960s. In large part this increase was a product of the postwar "baby boom." In part it resulted from state governments' expansion of public universities in response to demands from workers who wanted their children to realize the "American dream," a dream they thought was attainable through education. Universities were also expanded in response to corporations that sought more skilled workers, both for the workers' skills and in order to increase their number. Historically, companies have promoted education in order to "produce surpluses of skilled labor, thereby increasing the power of employers over employees."[66]

College graduates have different expectations from their jobs than do high-school graduates, and this created two problems in the late 1960s and 1970s. First, college graduates were not taking blue-collar jobs. While they filled certain jobs, they also left other jobs unfilled—jobs that corporations needed filled. Second, not enough "good" white-collar jobs were available for all the graduates, as was manifest in the widespread white-collar job dissatisfaction reported in a government study.[67] In 1972 such worker alienation seemed to be a problem that could not be resolved in an easy way, and the problem was expected to grow. A 1973 Bureau of Labor Statistics report projected that 9.8 million college graduates would enter the labor force by 1980, but that only 9.6 million jobs would require college degrees. Of these, 2.6 million were expected to have resulted merely from the upgrading of requirements on jobs for which a degree previously had not been required.[68]

The second problem caused by increased enrollment was that workers were discovering that the relationship between education and income had been spurious. As more people gained a college degree, the degree no longer proved to be the guarantee of a high wage. The power of workers to demand a higher wage is related to their uniqueness and scarcity. Even by the early 1960s increases in education were no longer translatable into higher wages across the board.[69] Perhaps more striking, by 1971 a college degree no longer even guaranteed a job. The United States Bureau of Labor Statistics reported that between 1969 and 1971 the rate of unemployment for college graduates increased by 150 percent, to 2.3 percent.[70] In effect, higher education was ceasing to serve as a mechanism for legitimating inequality, because the inequality less and less appeared to be the consequence of individual merit.

The two problems manifested themselves quickly, as the rate of increase in college enrollments declined. In 1971 the increase was 4.1 percent, whereas it had been expected to be 6.2 percent. At four-year colleges, there was an actual decline in first-time freshman enrollments.[71]

As colleges were no longer turning out graduates destined principally for elite positions, they had to take on an unaccustomed task of socializing students for subservient occupational roles. In effect, they had to fulfill two incompatible obligations simultaneously: train the elite to be independent and creative and train the mass to be obedient and orderly. For the second task, they had to take on the character of high schools, which might have been necessary even had there been no expansion, because the structure of jobs in the United States was changing. White-collar work increasingly resembled blue-collar work, with a compartmentalization of skills, a loss of control over the production process, and an inability to control one's own time. The expanding use of technology in the office also made the vaunted white-collar professional in many cases little more than an appendage to a computer.[72] In a manner similar to the late nineteenth-century process of industrialization, when craft workers were essentially de-skilled and the work process was broken into discrete parts, the white-collar worker today has lost much autonomy. The higher education of such workers needed to change in a corresponding way.

Universities seemed to lose a sense of purpose in the 1960s, and the aimlessness contributed to growing student alienation. In campus demonstrations that began in 1964, students not only focused on the war in Vietnam and on the institutional racism they found at many universities, but they also struggled against the inclination of higher-education institutions to take on the characteristics of the workplace—through depersonalization, large classes, and bureaucratic rule-making.[73] Ultimately, the protests were an expression of anger over a false dream universities had promised the students, a dream of upward mobility and control over their own lives.

Some educators at this point began to see the declining enrollments and the campus turmoil as patches of the same quilt. They perceived a widespread "crisis of confidence" in higher education, as a Carnegie Commission study termed it.[74] That is, to the extent that colleges and universities lost their ability to function as structures for developing skills and for legitimating the social order, their own legitimacy came into question.

The crisis was not limited to higher education. Throughout society in the late 1960s, people were challenging the legitimacy of major institutions, including corporations, the military, the health profession, and Congress. The crisis of legitimacy, as several writers have characterized it,[75] had deep roots in the very organization of state and society.[75] As Alan Wolfe explains the phenomenon:

> So long as a society remains in any degree capitalist, the state will be called upon to engage in the accumulation process to some degree. But at the same time, in order for capitalist decisions to be acceptable to the citizenry at large, democratic desires must in some way be taken into account.[76]

The state, then, had to convince the citizenry that it was not acting on behalf of the few when it helped capitalists, even though capital was owned only by the few. Its very claim to the right of rule was based on its assertion that it acted in everyone's interest. Though a legitimacy crisis was always a possibility, given the character of the state, crises were rare because of devices the state had been able to use to diminish the inconsistency between serving the few and helping the many. Support for education was one of those devices because of the seemingly universal benefit education offered. Thus it was a major concern for Congress that the legitimacy of higher education was in doubt in the late 1960s because throwing money at the institutions of higher education might have been one way that Congress could have resuscitated its own legitimacy. Instead, Congress needed to restructure higher education, so that it could both serve larger legitimating functions in the country and more narrow legitimating functions for Congress.

The crisis of legitimacy is a starting point to explain why Congress did not merely respond to the pleas of higher-education associations for institutional aid. It also helps us to understand why members would have been receptive to the Carnegie-Rivlin-Moynihan approach. An emphasis on equal educational opportunity allowed Congress to claim that it would be providing universal higher education with no economic barriers. In doing so it could assert its own claim to legitimacy—a claim that would not have been as strong had it endorsed the "middle-class" bill sponsored by Representative Green. That claim was critical because Congress also sought to restructure higher education in a way that would enable it to be a legitimating mechanism for the society at large. To this end Congress encouraged the development of community colleges.

Jerome Karabel explains that even by the early 1970s community colleges had altered the way in which the education system served to stratify the working class. The two-year institutions had transformed the mechanism from a three-tiered device into a four-tiered one: high school, community college, four-year college, graduate/professional school. He found that in contrast to four-year institutions, students in community colleges have parents who are significantly less educated, poorer, and more likely to be non-professional.[77] This pattern might indicate that community colleges are making opportunities available to the previously disadvantaged, if the students go on to four-year institutions. But fewer than half of those who enter community colleges even receive an associate (two-year) degree.[78] "Cooling out," Karabel explains, is a process that attempts to convince "latent-terminal" students—those who want to attend four-year schools but are deemed unfit—that they should terminate their higher education. It operates through remedial classes and the counseling of students against "unrealistic aspirations."[79]

With entry to four-year institutions restricted and admission to some form of post-secondary education universal, the higher-education system could begin to serve again as a means of legitimating inequality through meritocracy while it affirmed democracy.[80] Community colleges would also enable four-year institutions to re-focus their purposes because obedience-oriented socialization could be located principally at the community-college level.[81] In practice, this grand scheme was not quite so elegant. Many four-year colleges had already been expanded to accommodate large numbers of students. Some were re-designed in the 1970s as junior-senior colleges. But most continued to be open to non-elites, because of bureaucratic desires within the institutions and public pressures from without.

Congressional Initiative and the Legitimacy Crisis

Earlier in this chapter members of Congress were seen as having had a broader sense of the "problem" in 1972 than did the higher-education interest groups. The legislators did not articulate this sense fully, but their comments suggest that they appreciated intuitively the nature of the legitimacy crisis. Moreover, their behavior indicates that it was the legitimacy crisis they sought to overcome through reform of the higher-education system. It appears that they used the rubric of equal educational opportunity in this effort for several reasons. First, they may have believed in the concept. Second, it embodies the dominant ideology of competitive individualism and reward for merit, and the members seek "legitimate" rationales for undertaking major innovations. A rationale that is consistent with the dominent ideology will have built-in legitimacy.

This rationale might explain their emphasis on equality of educational opportunity, but it only partially explains why they took the trouble to restructure higher education so that it could again contribute to the maintenance of the social order. Moreover, ideology would seem to fly in the face of the traditional characterization of legislators as parochial and responsive only to immediate problems

One possibility is that the traditional view misses much about the contemporary Congress. Circumstance has forced members increasingly to focus on the total social formation, because people have demanded that they be responsible for an increasing number of problems in society.

Some members of Congress also have a sense of noblesse oblige. They think of themselves as members of the upper class. As such they feel responsible for helping to maintain the order of society, and perhaps even to help the poor, either because they fear what would happen if the poor were not helped or because they are genuinely altruistic. Notably, members who identified themselves as upper-class were far more inclined to be concerned about the ability of post-secondary institutions to function as mechanisms for equal opportunity than were the middle-class members. (See Table 5–4). Their sense of being upper-class may in some cases derive from personal wealth and in others simply from being a member of Congress. The concept of "upper-class" embraces a social as well as an economic dimension, and some of those who identified themselves as upper-class emphasized their unique status as "one of 435 people" who can claim the august title of United States Representative.

This sense, no doubt, would have been reinforced by the culture of Congress in the 1960s and early 1970s, which encouraged members to see themselves as congressional careerists.[82]

Institutional responsibility and noblesse oblige might have moved members to act in this case. But this conclusion returns the analyst to the source of the members' concern. The problem that they addressed did not arise in random fashion. The problem was rooted in the very organization of society, in the struggles between workers and owners over the nature of the production process and over their share of the surplus produced, and in the contradiction embraced by the state's dual purpose of serving the few who own capital while it tries to benefit the many who do not. Legislators may act from many motives and in response to a variety of pressures that are real or fabricated, self-generated or externally imposed. But they act within limits set by an acceptable ideology, by institutional arrangements, and ultimately by the agenda of crisis that is beyond their control.

The way in which they respond to crisis is not determined. Personal factors, group pressures, committee prerogatives, and presidential concerns, all have an impact on what Congress does. The legislator grappling with the larger problem often appears as an explorer, weary and lost, trying to clear a path through dense underbrush. But the legislator can be understood better as a deliberator groping for a solution to problems for which no one has clear answers. Legislators often have their own sense of the path, they are neither pawns nor narrowly self-seeking in all cases, and they act with a degree of autonomy—as their work on the 1972 Higher Education Act well demonstrates.

NOTES

1. It appears that the busing provisions were the main focus of President Nixon's attention as he contemplated signing or vetoing the legislation. See Lawrence E. Gladieux and Thomas R. Wolanin, *Congress and the Colleges: The National Politics of Higher Education* (Lexington, Mass.: D.C. Heath, 1976), pp. 217–219.
2. Public Law 92–318; 86 Stat. 235. The bill was signed into law on June 23, 1972.
3. U.S. Senate, "Education Amendments of 1972," Conference Report to accompany S. 659, 92nd Cong., 2nd Sess., Report No. 92–798, 22 May 1972, p. 167.
4. See Joel Havemann, "Education Report: Pending Bill Could Revolutionize Federal Programs for Higher Education," *National Journal*, 18 March 1972, pp. 472–481; also, "Senate Passes Landmark Aid to Higher Education Bill," *Congressional Quarterly Weekly Report*, 28 August 1971, p. 1844.
5. Homer D. Babbidge, Jr., and Robert M. Rosenzweig, *The Federal Interest in Higher Education* (Westport, Conn.: Greenwood Press, 1975), pp. 10–21; Frederick Rudolph, *The American College and University: A History* (New York: Vintage Books, 1962), pp. 247–262; Alice M. Rivlin, *The Role of the Federal Government in Financing Higher Education* (Washington, D.C.: Brookings, 1961).
6. Earl F. Cheit, *The New Depression in Higher Education: A General Report for the Carnegie Commission on Higher Education and the Ford Foundation* (New York: McGraw-Hill, 1970).

7. See, for example, Fred M. Hechinger, "Aid to Colleges: The Need is Great, But the Means Are Uncertain," *New York Times*, 14 September 1971, section IV, p. 9; John Walsh, "Higher Education Bill: Busing Bill a Cuckoo in the Nest," *Science*, 26 May 1972, p. 895.
8. Gladieux and Wolanin, *Congress and the Colleges*, p. 44.
9. Lauriston R. King, *The Washington Lobbyists for Higher Education* (Lexington, Mass.: D.C. Heath, 1975), pp. 19–20.
10. Ibid., pp. 21–22.
11. Gladieux and Wolanin, *Congress and the Colleges*, pp. 44–46.
12. Chester E. Finn, Jr., *Education and the Presidency* (Lexington, Mass: D.C. Heath, 1977), p. 48.
13. Norman C. Thomas, *Education in National Politics* (New York: David McKay, 1975), p. 40.
14. Carnegie Commission on Higher Education, *Quality and Equality: New Levels of Federal Responsibility for Higher Education* (New York: McGraw-Hill, 1968); *Toward a Long-Range Plan for Federal Financial Support of Higher Education, A Report to the President*, U.S. Department of Health, Education and Welfare, January 1969.
15. Gladieux and Wolanin, *Congress and the Colleges*, p. 52n.
16. Finn, *Education and the Presidency*, pp. 47–48.
17. Ibid., p. 45.
18. Daniel Patrick Moynihan, *The Politics of a Guaranteed Income* (New York: Random House, 1973). Also see his *Maximum Feasible Misunderstanding* (New York: Free Press, 1969).
19. Gladieux and Wolanin, *Congress and the Colleges*, pp. 63–64.
20. At least in the case of Moynihan's proposal for a National Foundation for Higher Education—an independent agency akin to the National Science Foundation that would have been charged with the responsibility for research generating experimental development—several accounts assert that Moynihan borrowed the Carnegie proposal for such an agency because it was consistent with his orientation. See Finn, *Education and the Presidency*, pp. 50, 67; Gladieux and Wolanin, *Congress and the Colleges*, p. 64.
21. Finn, *Education and the Presidency*, p. 52.
22. Ibid., pp. 53–54. See pp. 50–70 for a good review of the Working Group's process of decision making.
23. Gladieux and Wolanin, *Congress and the Colleges*, pp. 67–71, 75.
24. Seniority was based on service as of January 1971. Ideology was not used as a variable in stratifying the sample, but fifty-nine of the sixty-one members were asked to classify themselves. Likewise, class was determined by self-evaluation of the members' present status. The sample used the House Education and Labor Committee as a base. I interviewed 34 of the 38 Committee members. The remaining people in the sample were selected randomly from groupings structured according to party and seniority, and in sufficient numbers to have the total sample reflect the whole House.
25. Raymond Bauer, et al., *American Business and Public Policy* (New York: Atherton, 1963), pp. 408–413.
26. In 1973 Representative Green resigned from the Education and Labor Committee, although she was next in line for the chair, and moved to the Appropriations Committee, where she was last in seniority. She resigned from Congress at the end of 1974.
27. Gladieux and Wolanin report similar findings from their interviews. See *Congress and the Colleges*, p. 118.
28. Philip Brenner, "Committee Conflict in the Congressional Arena," *The Annals*, 411, January 1974, 88–91.
29. Havemann, "Education Report: Pending Bill Could Revolutionize Federal Programs for Higher Education," pp. 472, 477–78.
30. Indeed, a 1972 HEW study that compared the House (Green) and Senate (Pell-Brademas) bills indicated that there would be inconsistent impacts on both public and private institutions. For example, the University of Maryland would have been expected to gain $150,000 more from the House version than from the Senate version; but the University

of California, Berkeley would have gained $100,000 less from the House bill. Yale University stood to gain $75,000 from the Senate bill over the House bill; Harvard would have lost $5,000 from the Senate bill.

31. Stanley Elam, ed., *The Gallup Poll of Attitudes Towards Education, 1969–1973* (Bloomington: Indiana University Press, 1973), p. 49.

32. "110,000 Openings Went Begging in Freshman Classes This Fall," *Chronicle of Higher Education,* 13 December 1971, p. 1. Also Carnegie Commission on Higher Education, *New Students and New Places* (New York: McGraw-Hill, 1971), pp. 3–4; Carnegie Commission on Higher Education, *Priorities for Action: Final Report of the Commission* (New York: McGraw-Hill, 1973) pp. 77–78.

33. For a good discussion of this approach see David Gold, Clarence Lo, and Erik Olin Wright, "Recent Developments in Marxist Theories of the Capitalist State," *Monthly Review,* October 1975, pp. 32–35. Notable examples of the analysis are: Mark Green, *Who Runs Congress?,* 3rd ed. (New York: Bantam, 1979); G. William Domhoff, *The Higher Circles* (New York: Vintage, 1970).

34. Gladieux and Wolanin, *Congress and the Colleges,* p. 124.

35. Brenner, "Committee Conflict in the Congressional Arena," p. 90. The associations' behavior may also have been due to their calculation that working solely with Representative Green would yield the greatest benefit. See Gladieux and Wolanin, *Congress and the Colleges,* pp. 130–131.

36. Senator Pell had borrowed heavily from the Carnegie proposals when he first introduced his bill in 1969. Gladieux and Wolanin, *Congress and the Colleges,* p. 91. Also see John Walsh, "Higher Education: Reinforcement from the Carnegie Commission," *Science* 17 December 1971; Havemann, "Education Report: Pending Bill Could Revolutionize Federal Programs for Higher Education," p. 473.

37. Brenner, "Committee Conflict in the Congressional Arena," pp. 88, 91.

38. Lawrence E. Gladieux and Thomas R. Wolanin, "Federal Politics," in David W. Breneman and Chester E. Finn, Jr., eds., *Public Policy and Private Higher Education* (Washington, D.C.: Brookings Institution, 1978), p. 202.

39. Carnegie Commission on Higher Education, *The Open-Door Colleges* (New York: McGraw-Hill, 1970), p. 15.

40. Carnegie Commission on Higher Education, *Quality and Equality: Revised Recommendations* (New York: McGraw-Hill, 1970), p. 2.

41. Ibid., pp. 5, 21. Notably, the commission issued a report on institutional aid just weeks before the House-Senate conference was to begin. It recommended that a school receive $500 for each student at the school who was receiving federal aid. Carnegie Commission on Higher Education, *Institutional Aid: Federal Support to Colleges and Universities* (New York: McGraw-Hill, 1972), pp. 80–81.

42. Domhoff, *The Higher Circles,* pp. 179–201.

43. Samuel Bowles and Herbert Gintis, *Schooling in Capitalist America: Educational Reform and the Contradictions of Economic Life* (New York: Basic Books, 1976), pp. 19, 197–198, 206.

44. G. William Domhoff, "I Am Not an 'Instrumentalist'," *Kapitalistate,* Nos. 4–5, 1976, pp. 221–224.

45. Gosta Esping-Anderson, Roger Friedland, and Erik Olin Wright, "Modes of Class Struggle and the Capitalist State," *Kapitalistate,* Nos. 4–5, 1976, p. 189.

46. Gladieux and Wolanin, *Congress and the Colleges,* pp. 130–131.

47. This had been the pattern in particular with bills emanating from the House Education and Labor Committee, where the House tended to ignore committee recommendations. See Richard F. Fenno, Jr., *Congressmen in Committees* (Boston: Little, Brown, 1973), pp. 234–235.

48. Heinz Eulau and Harold Quigley, *State Officials and Higher Education* (New York: McGraw-Hill, 1970).

49. Gladieux and Wolanin, *Congress and the Colleges,* p. 24.

50. W. Norton Grubb and Marvin Lazerson, "Rally 'Round the Workplace: Continuities and Fallacies in Career Education," *Harvard Educational Review,* vol. 45, No. 4 (November 1975), p. 453.

51. Ibid., p. 457.

52. Elam, *The Gallup Poll of Attitudes Towards Education,* p. 163.

53. Gladieux and Wolanin, *Congress and the Colleges,* p. 20.

54. By saying that it functions in these four ways, I do not mean to imply that it must function these ways or that other mechanisms might not replace it if it ceased to function these ways. For a good discussion of this point see Stephan Michaelson, "Critique of *Inequality,*" *Harvard Educational Review,* 43, No. 1 (February 1973).

55. Bowles and Gintis, *Schooling in Capitalist America,* p. 205.

56. V. Lane Rawlins and Lloyd Ulman, "The Utilization of College-Trained Manpower in the United States," in Margaret Gordon, ed., *Higher Education and the Labor Market* (New York: McGraw-Hill, 1974), p. 217. Bowles and Gintis argue similarly that corporations preferred school-based education to apprenticeship for their workers—and so encouraged mass public education—because it made the allocation of workers easier under varying conditions; *Schooling in Capitalist America,* p. 158.

57. Rawlins and Ulman, "The Utilization of College-Trained Manpower," pp. 213–214.

58. Seymour E. Harris, *A Statistical Portrait of Higher Education* (New York: McGraw-Hill, 1972), pp. 54, 60.

59. Bowles and Gintis, *Schooling in Capitalist America,* p. 126.

60. Ibid., pp. 126–131; Philip Brenner, "Children Without Walls: A New Political Education," in Dorothy James, ed., *Outside, Looking In* (New York: Harper & Row, 1972), pp. 388–389, 393–395; David Cohen and Marvin Lazerson, "Education and the Corporate Order," *Socialist Revolution,* No. 8 (March–April, 1972), pp. 49–51; Joel Spring, *Education and the Rise of the Corporate State* (Boston: Beacon Press, 1972), Chapters 2 and 3; Marcus Raskin, *Being and Doing* (New York: Random House, 1971), Chapter 4.

61. Margaret Gordon, "The Changing Labor Market for College Graduates," in Gordon, *Higher Education and the Labor Market,* pp. 56–57.

62. Ivar Berg, with Sherry Gorelick, *Education and Jobs: The Great Training Robbery* (New York: Praeger, 1970). Also see Rawlins and Ulman, "The Utilization of College-Trained Manpower," pp. 200–203.

63. Bowles and Gintis, *Schooling in Capitalist America,* pp. 110–112.

64. Ibid., p. 103.

65. Cohen and Lazerson, "Education and the Corporate Order," p. 71.

66. Bowles and Gintis, *Schooling in Capitalist America,* p. 114.

67. U.S. Department of Health, Education and Welfare, *Work in America* (Cambridge, Mass.: MIT Press, 1973). Also see U.S. Senate, Committee on Labor and Public Welfare, Worker Alienation Act: Hearings Before the Subcommittee on Employment, Manpower and Poverty, 92nd Cong., 2nd sess. (Washington, D.C.: 1972).

68. Cited in Gordon, "The Changing Labor Market for College Graduates," p. 58. Similarly, another study found that 50 percent of 1972 high-school graduates expected to be professional and technical workers, but that in 1985 only 17 percent of the labor force was expected to be composed of such workers. See U.S. Bureau of Labor Statistics, Special Labor Force Report 161 (1974), cited in U.S. Department of Health, Education and Welfare, Office of Education, National Center for Education Statistics, "The Condition of Education, 1976," (Washington, D.C.: 1976), p. 244.

69. Rawlins and Ulman, "The Utilization of College-Trained Manpower," p. 204.

70. "The Condition of Education, 1976," p. 242.

71. Gordon, "The Changing Labor Market for College Graduates," pp. 62–63.

72. Michael Maccoby, "Character and Work in America," in Philip Brenner, Robert Borosage, and Bethany Weidner, eds., *Exploring Contradictions: Political Economy in the Corporate State* (New York: David McKay, 1974). Also see Harry Braverman, *Labor and Monopoly Capital* (New York: Monthly Review Press, 1974), Chapters 3, 15, 16; Bowles and Gintis, *Schooling in Capitalist America,* pp. 204–205.

73. Michael Miles, "Student Alienation and the Higher Education Industry," *Politics & Society,* vol. 4, No. 3 (1974).

74. Carnegie Commission on Higher Education, *Priorities for Action: Final Report of the Commission,* pp. 6, 176.

75. Alan Wolfe, *The Limits of Legitimacy: Political Contradictions of Contemporary Capi-*

talism (New York: Free Press, 1977); Jurgen Habermas, *Legitimation Crisis*, trans. Thomas McCarthy (Boston: Beacon Press, 1975); James O'Connor, *The Fiscal Crisis of the State* (New York: St. Martin's, 1973).

76. Wolfe, *The Limits of Legitimacy*, p. 6.
77. Jerome Karabel, "Community Colleges and Social Stratification," *Harvard Educational Review*, vol. 42, No. 4 (1972), pp. 526–530.
78. Ibid., pp. 530–540.
79. Ibid., p. 532. Also see Burton Clark, "The Cooling Out Function in Higher Education," *American Journal of Sociology*, vol. 65 (1960), pp. 569–576.
80. Fred Millar reports that Cleveland business leaders in 1950 encouraged the development of a community-college system there in anticipation of demands from the baby-boom generation and with a clear intention to maintain stratification: "Big City Elites and Educational Stratification: A Case Study of the Politics of Community Colleges in Cleveland, 1950–1970 (Ph.D. diss., Case Western Reserve University, 1975).
81. Bowles and Gintis, *Schooling in Capitalist America*, p. 212.
82. Joseph Cooper and William West, "The Congressional Career in the 1970s," in Lawrence C. Dodd and Bruce I. Oppenheimer, eds., *Congress Reconsidered*, 2nd ed. (Washington, D.C.: Congressional Quarterly, Inc., 1981).

6 Restructuring Congress: The Context of Reform

Despite the jokes made about it—despite the charges that it is a nineteenth-century institution muddling through the late twentieth century and that it is rarely influential even at the middle levels of power—the United States Congress still attracts the energy and exercises the bile of a host of reformers. In the last two decades advocates of congressional reform have proposed a variety of changes to achieve a wide array of goals, and during the 1970s Congress even adopted some of these proposals.

The changes that Congress instituted reveal the interests of the members and the effect of the external environment on those interests. This chapter looks at both the proposals and the actual changes in order to extend the analysis of how Congress has been studied and to provide another case study of the limits and possibilities of Congress.

Suggested reforms generally fall into two categories: personal and organizational. Personal reforms include those that focus on the characteristics and ethics of members of Congress and on the nature of congressional campaigns and campaign financing. Organizational reforms relate to the structure of Congress, its rules, and its traditions, such as seniority.

The categories are closely related. Both tend to be advocated for at least one of four reasons. First, there is the goal of *morality*: when legislators take bribes or misuse their official position for private gain, the institution as well as the public responds with anger and shock. The anger stems in part from the fear that this immorality can contribute to the deterioration of our societal system of morals.

Such concerns are related to a second goal of reformers: *legitimacy* of the government. To be legitimate, the government should, in theory, be an exemplar of private and public virtue through sound morals and adherence to the law—the foundation of society. Moreover, the government should be a neutral mechanism, above particular interests, so that it can moderate conflict between interests. Once captured by a particular set of interests, the government could no longer appear just and fair. Its decisions would not be accepted as legitimate by all sides in a conflict, and it would not be able to serve as a force for maintaining social harmony.

Related to legitimacy is a third purpose of reform: *efficiency*. As the government takes more responsibility for the smooth operation of all aspects of society, including the production and distribution of nonpublic goods, its legitimacy becomes linked to its ability to provide services efficiently. Congress is often viewed as an obstacle to the smooth operation of the government, either because it "gets in the way of" the executive or because its procedures are so cumbersome that it cannot make decisions quickly.

In this way the relative *power* of Congress vis-à-vis the executive represents a fourth concern of reformers. Some see a strong Congress as a bulwark against an imperial president and thus as a safeguard of civil liberties. Others, however, point to the congressional opposition to the expansion of civil rights under presidential leadership. Most analysts think of power as the extent to which one branch can achieve its goals in the face of opposition from another branch. There is a sense that Congress would express goals that might be antagonistic to those of the executive if it were not prevented from doing so by its lack of skill, information, and other resources—perhaps even courage. Implicit in this idea is the notion that Congress represents a set of interests that are different from those represented by the executive. Opposing views on which branch should be more powerful, then, reflect support for different sets of interests.

It is important to remember that each reform adopted by Congress represents a decision. The bases of Congress's choices were varied and reflected many different interests of the members. One important factor that analysts often de-emphasize, however, is the external congressional environment. Political scientist Claus Offe provides a guide for including the external environment in an analysis of congressional reform:

> For what the state does if it works on a problem is a *dual* process: it organizes certain activities and measures directed toward the *environment* and it adopts for *itself* a certain organizational procedure from which production and implementation of policies emerge.[1]

Even with respect to its own operations, then, Congress makes choices related to production and struggle in the society. But Congress is neither omniscient nor always of one mind about its relationship to the environment, as we will see, and the resulting reforms are not always consistent.

Personal and Organizational Reforms

Personal Reforms

One popular view of Congress is that the legislators themselves are the problem. Randall Ripley summarizes this position:

> The machinery of Congress is not inherently deficient. . . . What may be deficient is resolve on the part of a sufficient number of members to make the machinery, the ties to other publics and agencies, and the "system" work. . . . The critical question is how the people responsible for making the institutions function behave.[2]

The foibles and peccadilloes of senators and representatives make good copy for journalists and are the stock-in-trade of muckrakers. For example, Warren Weaver, Jr., reviews such "human flaws and appetites" in a chapter entitled "Swinging on the Hill."[3] Drew Pearson and Jack Anderson make their case against Congress by focusing on members' personal attributes.[4] Even members of Congress rail against their colleagues for lack of courage, determination, and intelligence. Richard Fenno, Jr., reports that during congressional campaigns members often "refurbish their individual reputations as 'the best congressman in the United States' by attacking the collective reputation of the Congress."[5]

Emphasis on the personal may reflect moral outrage as much as mere titillation. As an increasing number of cases of improper behavior, such as Abscam, come to light in the wake of Watergate, the very legitimacy of Congress (and the rest of the government) comes into question. The larger ramifications of individual lawlessness have been the subject of Ralph Nader's Congress Project Studies. Nader's study of the House and Senate Banking committees, in examining how the committees tend to operate in biased fashion, focuses on recruitment to the committees and the problems associated with campaign finances.[6] Similarly, Mark Green surveys the way in which Congress supports special business interests that provide members with campaign contributions, retain their law firms, and favor them with direct payments.[7]

The Nader studies also contend that recruitment to Congress contributes to a bias in favor of the wealthy and big business and against minorities, labor, and women. Lawyers predominate, as do men and white Anglo-Saxons.[8] The reformers argue that this recruitment bias reduces the sensitivity of lawmakers to demands from those unlike themselves.

The major issue concerning bias in the recruitment process has been campaign finances. With House races often costing each candidate more than $100,000 and Senate races running over $1 million, charges of earlier reformers—that only the rich could afford a seat in Congress without incurring unmanageable political debts—have become quite cogent. As Senator Joseph Clark (D-Pa.) has said, "The pernicious consequences of reliance on a few wealthy contributors for large donations is [sic] obvious."[9] Congress appears to be less than impartial; the government's credibility is therefore weakened when it claims to rule without bias, to be above class, and to serve as a neutral surrogate battleground for the resolution of social conflicts.

Robert Peabody and his co-authors report that the National Committee for an Effective Congress has long been lobbying for public financing of campaigns in order to diminish the pernicious effects of private contributions.[10] More recently, Common Cause has taken the lead in lobbying energetically for public financing of congressional campaigns. It was successful in 1971, 1974, and 1976 in securing passage of legislation that required disclosure of donors to congressional campaigns and that set limits on contributions.[11]

In a related effort, the House and Senate passed different versions of legislation in 1976 to tighten the regulations that govern the registration of lobbyists and the disclosure of their activities. But the bills would have seriously infringed the right of most citizens to petition Congress. Later versions corrected this flaw but left the bills less effective, and to date there is still no new lobby-registration law.[12] Like large campaign contributions, undisclosed lobbying diminishes the appearance of neutrality that Congress must maintain in order to secure its legitimacy.

Most observers have attributed the passage of new codes of ethics in Congress most immediately to the notoriety that attended disclosure of the Wayne Hays sex affair and the alleged sexual misconduct of two other representatives, and to the scandal over the alleged payments of several thousand dollars to members of Congress by the Republic of Korea and Washington-based businessman Tongsun Park. In 1977 the House passed a code of ethics that limited members' outside earned income to 15 percent of their congressional salary. Members were further restricted to earning no more than $750 for any one speech or article. No limits were placed on income derived from investments.[13]

Reforms primarily intended to secure the legitimacy of Congress have been seen also as a way to strengthen the legislature vis-à-vis the executive. For example, the Nader banking-committee study admonished Congress to eliminate the influence of special interests because "There is simply no way for Congress to regain power unless it somehow regains public esteem."[14]

Organizational Reforms

In 1974 Representative Richard Bolling (D-Mo.) sounded the theme of his newly created Select Committee on Committees when he declared, "Hampered by decentralized authority, lacking informational resources, stymied by obsolete rules and denying the Speaker his rightful tools, the House of Representatives cannot do its job. It is still, sadly, out of order."[15] Charged with restructuring the committee system in the House of Representatives, the Bolling Committee—as it came to be known—focused on some of the most popular proposals for reform of the House. Indeed, proposals for altering the committee structure, along with plans for altering the rules, procedures, and informal mechanisms of Congress, are the preponderent type of reform suggested by advocates of change. Five items headed the list of organizational reforms most frequently advocated: overturning the seniority system, changing rules in order to "democratize" Congress, increasing party discipline, altering the committee structure, and improving the information resources available to Congress.

Seniority. The seniority system has been a favorite target of reformers for decades. It is not in fact a system but a tradition of awarding the chair of a committee to the person in the majority party who has the longest continuous service on the committee. Advocates of other mechanisms for selecting the chair, such as by a vote of the whole party caucus, have charged that seniority rewarded senility and rendered Congress incapable of handling complex problems, made Congress unrepresentative because senior members came disproportionately from the South and rural areas, and contributed to the defeat of liberal legislation because it denied the forces that supported liberal Democratic presidents a means of disciplining conservative Democrats.[16]

The opponents of the seniority system were trying to achieve many goals. Some sought to increase the legitimacy of Congress by removing suspicions that it was not open to all interests equally and enabling it to handle complex problems. Others, in an era of activist presidents, have viewed ending the seniority system and increasing the legitimacy of Congress as a step toward the more important goal of strengthening Congress's power vis-à-vis the president. Most opponents of seniority, though, tended to believe that ending it would aid liberal causes espoused by the presidents. This latter view may have been shortsighted, because in the 1970s the seniority system brought to positions of power liberal members elected after 1958.[17]

While the seniority system is still much in evidence, it eroded a bit during the 1970s. In 1971 the House Democratic caucus adopted changes proposed by an ad hoc committee (the Hansen Committee) that it established in part to examine reform of the seniority system. Under the 1971 procedures, chairs were to be voted on separately (rather than as a slate) if ten members requested such a vote, and no member could chair more than one subcommittee. By 1975 the caucus had adopted a rule that automatically brought up each chair for a secret-ballot vote. This rule contributed to the caucus's unprecedented ouster of three committee heads—W. R. Poage (D-Tex.), F. Edward Hebert (D-La.), and Wright Patman (D-Tex.).[18] The power of senior members was further diminished by another rule, also passed in 1975, that prevented senior members from securing all of the positions on key subcommittees for themselves.

Rules. The rules of the House and Senate have also served as a target for reformers of Congress. Critics have often depicted the rules as obstacles to liberal legislation because they have permitted a few strategically placed members—who are often conservative—to kill legislation of which they disapprove. Reformers argue that, like seniority, the rules of the legislature favor rural and conservative areas and prevent Congress from being representative of all interests and responsive to contemporary problems.

Reformers have focused on changing procedures in order to "democratize" Congress, in the words of one Nader study.[19] This term has had two meanings—allowing the participation of more members within Congress on one hand and opening the legislative process to public scrutiny on the other.

In seeking the participation of more members, reformers focused on the power of the Rules Committee in the House, the internal rules that govern committees, the filibuster in the Senate, and the way in which members are assigned to committees and subcommittees. For example, the Nader study of the Judiciary Committees called for increased authority for subcommittee chairmen, an increase in the number of subcommittees, and clear jurisdictional definitions for subcommittees of the House Judiciary Committee.[20] Under Emanuel Celler, this committee had had vaguely defined subcommittees, with bills assigned solely at the chair's discretion. Similarly the Nader critique of the banking committees called for "more active use of subcommittees."[21]

Reform of committee rules—what came to be known as the "subcommittee bill of rights"—was also the focus of demands from the liberal Democratic Study Group in the early 1970s.[22] Prior to 1971, committee heads could rule committees by controlling the subcommittees through the appointment of staff and assignment of legislation, or in some cases (as in Ways and Means) by not creating subcommittees. Senior members of a committee often would take up most of the positions on a few subcommittees, which would then be assigned the committee's major legislation. Reformers hoped that allowing more members to participate in key decisions and enabling subcommittee chairs to act with some independence would make the House more responsive to new problems and would encourage members who were frustrated by the long wait for power. The rules adopted by the House Democratic caucus in 1971 went a long way toward meeting these demands for change.[23]

In the Senate there was less pressure for such change; under Lyndon Johnson's leadership, committee assignments had been liberalized and junior members had been given the opportunity for choice positions. Also, senators felt more effective than their counterparts in the House simply because of the smaller size of the Senate.[24] Democratization has centered on eliminating the filibuster, which, it has been argued, allows a few "unrepresentative" members to thwart the majority will of both Congress and the nation.[25] In 1975 the Senate changed Rule 22 concerning cloture to reduce the number of votes needed to cut off debate from two thirds of those voting (or sixty-seven if all senators were voting) to sixty senators.

Ironically, curbing debate may conflict with efforts to democratize Congress by opening up the process to the scrutiny of voters. While filibusters prevent the passage of legislation, they also generate awareness of an issue and so can bring the public into deliberations through letter writing and mass organizing.[26] As conservative *New York Times* columnist William Safire complained about a Senate rule further limiting debate, "There ought to be a way for a dissenting group of lawmakers . . . to dramatize and draw public attention to what may be a mistake."[27] Appropriately, Safire went on to link the cut-off of debate to secrecy in the House of Representatives.

Secrecy in congressional proceedings had been most extreme during the mark-up of a bill—when a committee drafts a final version, incorporating amendments and striking bargains—and during conference-committee meetings. Reformers argued that opening these sessions to public scrutiny might diminish the invidious influence of special interests, compel legislators to be more responsive to the average voter in their districts, enable members to receive "better" information and produce improved "products," and reassure the public that the process was fair, thereby enhancing the legitimacy of Congress.[28] In 1973 the House voted to open up its mark-up sessions unless a majority of a committee voted to close a session. The Senate adopted a similar rule in 1975. Both houses also changed their rules in 1975 to permit open conference-committee proceedings.

Party discipline. At least since the appearance of Woodrow Wilson's *Congressional Government* in 1884, proponents of reform in Congress have called for less independence for individual members and committees and more adherence to party programs. This has been true for those who favor a stronger Congress as well as those who support a strong executive. Richard Bolling, for example, suggested that party discipline is the *sine qua non* of a strong House:

> The current situation may be tolerated only if Democrats are so uninterested in the programs and policies of their party they are willing to continue to

entrust the helm to inept or unfriendly helmsmen. I believe most Democrats in the House are anxious that the House itself should regain effectiveness.[29]

Under the direction of a strong Speaker of the House, this argument goes, the House not only could act with some unity and so challenge an executive more effectively but also would be more accountable to the voters, who would be able to identify the party as the source of their pleasure or displeasure.[30]

In contrast, other writers who advocate greater party discipline in Congress tend to favor strong executive leadership. James MacGregor Burns articulated this position in 1949:

> Only by vitalizing our two-party system, by playing national party politics more zealously, and by centralizing control of our parties, will Americans be able to stabilize presidential leadership and foster teamwork in the federal government.[31]

Both camps have focused on the House Rules Committee as an obstacle to the achievement of their objectives.[32] Notably, Burns contrasts a president "representing the overriding interests of the nation" to the Rules Committee, which is composed of "representatives who advance local and regional ends."[33] Though Robert Peabody found that the Rules Committee was often used as a scapegoat by members—that they support the committee's decisions but criticize it to take the heat away from themselves[34]—the committee did continually pose a potential obstacle in the House because legislation must flow through it. To overcome this obstacle, it had been commonly suggested that the Rules Committee be elected by the caucus every two years, that the twenty-one-day rule in effect for the 81st and the 89th Congresses be made permanent, or that the Speaker be permitted to call up legislation out of the committee and be authorized to appoint new members to the committee.[35] In this way, it was argued, the committee would become an arm of the majority party through either the caucus or the leadership.

Again, both camps have argued that stronger leadership is a necessary part of revamping the parties in Congress. Representative Bolling argues, for example, that "the place to effect change is within the Democratic caucus. . . . It is here that power should be given to the titular party leader, the Speaker."[36] He proposed that the Speaker be given authority to nominate all members of the powerful Ways and Means Committee and Rules Committee and to nominate the chair of each committee.[37] Under the Speaker's leadership, the caucus would punish all members who do not follow party policy.

In the 94th Congress the House Democrats moved significantly to expand the powers of the Speaker and the caucus and to weaken the Rules Committee. Previously the Democratic members of the Ways and Means Committee had also sat as the Committee on Committees, the group that effectively decided on committee assignments for all Democratic members. By large majorities, the caucus voted to turn committee assignments over to the Democratic Steering and Policy Committee and to give the Speaker the power to nominate all Democratic members of the Rules Committee, subject to caucus approval. The Steering and Policy Committee, created in 1973, is composed of the four top Democratic Party leaders in the House, eight members appointed by the Speaker, and twelve members elected by regional subgroups of the caucus. Whether the Speaker and the caucus will emerge as powerful enforcers of party discipline in the House is still uncertain. Speaker Carl Albert was reticent about using the power given to him, and Speaker Thomas P. O'Neill and Majority Leader James Wright, elected in 1977, at first did not try to press party discipline on the members. By 1979, however, representatives were demanding strong leadership and less individual autonomy for themselves and encouraged the Speaker to "reward and punish" members through committee assignments.[38] But there has been little growth in party discipline among Democrats, and it was the Republicans who increased their unity under President Reagan in 1981.[39]

Committee structure. Echoing Woodrow Wilson's aphorism that Congress on the floor is Congress on display, and Congress in committee is Congress at work, Richard Bolling observed in 1974, "Central to the operation of the House is the committee system." He then went on to indict the committee system as the principal cause of "the failure of the modern House to provide vigorous national leadership."[40] During the past ten years, the organization of Congress has become perhaps the prime focus of reformers, who have concentrated on three areas: the number of committees and subcommittees in the House and Senate, the jurisdiction of each committee, and the nature of the congressional budgetary process.

Conventional wisdom in the 1970s was summed up by *Washington Post* reporter Walter Pincus when he asserted that "Congress must cut back on committees and subcommittees." He argued that in seeking to overcome its "lack of professional expertise," Congress had generated a problem for itself by creating "170 or more committees and subcommittees in each house. . . . Almost every subcommittee, to justify its existence, churns out reports or legislation which clog the mails and the floor calendar and accomplish little except to send Congress off in hundreds of different directions."[41]

The proliferation of committees and subcommittees since the 1946 Legislative Reorganization Act—which reduced the number of committees in both houses by more than 75 percent—contributed to an increased workload for members, to the point where they could not give appropriate attention to any matter. The Senate Select Committee to Study the Senate Committee System found that in 1976 senators averaged more than fourteen subcommittee assignments each.[42] Those who advocate a reduction in the number of committees argue that under these conditions Congress cannot effectively challenge the executive because the members' attention is so divided. In addition, reducing the number of committees might enhance the legitimacy of Congress: if there were only eight or ten committees, they would be forced to draw their members from a broader base and would appear to be more representative.[43]

In contrast, John Bibby and Theodore Lowi—coming from apparently different political perspectives—have argued that the present structure, or even one with more committees, would best keep Congress strong vis-à-vis the executive. Lowi argues that since 1946 the power of committee chairpersons has increased as committee jurisdictions have grown. Increasing the number of committees, he speculates, would spread the power and allow vigorous members the opportunity to get into the action.[44] Bibby contends that the power of the House derives from its "mastery of technical detail" growing out of the larger number of specialized committees.[45]

Advocates of committee consolidation would counter that their proposals perpetuate subcommittees. With the "subcommitee bill of rights" in the House, power is shared among Democrats. Furthermore, subcommittees provide the detailed specialization necessary for technical mastery. However, they note, the present organization of committees does not maximize the possibilities of mastery because overlapping jurisdictions lead to redundancy and wasted effort and prevent rational use of subcommittees. This view leads them to call for jurisdictional changes in tandem with a reduction in the number of committees.[46]

Proponents of jurisdictional changes emphasize that they want to bring coherence to the congressional policy-making process and reduce the fragmentation that the current committee system promotes. For example, the Senate Select Committee to Study the Senate Committee System stated:

Areas such as energy, environment, health, transportation and urban problems have become increasingly important and interdependent. Thus the Senate in the 1970s has been faced with numerous areas of legislation and oversight subject to wide overlap and competition in the historic jurisdiction of its committees.[47]

Currently, a policy area such as education might be covered by five or six legislative committees, in addition to several appropriations subcommittees. This encourages "piecemeal or inconsistent legislation and results in unnecessary delay. Different committees oftentimes promote divergent approaches to these problems."[48] Thus proposals for jurisdictional change tend to accompany plans for reducing the number of committees, as jurisdictions become aggregated into policy areas.

While such overlapping is often described as "irrational," some reformers have seen advantages in jurisdictional fuzziness. Lowi, for example, argues that expanding the number of standing committees "would very probably also loosen and expose the rigid and intimate relations between the present standing committees and executive agencies. . . . Overlapping jurisdictions produce healthy political competition."[49] Similarly, Lewis Anthony Dexter contends that jurisdictional overlapping promotes creativity. Jurisdictional change is an appropriate technique for rationalizing "routinizable aspects of managing," he remarks. "The Senate-in-committee, however, is not engaged in a routinizable process."[50]

Whatever "rational" benefits might accrue from jurisdictional change accompanied by a reduction in the number of committees, such proposals run into political difficulty because they take away chairs from members, reduce the number of chairs that are available, and deprive members of control of policies on which they now ride herd. Thus the Bolling Committee proposals and the original plans of the Senate Select Committee were scuttled, though the Senate finally enacted significant reforms.

In 1977 the Senate passed a resolution that decreased the number of committees from 31 to 19. The resolution categorized committees as "major" and "minor," and limited each senator to membership on only two major committees and one minor committee, and to no more than three subcommittees on each major committee and two on a minor committee.[51] By reducing the number of committees, the Senate necessarily changed committee jurisdictions. No longer was there a Commerce Committee and an Aeronautical and Space Sciences Committee; they were merged into a Committee on Commerce, Science, and Transportation. A Committee on Energy and Natural Resources, responsible for energy policy, replaced the Interior Committee. Even committees that remained unaffected by the reduction had their jurisdictions altered. For example, the Agriculture Committee lost responsibility for agricultural colleges and obtained responsibility for the school-lunch program.

The House was far more ruthless in rejecting the Bolling plan in 1974. The plan would have left unchanged at twenty-two the number of standing committees, but the committees would have been significantly different. For example, the proposal called for the division of the Education and Labor Committee into two committees. The Post Office and

Civil Service Committee would have been absorbed by the new Labor Committee.[52]

Instead the House adopted an alternative proposal recommended by the Hansen Committee. This proposal made minor modifications in committee jurisdictions. For example, it renamed the Public Works Committee the Public Works and Transportation Committee and gave it formal jurisdiction over urban mass transit, with which the committee had already been involved de facto because of its responsibility for the highway trust fund.[53]

The third area of organizational concern for reformers—after reducing the number of committees and altering committee jurisdictions—had been the congressional budgetary process. Typical was Aaron Wildavsky's indictment of the pre-1974 process as "mindless because most of the budget is not subject to scrutiny and irrational because all the possible relevant comparisons are excluded from view."[54] Critics contended that the incremental quality of the budgetary process prevented rational planning of the federal budget and contributed to inflation and the less than optimal allocation of federal expenditures. Reformers also charged that the decentralized, uncoordinated nature of the congressional budgetary process not only drained the federal government but weakened Congress vis-à-vis the executive. Louis Fisher, for example, contended, "Unless Congress can improve its budget capability it will remain a patsy, forever being bulldozed around by executives' assaults and encroachments."[55]

As Allen Schick reports, there had been three types of reform proposals intended to redress Congress's weakness in the budgetary process. The first covered "resource improvements through the acquisition of more staff, information, and time," the second "power improvements that constrain executive discretion," and the third "institutional improvements to make Congress more responsible for total spending, for determining priorities and to end the fragmentation of budget choice in Congress."[56]

In 1972 the newly created Joint Study Committee on Budget Control undertook an examination of the many proposals for reforming the budgetary process. Its efforts were given urgency by President Nixon's series of impoundments in 1973 and 1974. In 1974 Congress passed the Congressional Budget and Impoundment Control Act of 1974.[57] The act appears to address the three areas of concern that Schick described. It created the Congressional Budget Office (CBO), which was seen "as an authoritative clearinghouse of information and ideas about federal spending." The CBO's services were made available to all members of Congress, and it was hoped that it would provide members with technical support that could be used to challenge presidential assertions of budgetary power, such as the impoundment of funds. Under Title X of the act, Congress is given specific procedures by which it can block impoundments, particularly those undertaken with the purpose of thwarting the congressional intent underlying an appropriation.

Finally, the act established two budget committees, one in each house, which have jurisdiction over the budgetary process. Through two resolutions that they must report out—one in March, before annual authorization bills are passed, and one in September, after passage of appropriations bills—the committees are expected to determine total appropriations within tax and debt levels that have been set by Congress. In this way, the total budget can be debated and potentially controlled by the whole Congress, in a manner that permits Congress to relate means to ends.[58]

Information Resources. Perhaps because it is seemingly the least controversial and easiest problem to solve, reforming the information logjam facing Congress was high on the list of proposed changes in the 1960s and 1970s. A 1964 survey of members' complaints about Congress found that "the most frequently mentioned problems were associated with . . . the lack of information, the volume of legislation to be considered, and the difficulty of making a rational choice from among many conflicting alternatives."[59]

The problem of information has been emphasized primarily by those who seek to strengthen Congress vis-à-vis the executive, because Congress tends to be dependent on the executive for information necessary to make policy. The executive branch can obtain information, process it, and use it because the executive is hierarchically organized and has a large field network and huge staff, that is, the executive-branch agencies.

As John Saloma notes, a related problem is that "increasingly large bodies of information within the executive are screened from Congress entirely."[60] This is best illustrated by the way in which the intelligence agencies withhold details from Congress and manipulate members by the release of selective information.[61] But it also occurs as presidents claim "executive privilege" for data that might be useful in congressional deliberations.

The decentralized nature of the legislative branch complicates the problem. Members ultimately must watch out for their own interests, and information is often sought for political as well as technical reasons. Thus each member tends to want his or her own capability to obtain and evaluate data.[62] Similarly, committees tend to prize their autonomy and view information as a source of power, which impedes the processing of data received from disparate sources and by different committees.

To reduce these perceived problems related to information, reformers suggested changes in three areas: staff, internal information processing, and support services. Regarding staff, they proposed increasing the size of members' personal staffs, increasing the size of committee staffs, raising staff salaries, and increasing the number of "professional" staffers available to members. Some also emphasized the need for adequate minority-party staffing.[63]

The purpose of increasing the staff would be to provide Congress with the personnel necessary for obtaining and using additional information. As one Nader study pointed out: "With a staff of 36 . . . during the Ninety-second Congress, House Judiciary simply could not keep abreast of developments within its legislative jurisdiction."[64]

The number of staffers in Congress has greatly increased in the last decade. But larger staffs for individual members have not necessarily contributed to their ability to process information necessary for legislating; the members tend instead to use the staff for other purposes, such as constituent services, that increase their chances of re-election.[65] By 1979 several members were complaining about an unforeseen and even more serious consequence: the growth of staffs had generated more legislation than Congress could handle. The professional staff on each subcommittee, and the growing number of legislative assistants on personal staffs, felt they had to justify their high salaries by developing new bills and amendments, which flooded Congress.

In 1966 Kenneth Janda argued that the "information gap" between the executive and Congress could be reduced substantially by retooling Congress with modern equipment and techniques for information processing.[66] He had obviously hit upon an idea whose time had come, as calls for introducing computer technology to Congress became the rage.[67] In 1971 the House Administration Committee created a House Information Systems staff. By 1973 it had developed several information systems that are in use today for such purposes as retrieval of information about a bill's status and even for mailing letters to categorized groups of constituents.[68]

While Congress had two major research arms—the General Accounting Office and the Legislative Research Service of the Library of Congress—some critics had argued that both had been stymied by the legislators themselves, through requests for information that prevented in-depth analysis.[69] In an apparent response to such criticism, the Legislative Research Service was expanded under the Legislative Reorganization Act of 1970 and given explicit authority to carry out independent investigations, to develop policy proposals, and to be involved in policy review. In 1972 Congress created the Office of Technology Assessment, with the vague purpose of evaluating how programs achieve their goals—especially in the area of technology—in contrast to the General Accounting Office's purpose of considering whether an agency is spending its money as it claimed it would.[70] In a sense the Congressional Budget Office, created in 1974, acts as a fourth information arm, supposedly linking the OTA with the GAO by taking into consideration the criteria of efficiency and program goals.

Institutional Consequences of Reform

Since 1971 the House has had an electric tote board, which records a member's vote when he or she inserts a plastic card into one of the vote registers on the House floor. One day, in the late spring of 1981, the board went on the blink. Members had to shout out their vote, as they still do in the Senate. Mass confusion resulted because in ten years there had been so much turnover that only a few older members remembered how to vote without the cards.

Congress in 1981 was a different institution than it had been in 1971, and much more than its membership had changed during the 1970s. The changes were not all consistent. Some tended to centralize the decision-making process, others to decentralize it. In the short run, the decentralizing reforms appeared to be more prominent, and by the end of the decade Congress seemed to be a less coordinated, more individualized body. The centralizing reforms, however, may ultimately be more significant.

The Centralizing Potential of Reforms

Consider the one personal and five organizational categories of reform that the last section examined. Many of the changes covered in the six categories provide Congress with new ways of operating that might make central planning easier. They tend to centralize decision making in fewer hands and to insulate Congress. Centralized decision making decreases the points of access, and insulation discourages small groups from pressuring Congress. Both tendencies overcome the two features of Congress that hindered its planning ability: its capture by particular interest groups and its inability to coordinate discrete actions into broad-based policy. A review of the reforms discussed earlier will indicate that overcoming these features has been a consistent orientation of the reforms, though in advocating them reformers emphasized personal and institutional objectives.

Ethics and campaign-finance reform.   The irony of legislation aimed at insulating members from the pernicious control of wealthy individuals is that it is likely to push Congress closer to large national corporations. Veteran political journalist William Greider explains that the limit on outside earned income encourages non-millionaire members to seek in other ways the high status they believe is appropriate to them.[71] For example, many have responded favorably to personal visits by members of the Business Roundtable, a group of the top officers in the country's leading corporations.[72] Moreover, limits on campaign financing have diminished the significance of local business figures, and as a group members of Congress are more likely to listen to a few corporate executives than to many wealthy locals representing a variety of interests.

The loophole in the campaign-finance laws that has had the greatest impact permits contributions from Political Action Committees (PACs). A particular PAC may not contribute more than $5,000 to a candidate for each election, but wealthy donors may contribute to several PACs, all of which may support a particular candidate. Corporations and unions can also create several PACs, provided that each is independent. This regulation favors corporations, because they are permitted to solicit voluntary contributions from employees and stockholders. There were 2,800 PACs in 1980, and the greatest resources flowed from corporation/industry-sponsored PACs.[73] In addition, the law did not limit the amount a PAC might spend in a negative campaign against a candidate, so long as it did not endorse or coordinate its efforts with the candidate's opponent. This stipulation enabled groups such as the National Conservative Political Action Committee to direct large sums against Democratic Senators George McGovern, Frank Church, and John Culver in 1980, which contributed to their defeat.[74]

Seniority. The cases where House seniority was bypassed have usually involved somewhat autocratic chairmen who indicated that they wanted to chart independent courses for their committees. More important, the rules changes that facilitate the removal of a chair simultaneously enhance the power of the Democratic Steering and Policy Committee, which tends to centralize power in this organ.

Rules. Conflict tends to be contagious, political scientist E. E. Schattschneider observed in 1960.[75] A raging battle will bring in a wide array of interests that will need to be accommodated in resolving the conflict. Notably, several new rules should decrease conflict in Congress by making an extended Senate filibuster more difficult and by depriving House members of procedures that can be used for delay.[76] These changes will make Congress more "efficient" because fewer interests will need to be accommodated.

Party discipline. A disciplined party will force interest groups to deal with legislators through the party caucus. To the extent that a small group of members can lead the caucus, the points of access for groups are limited. With the Speaker now responsible for appointments to the Rules Committee, limited access diminishes an important competing center of power that had thrived in the less centralized House. (By 1979 members were demanding that the House and Senate leadership actively use the levers that the reforms had provided, but even in 1981, when there were serious "defections" by a group of forty-seven House Democrats nicknamed "boll weevils," the House Democratic leadership was reluctant to use these levers.)[77]

Committee structure. The direction of change has been to reduce the number of committees. Fewer committees facilitate coordination between committees, and in the Senate the smaller number of committees has allowed broad policy matters, such as energy, to be reviewed under one roof by consolidating relevant subjects into the jurisdiction of one committee. Both the House and the Senate attempted the coordination of key legislative matters, such as a new charter for the Central Intelligence Agency, through a process of sequential consideration by several committees. The House also developed a new organizational form to bypass committees and to allow broad policy formation: the ad hoc committee.[76] Although its use was limited, the leadership held it out as a potential threat to standing committees that resisted coordination. Ad hoc committees differ from select committees in that their members are appointed directly by the Speaker. Fewer committees and the growing intervention by the party leadership in committee operations can effectively reduce the points of access for groups and lessen the extent to which Congress is "captured."

The budgetary process reform was explicitly intended to enable Congress to engage in planning. But it was not until 1981 that the budget process approximated its potential. At that point the process even shocked many members when they realized that central planning meant a loss of autonomy for decentralized units.[79] Because the 1974 Budget Control and Impoundment Act requires Congress to pass two resolutions—one in May and one in September—to guide decisions by authorizing committees and by the House and Senate Appropriations committees, appropriations need to be reconciled with the final budget guidelines, which are drafted by the budget committees. In 1981, following President Reagan's lead, the committees established guidelines that not only set limits on spending but effectively reorganized federal government programs. In doing so, the budget committees seemed to bypass much of the legislative obstacle course that such major programmatic revisions previously had run.

Information resources. Congress is still far from bureaucratic because it is not hierarchically structured, but the enormous growth of staff in the 1970s has created a phenomenon familiar to most people who deal with bureaucratic organizations. Layers of staff have come to buffer interaction between the public and the members. The barrier allows legislators to disclaim responsibility for decisions by blaming staff, and it protects them from confronting groups directly. The access of smaller groups decreases, and members can more easily overlook local problems. The nature of the staff also plays a part: as the experts on Capitol Hill have become more professional, they have come increasingly to resemble their counterparts in the executive branch and in large national corporations. They are drawn from the same elite universities, reach conclusions by applying the same technical criteria, and often associate with each other by mingling in the same professional circles.[80]

In sum, reforms in these six categories discourage pluralism and conflict and encourage centralization of decision making in Congress. Campaign-finance reform propels members to divorce themselves from local interests as they come to depend on national funders. Reforms that permit party leaders to discipline members who deviate from a party program, that allow the majority party to select committee heads on some basis other than seniority, that deprive "deviants" of devices such as the Rules Committee or the filibuster with which to impede the efficient flow of legislation, and that reduce the number of power centers—especially in the budgetary process—by decreasing the number of committees are reforms that centralize the decision-making process in Congress. To be sure, the reforms might have other consequences. An end to seniority might lead to conflicts over committee chairmanships that could engage interest groups and raise significant issues,[81] but it also appears to be a *sine qua non* for strong party leadership and control.

The Decentralizing Effect of Reforms

Whatever its potential for centralization, Congress remains today an "open, egalitarian, and fragmented" institution, as political scientist Roger Davidson has characterized it.[82] In the House most decisions are made at the subcommittee level, a phenomenon that developed in the 1970s following adoption of the "subcommittee bill of rights." Indeed, subcommittee reforms in the early 1970s reinforced the decentralized nature of the House because the reforms provided these units with greater autonomy and authority to act. Subcommittees' independence has made coordination more difficult. Their large number means that interest groups have more access points in Congress, so that more groups have become involved.[83]

Similarly, in the Senate the growth of staff, and especially of specialized committee staff responsible to individual senators, has contributed to a decline in coordination. Individual legislators act as their own policymakers, isolating themselves from committee or party leadership. The autonomy of senators has been further enhanced by a breakdown of norms—such as deference to senior members—that had earlier restrained independent action.

In its actions, Congress has made an implicit choice for decentralization, despite its overt decisions in the 1970s to create mechanisms to facilitate central planning. This pattern of action reflects many of the causes that political scientists have identified for the reform movement itself: members wanted prestige, power, and resources to make independent decisions.[84] Decentralization immediately addressed these desires. It enabled legislators to claim credit for decisions, to use information resources to elective advantage, to speak with authority, to control a larger staff, and to pursue policy interests. The impetus for decentralization also came from external sources, Roger Davidson observes: "As the number and range of public issues have grown, workgroups have proliferated on Capitol Hill, mainly subcommittees, task forces, and special or select committees."[85] From this perspective, decentralization was an institutional adaptation to the need for handling more problems, for enabling Congress to work more efficiently.

In light of these apparently overwhelming reasons to decentralize, it is all the more striking that Congress made any decision to centralize its operations. If the enhancement of personal interests were such a significant motivation to decentralize, the members would not have approved centralizing reforms that could limit their personal discretion, give greater authority to party leaders, and insulate them from the electorate. What accounts for the seeming anomaly is that members were attempting to grapple with a set of problems created by the external environment. Davidson appropriately points to the external environment in describing a motive for efficiency. But the problems went beyond a concern for administrative neatness, for a "technical" adjustment. The problems were political and their concerns had to be political. Centralization and decentralization were not competing strands; they were parts of the same quilt. To appreciate how the two tendencies might have addressed a common concern, let us examine the external context that set the agenda for reform.

The Context for Reform

There is no necessity that a Congress with centralized control act in concert with a president. But there is good reason to expect that centralization would weaken the checks and balances between Congress and the executive, because centralization creates fewer points of access for information. As the executive is already a major source of information for Congress, streamlining congressional operations would close off other sources and give the executive more influence.

An important consequence of such a change might be that interests represented by the executive would gain favor over those represented by Congress. Analysts have often described congressional interests as "local" and executive-branch interests as "national."[86] As the next chapter argues, this dichotomy has been overdrawn, in part because what is uniquely local in our increasingly homogeneous country is difficult to discern.[87] But to the extent that multiple access points in Congress provide it with non-executive-branch information, centralization would do the opposite. It would favor, in Bertram Gross's phrase, "a few efficient gatekeepers operating as loyal junior members of an oligarchy dominated by Macro-Business, the Super-Rich and Chief Executive-National Network."[88]

If the beneficiaries of centralization were to be national corporations, it is important to appreciate the problems they were experiencing. The unsolved problem for national corporations at the start of the 1970s—a problem to which Congress seemed to contribute because of its structure—was that the anarchic "market" had become an intolerable mechanism for organizing society. For thirty years after the New Deal several factors pasted over the cracks in the market system: military spending provided quick fixes; exploitation of the Third World provided inexpensive raw materials and, later, cheap labor; and the devastation of Japan and Europe in World War II provided the absence of international competition. Prosperity in the United States served as the basis for the system's legitimacy and sanctioned the government's mode of operation as a broker state, parcelling out benefits to interest-group claimants who continued to "do their own thing."[89]

By 1970 the paste itself had cracked. The economic crisis discussed in Chapter 4 and the legitimacy crisis discussed in Chapter 5, which set the contexts, respectively, for congressional policy towards Cuba and the development of the Higher Education Act, together set the context for congressional reform in the 1970s. Government planning had become imperative, but the machinery of government was badly structured to achieve planning. Two features of Congress made it an especially bad planning instrument: it was "captured" at key junctures and its decentralized parts were uncoordinated.

One popular view of Congress, as noted in Chapter 2, holds that Congress is no more than the agent of special interests, whether these be corporations, labor unions, or even another country, such as Nicaragua.

Even on Capitol Hill some members are jokingly referred to as the Senator from ITT or the Representative from Texaco. But legislators generally do not get "captured" in the sense that they are bought off or bribed. As members of subcommittees, they frequently become part of a subgovernment, which also includes a corresponding executive-branch agency and the "client" served by the agency. The client may be a company, a union, or a manufacturing sector.[90] Each unit of the subgovernment tends to support the other and to reinforce the relationship. Staffs circulate between the units, as do key members. There tends to be personal interaction among the units at Washington social functions, and they look to each other for "reliable" information. Because they are all grappling with the same "technical" problems, they come to see themselves as the only people who appreciate these problems, and they insulate themselves from people not in the subgovernment.

Subgovernment decision making tends to be incremental, paralleling political scientist Aaron Wildavsky's description of the old budgetary process.[91] In Congress, the units of a subgovernment tend to be responsible for discrete issue areas. Few parts of Congress have responsibility for developing broad-based policy. Subgovernment units, in fact, may try to subvert the development of broad-based policy for fear of losing control over legislation in their area.

In the face of economic turmoil, the subgovernments operated to extract more benefits from the government for their particular problems. This not only contributed to the problem by fueling inflation, but it also began to weaken the government. As James O'Connor argues, these two phenomena are linked. He explains that as the monopoly sector grows, it carries with it an ever smaller percentage of the work force. Workers then must find employment in the "competitive" sector of the economy where wages are lower, which means that they cannot afford to purchase social services from private suppliers. Moreover, the high-technology industries cannot afford individually to invest in research and development, and they turn to the government. Having assisted these industries, the government also feels compelled to provide services to workers so that it can retain an appearance of neutrality and maintain its legitimacy. Thus in an effort to reconcile the needs of a private economy with its own need for legitimacy, the federal government's resources become drained at an ever accelerating rate.[92] This diminishes the ability of the government to plan the economy.

By the 1970s, historian Otis Graham reports, national leaders recognized that government reorganization would be necessary to enable planning to take place. They saw that the "Broker State system cannot pilot this or any complex modern society through straits permanently narrowed by population pressures, material shortages, international interdependence, and recurrent war."[93] Planning required the break-up of the subgovernments, and President Nixon quickly moved to weaken them. He attempted to create a "super Cabinet" that could bypass the bureaucracy and operate out of the White House, and he authorized the Office of Management and Budget and the Domestic Council to engage in planning. His expansion of revenue-sharing further removed from the subgovernments the source of their cohesiveness—government grants.[94]

In this context consider the congressional reforms described earlier in the chapter. Many of the analysts are correct that there were personal and institutional reasons for reform. But such reasons alone do not explain the larger politics of reform. As Bertram Gross observes, reformers who propose to make congressional operations more "efficient" seem to assume that such a change "is a supreme value of and in itself."[95] They ignore how a more efficient Congress would relate to its environment, in part because they tend to ignore historical experiences.

However, a similar reform in 1946 came at another critical juncture, as the federal government had clearly become responsible for the maintenance of the stability and expansion of markets and access to resources for private investors. In the executive branch there were fears that without planning the economy would return to depression, and these fears led to the development of the Employment Act of 1946, the National Security Act of 1947, and National Security Memorandum 68.[96] The latter two enabled the executive partially to plan the economy through military budgets with little congressional control. Still, a Congress fragmented into more than eighty committees in each house might have upset the "rational" designs of the executive, and the reorganization act addressed this potential by drastically reducing the number of committees.[97]

Correspondingly, the 1921 Budgeting and Accounting Act required the executive to coordinate the segmented budgets of the different departments into one unified budget at the end of a period of great growth and turmoil in the economy. The federal government had been involved through some efforts at planning and regulation, but as its own budget grew in size, planning had to become more systematic.[98] Compare the statements by reformers reported above calling for a coordinated congressional budget process with the following comments in 1919 on the need for a budget act:

> The estimates of expenditure needs now submitted to Congress represent only the desires of the individual departments . . . without making them, as a whole, conform to the needs of the Nation as represented by the Treasury and prospective revenues.[99]

Corporations did not pin all of their hopes on a restructured Congress that could reduce federal expenditures and that would channel money into "productive" areas instead of into the rat hole of the subgovernments. As in other eras, corporations proposed many solutions to the stagnation they experienced, each of which became an aspect of the whole. Foreign investment was one such effort, as we discussed in Chapter 4. Corporate merger was another. In the late 1960s and early 1970s conglomerates came on the scene. These were legal monsters that combined under one corporate name previously independent companies making quite different products. The theory was that internal diversity would strengthen the whole unit, while common corporate management would generate efficiency. It was the same sort of centralizing model that some reformers recommended for Congress. The ideas of congressional reformers were imaginative but not always novel—Congress listened to them partly because these ideas captured a prevailing orientation among national corporate elites. Centralizing Congress was both a solution to the problems corporations faced, and a solution that was consistent with others they were considering.

From the perspective of the individual member of Congress, this larger picture was not as evident as it appears in hindsight. Some legislators well appreciated that the organization of Congress was diminishing the ability of the whole government to resolve major problems. But most focused their attention more narrowly. They perceived a growing din of complaints and voter dissatisfaction, which were manifestations of a failing economy. As a consequence, members needed to devote more attention to re-election.

The reforms, in part, were their reaction to these circumstances. Both those reforms that created greater decentralization and those that were potentially centralizing offered an individual member a means of handling the problem of voter dissatisfaction. Decentralizing reforms would allow the individual representative or senator to shine, to stand out and claim credit for district-related or symbolic benefits. Centralizing reforms met this re-election interest of the members less well, although they might have been useful in insulating a member from blame for unpopular decisions such as those involving budget cuts, reductions in government service, military intervention in the Third World, or re-distribution of wealth away from the middle class. Party leaders, budget committee members, and even the president could be held responsible for the decisions, and they could take the heat.

Reform not only served the needs of individual members directly but also was a strategy for bolstering them indirectly, by strengthening the legitimacy of Congress itself. By 1973 members were feeling the loss of Congress's legitimacy—as discussed in Chapter 2–through the anti-incumbent sentiment evident at the polls. Since 1972 more members have retired voluntarily than in any comparable period since World War II.

Reform was good public relations. It held out the image of rejuvenation, action, and responsiveness. Other organizations—such as the national Democratic Party—were going the same route, creating reform commissions and instituting changes to regain legitimacy. Just as major institutions in this period suffered a crisis of legitimacy, a crisis shared by Congress, so too was reform in the air, which encouraged congressional efforts. Despite the freedom of the press, the media that dominate opinion in the United States share a remarkable ideological consistency, partly because they are privately owned.[100] This ideology contributed to the elite consensus about the need for reform.

Meanwhile, the rapid turnover in Congress was bringing in members who were ideologically diverse but who shared a vague commitment to "modernize" the legislature, to abolish some of the patterns that had made the old Congress an object of scorn. The old patterns, of course, were the very ones that had facilitated the "capture" of Congress and made it a weak planning instrument. The newcomers thus added fuel to the reform movement.

The context of reform, then, went beyond the frustrations of junior members and their desires for power or glory and beyond the needs of the organization to handle an increased workload more efficiently, although each undoubtedly had an impact. Reform in Congress came at a time when the economy was in crisis and major institutions had lost legitimacy. It is this context that appears to have been determinative.

Conclusion

As the first section of this chapter makes clear, critics had been proposing changes in Congress from the moment Congress adopted its last set of reforms in 1946. Similarly, there was little new about the frustrations of junior members or about the congressional workload that would have dictated reforms in the 1970s. It was the 1961–1965 period that saw the growth of federal agencies, which might have generated an immediate imperative for corresponding congressional reorganization. Yet major reforms occurred a decade later.

The reform decade in Congress resulted from the conjunction of a set of pressures that included traditional desires of the members, and significantly it involved the economic and legitimacy crises of the period. These crises affected the electorate and brought new members to Congress who were reform-oriented. The crises created pressures on all the members, who sought relief through the symbolism of reform and through the particular reforms that might have alleviated the pressures.

Notably, the reforms that members adopted were those that they might have expected would both serve their personal interests and address larger problems. This dual service was true of the decentralizing as well as the centralizing reforms.

Decentralizing Reforms

The "subcommittee bill of rights" and the growth of staff served personal interests of autonomy for each member. These changes were also a means of grappling with the crises, because they provided a way of breaking up the existing subgovernments. The new power of House subcommittees and the staff expertise in the Senate gave new members power over issue areas that had been handled by old networks.

Centralizing Reforms

Disciplined parties, a centralized budget process, increasingly professional staff, fewer committees, and a centralized information process allow members to avoid blame and to manipulate voters. These reforms also weaken the subgovernments and, along with campaign-finance reform, link Congress more closely to other national elites. Members of Congress might have thus taken on the same perspective as those elites, which would facilitate central planning for national corporations.

The reforms Congress selected served the personal interests of the members, the institutional interests of legitimacy, and the larger systemic interests of planning. But of course each reform could not function so ideally as to serve all three sets of interests. Decentralizing reforms, for example, served members' personal interests more than they served institutional or systemic interests. Conversely, centralizing reforms better addressed systemic problems. The different effects of the various reforms led members to balance their interests and to create inconsistencies in doing so. Thus the Senate rejected a major reduction in the number of its committees—even though it decreased the number of standing committees and altered the jurisdictions of several committees—despite its awareness that even fewer committees would have enhanced coordination and reduced the number of veto points.[101] Similarly, the House rejected entirely a proposed restructuring of its committees and resisted efforts to consider new proposals. In both cases, personal interests of the members appeared to outweigh the alleged benefits for the institution or the larger system.

From today's vantage point, it seems as if many of the reforms of the 1970s do not address the economic and legitimacy crises that have been carried over from the last decade. This does not mean, however, that reforms were not intended to resolve systemic problems. Grappling with the crises was a process of guesswork. Members had few guides by which to judge the effect of each reform. They were thus bound to choose strategies that were inconsistent, because they were unaware of the inconsistency or they blindly hoped that something would work. They also chose strategies that were simply bad guesses.

The "subcommittee bill of rights" may have been a bad guess from the perspective of the crises members were trying to overcome and from that of their personal needs. Members found in the late 1970s that autonomous subcommittees, with their resources, produced more legislation than the House could handle, and the members did not like much of the legislation. The subcommittees and staffs seemed almost to generate legislation to justify their existence rather than in response to real problems. The increased legislation became a burden to members because it absorbed valuable time. Moreover, the subcommittees quickly formed new subgovernments and the old pattern of subgovernment incrementalism prevailed.

Congressional reform in the 1970s indicates that as Congress chooses its mode of operation, it both is independent of the private sector and embodies the conflicts of the private sector in its choices. Members choose freely in pursuit of their interests, and herein lies the possibility of Congress. But their interests are constrained, because Congress's actions are part of the web of production and struggle that shapes society.

NOTES

1. Claus Offe, "The Theory of the Capitalist State and the Problem of Policy Formation," in Leon Lundberg, et al., *Stress and Contradiction in Modern Capitalism* (Lexington, Mass.: D. C. Heath, 1975), p. 135. For a good case study applying this notion, see Charles G. Benda, "State Organization and Policy Formation: The Reorganization of the Post Office Department," *Politics & Society,* 9, No. 2 (1979).
2. Randall Ripley, *Congress: Process and Policy,* 2nd ed. (New York: Norton, 1978), pp. 395–396.
3. Warren Weaver, *Both Your Houses: The Truth About Congress* (New York: Praeger, 1972), p. 46.
4. Drew Pearson and Jack Anderson, *The Case Against Congress* (New York: Simon & Schuster, 1968).
5. "If As Ralph Nader Says, Congress Is 'The Broken Branch,' How Come We Love Our Congressmen So Much?" in Norman Ornstein, ed., *Congress in Change: Evolution and Reform* (New York: Praeger, 1975), p. 280; Richard F. Fenno, Jr., *Home Style: House Members in Their Districts* (Boston: Little, Brown, 1978), pp. 164–168. For a report on how members view ethics, see Edmund Beard and Stephen Horn, *Congressional Ethics: The View from the House* (Washington, D.C.: Brookings Institution, 1975).
6. Ralph Nader Congress Project, *The Money Committees* (New York: Grossman, 1975).
7. Mark Green, *Who Runs Congress?,* 3rd ed. (New York: Bantam, 1979). See also Morton Mintz and Jerome Cohen, *America, Inc.* (New York: Dell, 1972), Chapter 6.
8. For data on the composition of the 97th Congress, as an example, see Congressional Quarterly *Weekly Report,* 24 January 1981, pp. 198–199. Also see Richard Zweigenhaft, "Who Represents America?" *Insurgent Sociologist* (Spring 1975), pp. 119–130.

9. Joseph Clark, *Congress: The Sapless Branch*, 2nd rev. ed. (New York: Harper & Row, 1965), p. 219. Also see Green, *Who Runs Congress?*, Chapters 1 and 8.
10. Robert Peabody, Jeffrey Berry, William Frasure, and Jerry Goldman, *To Enact a Law: Congress and Campaign Financing* (New York: Praeger, 1972).
11. James Wagner, "New Federal Election Law Has Its Critics," Congressional Quarterly *Weekly Report* 23 October 1976, pp. 3032–3035.
12. Alan Berlow, "Detailed Analysis of Lobby Disclosure Bill," Congressional Quarterly *Weekly Report,* 17 November 1979, pp. 2584–2586. Also see U.S. Senate, "Lobby Reform Legislation," Hearings on S-774 Before the Committee on Government Operations, 94th Cong. 1st Sess., 22 April 1975.
13. Thomas P. Southwick, "House Adopts Tough Ethics Code," Congressional Quarterly *Weekly Report* 5 March 1977, pp. 387–391. Other provisions include full disclosure of each member's personal finances, a ban on unofficial office accounts, and restrictions on gifts from lobbyists. Also see "Special Report on Financial Disclosure," Congressional Quarterly *Weekly Report,* 1 September 1974, pp. 1823–1892. In 1981 the House raised the limit on outside earned income to 30 percent of a representative's salary, which was then $60,662.
14. Congress Project, *Money Committees,* p. 361. Also see Walter Pincus, "Basic Reforms Now for a Dated Congress," *Washington Post,* 9 January 1977, p. C1.
15. Richard Bolling, "Committees in the House," *The Annals,* No. 411 (January 1974), p. 2. These charges repeat those that framed his earlier critiques: *Power in the House* (New York: E. P. Dutton, 1968) and *House Out of Order* (New York: E. P. Dutton, 1966).
16. Philip Brenner, "Committee Conflict in the Congressional Arena," The *Annals,* No. 411 (January 1974), pp. 87, 99–100; Green, *Who Runs Congress?*, pp. 65–66. For a discussion of the history of seniority, see Barbara Hinckley, *The Seniority System in Congress* (Bloomington: Indiana University Press, 1971).
17. Norman Ornstein and David Rohde, "Seniority and Future Power in Congress," in Ornstein, *Congress in Change,* p. 72. Also see Barbara Hinckley, *Stability and Change in Congress,* 2nd ed. (New York: Harper & Row, 1978), pp. 74–80.
18. "Congressional Reforms Made in 1975," Congressional Quarterly *Almanac 1975* (Washington, D.C.: CQ Press, 1976), pp. 26–29.
19. Congress Project, *Money Committees,* pp. 362–363.
20. Ralph Nader Congress Project, *The Judiciary Committees* (New York: Grossman, 1975), pp. 368–369.
21. Congress Project, *Money Committees,* p. 362.
22. Norman Ornstein, "Causes and Consequences of Congressional Change: Subcommittee Reforms in the House of Representatives, 1970–73," in Ornstein, *Congress in Change,* pp. 90–100. For a history and analysis of the DSG, see Arthur Stevens, Arthur Miller, and Thomas Mann, "Mobilization of Liberal Strength in the House, 1955–1970: The Democratic Study Group," *American Political Science Review* 68, No. 2 (June 1974).
23. David Rohde, "Committee Reform in the House of Representatives and the Subcommittee Bill of Rights," *The Annals,* No. 411 (January 1974).
24. As the Senate became the breeding ground for presidents, the vaunted "establishment" that Senator Joseph Clark once decried became less imposing. Compare his *The Senate Establishment* (New York: Hill and Wang, 1963) with Nelson Polsby, "Goodbye to the Senate's Inner Club," in Ornstein, *Congress in Change,* pp. 208–215.
25. Walter J. Oleszek, *Congressional Procedures and the Policy Process* (Washington: CQ Press, 1978), pp. 166–167. But see Raymond Wolfinger, "Filibusters: Majority Rule, Presidential Leadership, and Senate Norms," in Raymond Wolfinger, ed., *Readings on Congress* (Englewood Cliffs, N.J.: Prentice-Hall, 1971).
26. Brenner, "Committee Conflict in the Congressional Arena," pp. 98–99.
27. William Safire, "The Tip and Bobby Show," *New York Times,* 10 January 1977, p. 21.
28. Leroy N. Rieselbach, *Congressional Reform in the Seventies* (Morristown, N.J.: General Learning, 1977), pp. 47–48. Also see Green, *Who Runs Congress?*, pp. 66–68; Ralph Nader Congress Project, *The Revenue Committees* (New York: Grossman, 1975), p. 287.

29. Bolling, *Power in the House*, p. 255.
30. *Ibid.*, pp. 265–266. For a review of the early sources of the concept of "responsible parties," see Austin Ranney, *The Doctrine of Responsible Party Government* (Urbana: University of Illinois Press, 1962). For a probing critique of the doctrine, see J. Roland Pennock, "Responsiveness, Responsibility, and Majority Rule," *American Political Science Review*, 46, No. 3 (September 1952).
31. James M. Burns, *Congress on Trial: The Legislative Process and the Administrative State* (New York: Gordian, 1966), p. 193. In *Deadlock of Democracy: Four Party Politics in America* (Englewood Cliffs, N.J.: Prentice-Hall, 1963), Burns addressed a subtheme of *Congress on Trial*, namely that the parties in Congress differed from the presidential parties and that the two should be brought into congruence to enhance democratic control.
32. James Robinson, "Proposed Reforms: Party Responsibility Versus Legislative Independence," in Joseph Clark, ed., *Congressional Reform: Problems and Prospects* (New York: Crowell, 1965).
33. Burns, *Congress on Trial*, pp. 136, 186.
34. Robert Peabody, "The Enlarged Rules Committee," in Robert Peabody and Nelson Polsby, eds., *New Perspectives on the House of Representatives* (Chicago: Rand McNally, 1963), pp. 143–44.
35. Robinson, "Proposed Reforms," pp. 155–166. Also see Leroy N. Rieselbach, *Congressional Politics* (New York: McGraw-Hill, 1972), p. 369.
36. Bolling, *Power in the House*, p. 265.
37. *Ibid.*, pp. 267–268. For the executive position see Rieselbach, *Congressional Politics*, pp. 366–369.
38. Mary Russell, "O'Neill Rebounds From Setbacks in Party and on Floor," *Washington Post*, 22 November 1979, p. A3.
39. Congressional Quarterly *Weekly Report*, 9 January 1982, pp. 61–63. Also see Dennis Farney, "In the Reagan Tide, Tip O'Neill Steers Safe Middle Course," *Wall Street Journal*, 27 April 1981, p. 1.
40. Bolling, "Committees in the House," pp. 2, 3. For a similar statement on the Senate see U.S. Senate, Temporary Select Committee to Study the Senate Committee System, *The Senate Committee System*, Committee Print, 94th Cong., 2nd Sess., July 1976, p. 5.
41. Pincus, "Basic Reforms Now for a Dated Congress," p. C-1.
42. *The Senate Committee System*, p. 6.
43. Norman Ornstein, "Toward Restructuring the Congressional Committee System," *The Annals*, No. 411 (January 1974), pp. 148–149, 153.
44. Theodore J. Lowi, "Congressional Reform: A New Time, Place and Manner," in Theodore J. Lowi and Randall B. Ripley, eds., *Legislative Politics, USA*, 3rd ed. (Boston: Little, Brown, 1973), p. 370.
45. John Bibby, "Reforming the Committees While Retaining the Unique Role of the House," in U.S. House, Select Committee on Committees, *Committee Organization in the House: Panel Discussions*, Vol. II, Part 3, 93rd Cong., 1st Session (1973), p. 528.
46. Robert L. Peabody, "Committees From the Leadership Perspective," *The Annals*, No. 411 (January 1974), pp. 142–144.
47. *The Senate Committee System*, p. 8. For similar statements with regard to particular committees, see Congress Project, *The Money Committees*, pp. 363–364 and *The Judiciary Committees*, pp. 369–370.
48. *The Senate Committee System*, p. 160.
49. Lowi, "Congressional Reform: A New Time, Place and Manner," p. 371.
50. Lewis Anthony Dexter, "The Advantages of Some Duplication and Ambiguity in Senate Committee Jurisdictions," in *The Senate Committee System*, p. 172.
51. Thomas P. Southwick, "Senate Approves Committee Changes," Congressional Quarterly *Weekly Report*, 12 February 1977, pp. 279–284. The original Select Committee proposals called for more drastic reductions in the number of committees. One would have decreased the number of standing committees to five. See "Senate Panel Develops Plan to Cut Committees from Eighteen to Five," *National Journal*, 21 August 1976, p. 1189.

52. U.S. House, Select Committee on Committees, "Committee Reform Amendments of 1974," Report to accompany H. Res. 988, 93rd Cong. 2nd Session, Report 93–916, Part II, 21 March 1974, pp. 25–27.

53. "Major House Committee Reform Rejected," Congressional Quarterly *Almanac 1974* (Washington, D.C.: Congressional Quarterly, 1975), pp. 634–641. The most significant provisions of the Hansen Committee resolution concerned the rules of the House and the power of the Rules Committee.

54. Aaron Wildavsky, "The Annual Expenditure Increment," in *Committee Organization in the House*, p. 641. Wildavsky notes (pp. 640–641): "The largest determining factor of the size and content of this year's budget is last year's budget. . . . Budgeting, therefore, is incremental, not comprehensive."

55. Louis Fisher, "Congress, the Executive and the Budget," *The Annals*, No. 411 (January 1974), p. 113.

56. Allen Schick, "Congress Versus the Budget," in *Committee Organization in the House*, p. 625.

57. John W. Ellwood and James A. Thurber, "The Politics of Congressional Budget Process Re-examined," in Lawrence C. Dodd and Bruce I. Oppenheimer, eds., *Congress Reconsidered*, 2nd ed. (Washington, D.C.: CQ Press, 1981); Allen Schick, *Congress and Money: Budgeting, Spending and Taxing* (Washington, D.C.: Urban Institute, 1980).

58. Allen Schick, "The Three-Ring Budget Process: The Appropriations, Tax, and Budget Committees in Congress," in Thomas E. Mann and Norman J. Ornstein, eds., *The New Congress* (Washington, D.C.: American Enterprise Institute, 1981), pp. 325–327.

59. Roger Davidson, David Kovenock, and Michael O'Leary, *Congress in Crisis: Politics and Congressional Reform* (Belmont, Calif.: Wadsworth Publishing, 1971), pp. 76–78.

60. John S. Saloma III, *Congress and the New Politics* (Boston: Little, Brown, 1969), p. 213. Also see Rieselbach, *Congressional Politics*, p. 385.

61. Loch Johnson, "The U.S. Congress and the CIA: Monitoring the Dark Side of Government," *Legislative Studies Quarterly*, 4 (November 1980); Philip Brenner, "Congress and the Investigation of Intelligence," *Cuba Review* (June 1976), pp. 9–12.

62. Saloma, *Congress and the New Politics*, pp. 214–215. Also see Kenneth Janda, "Information Systems for Congress—Revisited," in *Committee Organization in the House*, pp. 724–729; and Norman J. Ornstein, "Information, Resources, and Legislative Decision-Making" (Ph.D. diss., University of Michigan, 1972).

63. For example, see *The Money Committees*, pp. 459–460, and Rieselbach, *Congressional Politics*, p. 383. Also see John S. Saloma III, "Proposals for Meeting Congressional Staff Needs," in *Committee Organization in the House*, pp. 683–684.

64. *The Judiciary Committees*, p. 371.

65. Irwin B. Arieff, "The New Bureaucracy: Growing Staff System on Hill Forcing Changes in Congress," Congressional Quarterly *Weekly Report*, 24 November 1979, pp. 2631–2654. Also see Harrison W. Fox, Jr., and Susan Webb Hammond, *Congressional Staffs: The Invisible Force in American Lawmaking* (New York: Free Press, 1977), Chapters 1, 2, 6; Michael J. Malbin, *Unelected Representatives: Congressional Staff and the Future of Representative Government* (New York: Basic Books, 1980).

66. Janda, "Information Systems for Congress," in Alfred de Grazia, ed., *Congress: The First Branch of Government* (Garden City, N.Y.: Doubleday, Anchor Books, 1967), pp. 421–422.

67. Saloma, *Congress and the New Politics*, pp. 218–232; Rieselbach, *Congressional Politics*, pp. 386–388.

68. The Senate has a similar system in operation. On the House see Frank B. Ryan, "Information Systems Support to the U.S. House of Representatives," in *Committee Organization in the House*, pp. 730–736.

69. Charles Dechert, "Availability of Information for Congressional Operations," in de Grazia, *Congress: The First Branch of Government*, pp. 161–162.

70. "Congress Has Four Major Research Arms . . . And It May Use Them All on a Project," Congressional Quarterly *Weekly Report*, 24 November 1979, pp. 2650–2651.

71. William Greider, "Do We Want a Congress That's Clean?" *Washington Post*, 5 November 1978, p. D2.

72. Thomas Ferguson and Joel Rogers, "The Knights of the Roundtable," *The Nation*, 15 December 1979, pp. 620–625.
73. Larry Light, "The Game of PAC Targeting: Friends, Foes and Guesswork," Congressional Quarterly *Weekly Report*, 21 November 1981, pp. 2267–2270. Also see Gordon Adams, *The Iron Triangle: The Politics of Defense Contracting* (New York: Council on Economic Priorities, 1981), Chapter 8; Edwin M. Epstein, "Business and Labor under the Federal Election Campaign Act of 1971," in Michael J. Malbin, ed., *Parties, Interest Groups and Campaign Finance Laws* (Washington, D.C.: American Enterprise Institute, 1980).
74. Larry Light, "Democrats May Lose Edge in Contributions from PACs," Congressional Quarterly *Weekly Report*, 22 November 1980, pp. 3405–3409.
75. E. E. Schattschneider, *The Semi-Sovereign People* (New York: Holt Rinehart, 1960), Chapter 2. Also see Brenner, "Committee Conflict in the Congressional Arena," p. 92.
76. Philip Brenner, "An Approach to the Limits and Possibilities of Congress," in Lawrence Dodd and Bruce Oppenheimer, eds., *Congress Reconsidered* (Washington, D.C.: CQ Press, 1980). Also see Philip Brenner, "An Examination of Conflict in the U.S. House of Representatives" (Ph.D. Diss., Johns Hopkins University, 1975), Chapter 4.
77. Irwin B. Arieff, "Conservative Southerners Are Enjoying Their Wooing As Key to Tax Bill Success," Congressional Quarterly *Weekly Report*, 13 June 1981, p. 1025.
78. David Vogler, "The Rise of Ad Hoc Committees in the House" (Paper presented at the annual meeting of the American Political Science Association, New York City, September 1978).
79. Dale Tate, "Institutional Fallout: Reconciliation's Long-Term Consequences in Question As Reagan Signs Massive Bill," Congressional Quarterly *Weekly Report*, 15 August 1981, pp. 1463–1466.
80. Michael J. Malbin, "Delegation, Deliberation, and the New Role of Congressional Staff," in Ornstein and Mann, *The New Congress*, pp. 150–154. Malbin's conclusion, based on the same observation about the staff's background, differs from the one here. He argues that the staff has given small and "ideological" groups greater access to Congress.
81. Brenner, "Committee Conflict in the Congressional Arena," pp. 99–100.
82. Roger H. Davidson, "Subcommittee Government: New Channels for Policy Making," in Ornstein and Mann, *The New Congress*, p. 131.
83. Ibid., p. 123.
84. For example, see Ornstein, "Causes and Consequences of Congressional Change: Subcommittee Reforms in the House of Representatives"; Lawrence C. Dodd, "Congress and the Quest for Power," in Lawrence C. Dodd and Bruce I. Oppenheimer, eds., *Congress Reconsidered* (New York: Praeger, 1977); Davidson, Kovenock, and O'Leary, *Congress in Crisis.*
85. Davidson, "Subcommittee Government: New Channels for Policy Making," p. 100.
86. Burns, *Congress on Trial*, p. 136; Samuel P. Huntington, "Congressional Responses to the Twentieth Century," in David B. Truman, ed., *Congress and America's Future*, 2nd ed. (Englewood Cliffs, N.J.: Prentice-Hall, 1973), p. 20; James O'Connor, *The Fiscal Crisis of the State* (New York: St. Martin's, 1973), p. 81.
87. For a similar assessment see Saloma, *Congress and the New Politics*, p. 257.
88. Bertram Gross, "Toward a House of Worse Repute, or How to Be a Rubber Stamp With Honor," in *Committee Organization in the House*, p. 768. Also see Bertram Gross, *Friendly Fascism: The New Face of Power in America* (New York: M. Evans and Co., 1980), pp. 67–71.
89. Theodore J. Lowi, *The End of Liberalism*, 2nd ed. (New York: Norton, 1979), Chapter 2.
90. Randall B. Ripley and Grace A. Franklin, *Congress, The Bureaucracy, and Public Policy*, rev. ed. (Homewood, Ill.: Dorsey, 1980). For a good case study of one important subgovernment, see Adams, *The Iron Triangle*, Chapters 1–3. Also see David Vogler, *The Politics of Congress*, 3rd ed. (Boston: Allyn & Bacon, 1980), pp. 295–297.
91. Wildavsky, *Politics of the Budgetary Process*, 2nd ed. (Boston: Little, Brown, 1974).

Also see Charles Lindblom, *Politics and Markets* (New York: Basic Books, 1977), pp. 314–317.

92. O'Connor, *Fiscal Crisis of the State*, pp. 25–63. O'Connor refines his analysis as he begins to examine the reasons for stagnation in the monopoly sector in "Productive and Unproductive Labor," *Politics and Society*, 5, No. 3 (1975).

93. Otis L. Graham, Jr., *Toward a Planned Society: From Roosevelt to Nixon* (New York: Oxford University Press, 1976), p. 301.

94. Richard P. Nathan, *The Plot that Failed: Nixon and the Administrative Presidency* (New York: Wiley, 1975), Chapter 2. Although President Nixon was unsuccessful in his attack on the subgovernments, President Reagan attempted a similar attack when he took office. For a view of the Reagan administration's perspective on the problems engendered by subgovernments, see William Greider, "The Education of David Stockman," *The Atlantic Monthly*, December 1981, p. 30.

95. Gross, "Toward a House of Worse Repute," p. 777. Gross had observed in an earlier work that procedural reform is never merely technical, because it has substantive impact. See his *The Legislative Struggle: A Study in Social Combat* (New York: McGraw-Hill, 1953), pp. 40, 418. Similarly, Lewis A. Froman, Jr., notes that organizational "rules and procedures are not neutral in their effects on the distribution of advantages and disadvantages." However, his focus was on politics within Congress itself. See *The Congressional Process* (Boston: Little, Brown, 1967), p. xi.

96. On the Employment Act see Stephen K. Bailey, *Congress Makes a Law* (New York: Columbia University Press, 1950); on the National Security Act and NSC-68 see Marcus G. Raskin, *The Politics of National Security* (New Brunswick, N.J.: Transaction Books, 1979), Chapter 2; also see Fred Block, "Economic Instability and Military Strength: The Paradoxes of the 1950 Rearmament Decision," *Politics & Society*, 10, No. 1 (1980). On the use of the military budget for planning, see Seymour Melman, *The Permanent War Economy* (New York: Simon & Schuster, 1974) and Richard Barnet, *The Roots of War* (New York: Atheneum, 1972), Chapters 6–8.

97. On the 1946 Legislative Reorganization Act see George B. Galloway, *History of the House of Representatives* (New York: Crowell, 1968), pp. 57–61.

98. Joseph P. Harris, *Congressional Control of Administration* (Garden City, N.Y.: Doubleday Anchor, 1965), pp. 57–68.

99. *National Budget System*, House Report No. 362, to Accompany HR 9783, 66th Cong., 1st Sess. (1919), p. 4, as quoted in Ibid, p. 66.

100. Herbert J. Gans, *Deciding What's News* (New York: Vintage Books, 1979), Chapter 9; Gross, *Friendly Fascism*, pp. 255–264.

101. *The Senate Committee System*, p. 8.

PART **III**

Conclusion

7 The Limits and Possibilities of Congress

Speaker of the House Sam Rayburn was said to have offered freshman representatives a classic piece of advice that became Congress's hallmark for generations: "In order to get along, you gotta go along." Even in 1972, when fifty-year veteran Representative Emmanuel Celler was asked in an interview what advice he would give to new members of Congress, he said, "Sam Rayburn's admonition would still serve them well." If followed, such advice no doubt would have had a conservatizing effect on Congress, and it probably did have such an effect.

Yet the 1970s found Congress making significant internal changes in its operation, attempting to restructure the system of higher education in the United States, and forging a new direction in American relations with Cuba. These dramatic initiatives suggest anything but a conservative legislature. Seen with other major actions, such as civil rights legislation, they even suggest that anything might be possible from Congress—that there are no real limits to what Congress can do. A brief review of the three case studies, in reverse order of their earlier presentation, helps focus the larger picture of the limits and possibilities of Congress.

Congressional Reform

Six major changes of the 1970s, in the following areas, were examined:

1. ethics and campaign finance;
2. the seniority system;
3. House and Senate rules;
4. party governance;
5. committee structure;
6. information resources.

While particular reforms might be explained by the self-interest of individual members, self-interest does not explain the pattern of reforms. Many of the changes had been advocated for years but were adopted only when members appreciated that a major problem existed, a problem that the reforms might address. The problem was twofold: a crisis in the process of accumulating profit required a government capable of making plans and enforcing them and, collaterally, Congress needed to regain its legitimacy so that its plans would gain adherence. Not all reforms served this end, in part because the self-interest of some was inconsistent with the interest of the whole, but the selfish interests had to be served in order to secure the major reforms. In part, some reforms did not contribute to Congress's legitimacy because the members guessed "incorrectly"; they believed that a decentralizing reform such as the "subcommittee bill of rights" might enhance Congress's capability by making it more specialized and efficient.

Higher Education Act

In 1972 the higher-education system in the United States was in crisis. Colleges and universities were suffering from a "depression," in which costs were outpacing revenues. Moreover, the institutions were losing their social importance because college graduates and university postgraduates were finding only menial jobs that were not commensurate with their years of training. Several groups advocated that Congress respond to the crisis by authorizing the federal government to increase direct financial aid to the institutions in massive amounts. Instead Congress passed a bill that directed aid to students, especially poorer ones, and supported the growth of community colleges. Interviews with members indicated that they rejected implicitly the pleas of interest groups because aid to institutions did not seem to address a larger problem about which the members were concerned. They were concerned about saving an important mechanism of social control, which could legitimately channel people into a stratified society without generating significant opposition. Thus they focused on equal educational opportunity and seemed to give favor to the poor, even though the impact of the act was understood to be that the reformed education system would maintain inequality. Such a reform was also in the interest of corporations, which wanted well-trained personnel and social harmony. But it does not appear that the members were responding to corporate appeals, though they used the rationalizations of the corporation-oriented Carnegie Foundation. The rationalizations seem to have resonated well with the members' own perception of the problem, and it was to this perception that they responded.

Normalization of Relations with Cuba

For at least twenty-five years after World War II, congressional-executive relations in making foreign policy were aptly characterized as "the president proposes and Congress disposes." The pattern began to change in the 1970s, and congressional efforts to spur a move towards normalization of relations with Cuba were one part of the changing pattern. Several senators and representatives sponsored legislation to repeal the trade embargo against Cuba, made speeches, held conferences, and even traveled to Cuba from 1971 to 1975, and in 1977 and 1978. In the earlier period they were opposed by the president and had little to gain personally, but they perceived a problem for the United States to which normalization of relations with Cuba seemed to be part of a solution. The problem centered on the turmoil of the international economy, which was causing economic dislocation in the United States. In Congress several members believed that stabilizing international trade for American corporations would alleviate the problem. But American relations with Latin America were at a low point in the early 1970s, which seemed to hinder corporate activity in the region. For Latin Americans antagonism to Cuba was an important symbol of the American attitude, and it was this negative symbol that the members of Congress who sought normalization tried to remove. There was no strong lobby that pressured members to change the American policy, though members heard from corporations that sought the change. Members also heard from those who opposed it, but they listened to advocates of change because this view coincided with their own. By 1977 the international economy had improved only slightly, but normalization of relations with Cuba became a less important element in addressing the problem, and the impetus for undertaking this "costly" effort evaporated in Congress.

In each of the cases, the congressional initiatives related to a problem in the larger political and economic system. Members learned of the problem in part through interest-group demands but focused on solutions that addressed the larger problem rather than the specific demands. The world of a legislator extends beyond the confines of Congress, the needs of the district, and the demands of interest groups and constituents. It is the world, as described in Chapter 2, with a material base shaped by the system of production and an ideological base related to the system of production. Traditional approaches to the study of Congress do not take into account these bases, and so leave out of consideration the way in which the larger context affects Congress.

The traditional approach leads scholars to make five assumptions about why members of Congress behave as they do. Recall the five assumptions from Chapter 1:

1. members of Congress are parochial and narrow;
2. most members care principally about their own re-election;

3. when they do not focus on re-election, members of Congress attempt to maximize other personal interests;
4. in order to pursue their interests, members of Congress concern
   themselves with internal institutional power, and this concern may
   become an end in itself;
5. some members of Congress care most about making good public
   policy.

At this point, on the basis of the case studies and by taking into
account the whole world of Congress, we can provide a critique of these
assumptions. This chapter will assess the limits and possibilities of Congress first by elaborating the critique of the assumptions. The critique will
suggest why the limits on Congress are not as constricting as people
generally believe, and why the possibilities are not as great as people tend
to expect. An examination of how members of Congress view themselves
and why they have this view, a consideration of the way in which this
view corresponds to the importance of the larger context that is assumed
by this book, and an outline of the functions of Congress that these
findings suggest follow.

A Critique of the Assumptions

Members of Congress Are as Nationally Oriented as Other Elites

An assessment of anyone's orientation is difficult to sustain empiri-
cally. The executive branch allegedly has a national orientation. But
when a thirty-year career official in the Washington bureaucracy is asked,
"Where are you from?" it is common to hear that his or her home is
Kansas. President Johnson rushed back to Texas when his term was over,
and President Carter returned to Plains, Georgia. Though the Texan and
the Georgian in them were evident, few critics contended that they were
parochial. But in the eyes of critics, the congressional style of maintaining
a local identification makes members of Congress suspect of being parochial. Parochialism seems rather to be a trait in the eyes of the beholder.

Indeed, efforts to measure orientation have turned up evidence that
contradicts the generalization. Using data from the 1960s, a period when
members of Congress were supposedly more parochial than they are today, Roger Davidson found that 28 percent of his sample in the House
saw themselves as representing a national rather than a local constituency. Another 23 percent offered no geographic area as the basis of their
representation and were classified as oriented to the nation and their local
constituency equally.[1] The surprise here is how large a group Davidson

found that was willing to express a non-local focus, because members tend to cultivate a local twang even when they address international problems. Thus one representative winked when he said that, among the other things he did on a path-breaking trip to Cuba was to investigate whether Cuban air conditioners could take replacement parts from a company that manufactured parts in his district.

The characteristics of members of Congress also are remarkably similar to those of other national elites. In the 97th Congress (1981–1983), nearly half of the 535 members had law degrees.[2] Members of Congress are far better educated than the general population and quite similar in education and background to people in the higher civil service.[3] They may spend time in their districts, but most of their time is spent in Washington, working with people who are nationally oriented, such as their staff. An important change in the 1970s was the increased professionalism of congressional staff, both at the committee and office level.[4] The staff now is drawn from elite universities and from the executive branch and tends to resemble its counterpart in national corporations and the bureaucracy. Their orientation not only affects that of the legislators but also is important because the staff has responsibility for much of the real policy work that occurs in Congress.[5]

Many analysts have conceded that members of Congress may no longer be country bumpkins, but these analysts continue to assume that members are parochial. The heart of this assumption is not the personal qualities of the legislators, but the assertion that elections necessarily promote localism in Congress because each member is dependent on his or her district.

The assertion suffers from several weaknesses. First, the prevailing notion of localism embodies a sense that one locality will demand and expect benefits for itself at the expense of other localities. But there is no necessity for benefits to be distributed or re-distributed this way. They could be conceived of in class terms, so that people who had similar needs in all localities became recipients. Legislators could claim credit for such benefits too.[6] Thus transforming broad-based legislation into segmented payoffs for each district may have less to do with parochialism than with congressional concern about the types of conflict that can occur over re-distributive policies.[7]

Second, the cost of elections has made members of Congress less tied to their districts, because a member can rarely raise the money for a modern campaign solely from constituents. In 1980 several candidates spent over $500,000 for House seats.[8] Sums over $1 million in a Senate race are no longer news. The money for these races comes from out-of-district and out-of-state, from national mail-order solicitations and from political action committees. Organizations that contribute over $1 million to candidates—such as the American Medical Political Action Committee or the United Auto Workers Voluntary Community Action Program— are not supporting candidates they think are tied to the narrow interests of their districts.[9]

It is not even clear that district interests are narrow. The concerns of constituents in one district depart less now from those in another district, because the electorate appears to be less interested in obtaining pork-barrel benefits for themselves than in solving broad national problems, such as inflation, that affect everyone.[10] What is clear is that constituents often punish severely a member who seems to have forgotten his or her roots, has become aloof, and has taken the constituency for granted.[11] Constituents evaluate their own representatives in terms of local activities, service, and personality and tend to dissociate the legislator from lawmaking activities of Congress.[12] Indeed, except for a few salient issues, they tend not to know how a legislator votes.[13] This leaves members of Congress relatively free to be non-parochial if they so choose and even to be unaware of how a broad-based policy might affect their districts. The history of United States-Cuban policy shows that members were not responding to constituent pressures, and the case study of the Higher Education Act illustrates that members had little sense of how the bill would affect their constituents.

Re-election Isn't All That It's Cracked Up to Be

"These damn liberals will be sorry," a prescient representative remarked in an interview during consideration of the 1970 Reorganization Act. "When they get their recorded teller vote, they'll spend half of their lives running back and forth to the floor." There is growing impressionistic evidence since then that the representative was right, that for many the costs of remaining in Congress, compared with the rewards they bring (regardless of the benefits a member might have sought), are too high. Not only have the sessions increased in length and become more hectic, but members complain about the seemingly endless search for campaign finances, the loss of privacy in their lives, diminishing public respect, and insufficient time to spend with their families.[14] In addition, members who might have been encouraged to wait around for many years in order to obtain committee chairmanships by virtue of seniority are now discouraged when they realize that the subcommittee reforms of the early 1970s have greatly reduced the power and prerogatives of the full committee chairmen.[15] With so many chiefs, now, it is difficult to work one's will except on specialized issues.

It goes without saying that members of Congress are not saints. They will not long suffer an unfavorable calculation of costs and benefits, and the mounting dissatisfactions seem to provide a reasonable explanation for the growing number of retirements from the House and Senate. As Joseph Cooper and William West observe, "Voluntary retirement in the 1970s has supplanted electoral defeat as the prime source of turnover in the House."[16]

Thus there should be significant doubt that all or most members of Congress organize their behavior around the singular goal of staying in office. The job is not sufficiently desirable to generate contortions; too many retired members have reported back that there is life after Congress. Perhaps in the early 1970s, when political scientist David Mayhew articulated the conventional wisdom about the importance of re-election, it was the primary consideration for legislators. But Mayhew was circumspect enough to suggest also that were voluntary turnover as high in Congress as in some state legislatures—or as high as it was in Congress eighty years ago—the assumption of the electoral connection might be invalid.[17]

Many members of Congress still care about re-election, but even those who are desperate about staying in office do not necessarily shape all of their behavior with this in mind—nor did they ever. More likely is it that they merely take the election into account in some way. The Higher Education Act found Senator Claiborne Pell seeking an omnibus bill in order to accommodate his plans to campaign throughout 1972: his concern with re-election may explain why twenty bills were packed into one. However, Pell's concern explains neither the significant features of the bill nor his insistence on aid to poor students rather than to colleges of middle-class students.

There is good reason for a legislator not to shape all behavior around re-election. There is evidence that incumbents can continue to be elected with a variety of nonpolicy techniques, which include servicing constituents and adapting their in-district styles to changing times.[18] It may be for these reasons that fewer congressional elections are close. And despite the losses by some nationally prominent legislators in 1980, the prevailing pattern of high return rates for incumbents was maintained.[19]

This reality is not lost on the members, who appear to act in ways that are not calculated to promote electoral success, as Charles Bullock, studying members as they choose their committees, has found:.

> Re-election, while a frequent concern, is not the overriding motive among freshmen and is even less common among nonfreshmen. Both groups display great interest in committees offering opportunities to participate in shaping public policy on controversial topics.[20]

Similarly, Chapter 6 found that several reforms in the 1970s—such as the creation of the Budget Committees—would encourage centralized decisions in Congress and thus rob members of the chance to promote themselves by taking credit for legislation. Such behavior is hardly the type one would expect from wary, election-conscious, vote-seeking legislators—that is, from the legislators portrayed by the second assumption.

The Rich Are Not Omniscient, and Legislators Are Not Easily Manipulated

Members of Congress may appear to be the pawns of wealthy contributors and to be ever on the outlook for money, luxurious trips, and flattery. But even if this were the case, it would not translate easily into an explanation of policy. At best it might explain how particular groups gain particular benefits. Mark Green and Jack Newfield, for example, have catalogued campaign contributions and honoraria for lectures that large corporations give to key members of committees that write legislation affecting these corporations: military contractors support Senators Sam Nunn (D-Ga.) and John Tower (R-Texas); banks and real-estate interests support Senator Jake Garn (R-Utah) and Representative William Stanton (R-Ohio); the medical lobby has helped Representative Phil Gramm (D-Texas) and Senator Steve Symms (R-Idaho).[21] No doubt this support may translate into a special tax provision here and an extra billion there. If the legislator is truly in a key position, it may mean an effective veto over the dismantling of a program or over the creation of a tough regulation. When linked to a strong subsystem, as Gordon Adams has painstakingly described the process of defense contracting, it might even mean commitments over many years that affect thousands of lives.[22]

However, even defense contractors do not have enough money to buy off large numbers of legislators. To explain congressional policy by the way members aggrandize their personal interests, one must rely on the notion of reciprocity, by which favors are exchanged for every legislator's gain. But this explanation for myriad congressional decisions is weak and it would require virtually every member to be beholden to a powerful external group. The evidence to sustain that contention is not there.

Moreover, members at times act against the interests of powerful groups. The history of the Higher Education Act of 1972 finds Congress in opposition to the well-organized higher-education associations when it passed a "landmark" plan essentially proposed by the Carnegie Commission on Higher Education. This group had only the power of its ideas. The commission had close ties to national corporations, but these ties were not a resource that was used to pressure members. Corporations themselves seemed to be little involved in the process. The case seems to have been one in which there was a meeting of minds rather than a crude model of pressure. Members of Congress used rationalizations that the

Carnegie Commission provided but were not pressured into using them. One would expect that even a simple model, in which members of Congress were the pawns of benefactors, would not be in the interest of the benefactors themselves, who, in pursuing their narrow self-interest, would need an organization that could take a detached view and act in their long-term interest.

Moreover, the interests of the wealthy rarely coincide, and their assessment of what is in their long-term interest coincides even less frequently. That is, a strategy for serving the long-term interests of owners of wealth—for making broad societal policy—is a guess about what will work. There will be several possibilities, and elites will ardently disagree among themselves. In this light, to depict a Congress that makes broad policy as the pawn of the national corporate elite is difficult. Members are more autonomous than is suggested by the assumption that they continually seek to maximize their personal interests. Ultimately this assumption offers little guidance as to what shapes the members' behavior when they initiate policy, as they did in the cases of Cuba and higher education.

Power for a Purpose, Not for Its Own Sake, Is the Quest

To some members, power is what one wins in the congressional process. As in a game, it is an end in itself.[23] Power for its own sake may motivate some members, but it is a questionable explanation for the behavior of most, for whom the congressional process is not a game: they appreciate that the decisions they make affect people's lives and even shape society. To examine the purposes for which members want to use their power becomes most important, because the struggle for power is linked to the uses of power.

Scholars who focus on power often treat it as a variable unrelated to its purposes and thus isolate it as a uniform object of desire. But they also consider the several purposes a legislator might have in seeking power.[24] It is said that a member of Congress might want power in order to be the one on top in an institution that disperses power unequally, to help in re-election, and/or to make policies that he or she believes are preferable.

The first purpose describes a situation of eternal conflict between subordinates and superiors, in which the subordinates continually try to wrest control from their superiors and the latter try to hold on. The situation is akin to what sociologist Ralf Dahrendorf describes as the basis of all conflict—the inequality of authority.[25] Such a situation might arise when one person is a bully and uses power to push others around. This case is not relevant to Congress, where norms sanction such behavior and members share a sense of superficial equality.[26] In a second instance, the inequality of power is a relationship where one actor prevents another from attaining the ends that he or she desires. But a focus on the inequality tells little about the nature of the competing ends each seeks: if the goals were not in conflict there would be no inequality of power, and the analyst is forced back to a consideration of political purposes.

Re-election becomes a never-ending circle. Members seek power in order to facilitate their re-election, and then they seek re-election in order to stay in power. To get out of the circle there must be some other purpose than power or re-election.

Consider finally that a member seeks power in order to make "good" policy. Indeed, several proponents of change in the 1970s sought power in Congress for the purpose of changing policy, not merely to hold power abstractly. Similarly, as the study of institutional reform showed, some members sought power in order to "rationalize" the legislative process as a way of regaining legitimacy for Congress as a whole. It is important to appreciate, however, that a member cannot make a bid for power regardless of the "good" policy he or she espouses. The "good" reforms analyzed served particular ends, related to class dynamics in the larger society. Members who can bid for power in order to achieve their policy ends are those who favor policies within an "acceptable" range.

The power to make policy is related to the policy that is to be made; this power equation in Congress is structured to prevent the random individual who gets power from doing merely anything that he or she wants. Robert Peabody observes, for example, that the membership has usually selected party leaders who fall in the middle on the ideological spectrum represented in Congress,[27] which is already skewed in a conservative direction. Powerful members on the most powerful House committees, too, tend to fall in the ideological middle. In the 97th Congress, the Ways and Means, Appropriations, and Rules committees were ranked as "exclusive" and were generally considered to be the most powerful. The Budget Committee was seen as equivalent in power but did not receive a designation as "exclusive." As Table 7–1 indicates, the most powerful Democratic members on the four committees had an average ADA score of 65, in the same range as the 57 rating for all House Democrats.[28] The average for the four chairmen was 47, lower than the House average. Consideration of these four committees leads us to the critique of the final assumption.

Most Members Care About Making Public Policy—Good and Bad.

Whatever their other concerns, most members also care about making policy. Even the representation of particular interests, such as tobacco farmers or aircraft manufacturers, has a consequence for the public interest—though different observers would assess in differing ways whether

TABLE 7-1 **ADA Ratings for Leaders of Four Powerful House Committees**

COMMITTEE/ SUBCOMMITTEE	CHAIRMAN	1980 ADA SCORE	MEAN SCORE OF COMMITTEE "LEADERS"
APPROPRIATIONS	Whitten (Miss.)	28	67
Commerce	Smith (Iowa)	72	
Defense	Addabbo (N.Y.)	72	
DC	Dixon (Cal.)	94	
Energy	Bevill (Ala.)	22	
Foreign Oper	Long (Md.)	83	
HUD	Boland (Mass.)	78	
Interior	Yates (Ill.)	100	
Labor	Natcher (Ky.)	50	
Legislative	Fazio (Cal.)	89	
Mil Construct	Ginn (Ga.)	33	
Transport	Benjamin (Ind.)	61	
Treasury	Roybal (Cal.)	89	
BUDGET	Jones (Okla.)	39	66
Econ Policy	Obey (Wisc.)	94	
Energy	Wirth (Col.)	78	
Enforcement	Mineta (Cal.)	83	
Entitlement	Simon (Ill.)	78	
Human Resources	Gephardt (Mo.)	56	
Nat'l Security	Mattox (Tex.)	50	
Reconciliation	Panetta (Cal.)	67	
Tax	Nelson (Fla.)	33	
Transport	Solarz (N.Y.)	78	
RULES	Bolling (Mo.)	72	68
	Long (La.)	50	
	Moakley (Mass.)	72	
	Pepper (Fla.)	61	
	Chisholm (N.Y.)	78	
	Zeferetti (N.Y.)	44	
	Derrick (S.C.)	56	
	Beilenson (Cal.)	94	
	Frost (Tex.)	50	
	Bonior (Mich.)	83	
	Hall (Ohio)	89	
WAYS AND MEANS	Rostenkowski (Ill.)	50	54
Health	Jacobs (Ind.)	50	
Oversight	Rangel (N.Y.)	78	
Public Asst	Stark (Cal.)	94	
Select Revenue	Cotter (Conn.)	44	
Soc Security	Pickle (Tex.)	22	
Trade	Gibbons (Fla.)	39	

SOURCE: Congressional Quarterly *Weekly Report*, 21 March 1981, pp. 514–517.

the consequent public policies were "good" or "bad." Making public policy is what members of Congress do, whether they are arousing or discouraging constituents' support for a policy; whether they chart new directions or endorse old ones; whether they are shaping, introducing, fighting over, or merely voting on legislation; whether they oversee the executive on a case-by-case basis, in a systematic way, or by closing their eyes. These several tasks are the components of policymaking. All members of Congress undertake a few of them, regardless of the committee on which they serve.

Those on powerful committees are especially active policy makers. The House and Senate Appropriations committees and the committees on Ways and Means and Finance are powerful because they shape so many aspects of public policy. A member may have sought membership on one of these committees for the sake of power, but once there he or she will necessarily make policy.[29] Members do not concern themselves with whether policy is good or bad; they attempt to achieve particular ends, which are good for some people and bad for others.

However, these goals are not only of their own making. They are developed within a context that establishes what sort of public policies might be acceptable. In this sense, acceptable policies are "good" policies. Consider how this process manifested itself in the congressional initiatives on Cuba policy and higher education.

Cuba policy. The congressional initiative to normalize relations between the United States and Cuba began to take hold when it became consistent with solutions to international economic and political problems that the United States experienced in the early 1970s. As a matter only of fair play, good sense given the proximity of the two countries, or self-interest on the part of corporations seeking new trade opportunities, the first initiatives gained little headway. Only when the old policy became a symbol of American imperialism, when national elites saw good relations with the Third World as a means of controlling turmoil in the international economy, and when Cuba had gained respect among Third World nations did congressional initiatives "make sense." Addressing these problems became the framework of the Cuba initiative, so that when the problems were solved by other means, the freedom for members of Congress to make the same proposals in 1976 that they had made in 1975 was constricted. The media, executive-branch officials, and corporate leaders no longer described the congressional initiative as good policy.

Higher education. The immediate context of congressional action to re-shape higher education in the United States was twofold: the financial crisis that colleges and universities faced and the approaching terminal date on authorizations for existing aid programs. Instead of focusing on this context and merely renewing the old programs, members chose to confront an even larger problem—the legitimacy and function of the higher-education system. As a matter of equity or societal obligation, proposals to fund in a major way the higher education of poor students had gained little headway before. But when this funding was framed to serve as part of a system for re-establishing higher education as a mechanism of social differentiation and skill training, the proposals found surprisingly ready acceptance. They became "good" public policy when they addressed problems of the market economy and accepted the logic of the market. Of course, not all proposals are so readily adaptable, nor were all the proposals acceptable.

In short, most members of Congress are involved in making policy and so must become concerned about it. It is not the concern primarily of those on policy committees, but of members on almost every committee. Yet in making policy, members are not free to do whatever they wish. They work within a context that limits what is possible. Even with the most dedicated policymakers, Congress cannot re-create the world.

Beyond Narrow Limits

The critique of the five assumptions suggests that the supposed limits on members of Congress are more excuses than real constraints. There is ample evidence that the five assumptions at least describe an aspect of the congressional world. Legislators certainly seek federal largesse for their districts and segment policy; no doubt they care about re-election and glory; members struggle for power within the Congress; and some may see themselves as the policymakers they really are, searching for "good" policy. But there is no compelling need for this behavior. The thrust of the critique has been that the behavior is not rooted in the nature of Congress or its members. Together the assumptions may describe the way Congress behaves, but the description should not lead to a deterministic trap that assumes this is the way it must behave. The possibility exists for each assumption to be relaxed, as was the case when Congress initiated a new policy towards Cuba, passed landmark higher-education legislation, and reformed itself during the 1970s.

To be sure, in those cases members acted from motives, such as prestige, embraced by the five assumptions. But the assumptions only capture the immediate world of the legislator, the daily pressures he or she feels, the direct sense of yearning and frustration that members of Congress experience. Although these immediate influences are real, they only mediate the ultimate limits on congressional behavior. They are a filter through which members of Congress come to constrain the policies they make. Members come to see "good" public policy as not merely any well-conceived policy. Good congressional policy must be consistent with the prevailing economic structure and must do no more than reinstate the soundness of the system by correcting its flaws.

This treatment of the assumptions is at quite a distance from the traditional scholarship that has generally articulated them. Rather than a group of parochial bumpkins, narrowly self-interested, Congress is in fact a body that can initiate broad societal policy responsive to the needs of the time. But Congress is also limited in the way in which it can respond and cannot do everything one might wish. That is, the possibilities are greater than is normally suggested by the conventional wisdom, and the ultimate limits are more severe. The next section considers an explanation for this irony.

Members of Congress Think What They Think Because They Do What They Do

How Members See Themselves

Political scientist Richard Fenno has discovered a fascinating paradox: people who express a low regard for Congress as a whole will often express a high regard for their own representative.[30] There may be several explanations for the paradox,[31] but the fact remains that the typical constituent sees his or her representative as a person with real attributes, feelings, and personality—as someone whom constituents can distinguish from the other members of Congress—and sees the institution as an abstract, distant body. It is part of the American culture to think about people this way, as individuals, because all people like to think of themselves as unique individuals too.[32] Indeed, each member of Congress is distinctive, with his or her own character and personality. To try to understand Congress by summing up its individual members, an analyst would be obliged to appreciate a diverse range of factors that influence them personally, including those that help to form their characters.[33]

Another way to understand the behavior of legislators—one that is less common—is to appreciate that they have a collective experience as members of the Congress. The experience affects each of them similarly, despite their distinctive personalities and characters, because what people do affects how they perceive the world.[34] The institution does not determine precisely what they do—they make history by making choices as individuals—but the weight of the institutional experience shapes their choices.

Both factors are important because they are the two sides of a dialectic. Recent scholarship on Congress has emphasized one side: that the intentions of the members determine the way they behave. In part this emphasis has been a reaction to an earlier literature that tended to emphasize the other side: that the institution *qua* institution shaped behavior through group sanctions.[35] This sociological approach was abandoned in part because scholars found that the institution was less rigid and more open to change than would have been expected from a systems analysis, which was the basis of the sociological approach.

The collective experience, however, need not be conceptualized as a set of institutional pressures. An alternative would be to appreciate that the institution is part of the larger political-economic context examined in Chapter 2. It may be a sense of the place Congress has within the larger context that the members share.

How Congress comes to develop that sense of the place deserves attention. Every day members make decisions that they know are "authoritative" for the whole country. It would be understandable, then, that members come to see themselves as rulers of the country. They come to see themselves as a national elite—regardless of their power within the institution—that has the respect and recognition that appropriately belongs to national elites, that has the responsibilities for governing that elites should have, that has the power to shape events, and that shares with other elites common perspectives on the problems all elites must confront.[36]

Abundant impressionistic evidence suggests that members of Congress feel that they are members of a national elite and hold national power—they do not merely feel that they hold personal power over particular people in a bounded setting such as the legislature.[37] This evidence was corroborated in a series of interviews, in which members were asked why they or other members wanted to be in Congress.[38] More than 30 percent said they wanted to be in Congress because of the power; 26 percent said it was because they liked to accomplish something; 23 percent noted the privileges, which several linked to "feeling important"; and the same percentage mentioned that it was because they felt respected or recognized. (See Table 7–2.)

These four reasons are closely linked. Members are quite realistic about one's inability to "accomplish something" without societal power. Those who said that they felt important related this feeling to their power as members of Congress or the power of the government. Similarly, those who said they felt respected said that they received respect and recognition because of their importance as members of Congress.

The power to which the members referred is not the same sort that political scientists traditionally analyze, where A is said to have power over B because A can get B to do something he or she would not other-

TABLE 7-2 **Reasons for Being a Member of Congress**

REASON	REPUB-LICANS	DEMO-CRATS	SENIOR*	JUNIOR	TOTAL
"Power"	3	8	5	6	11
"Accomplish something"	1	8	7	2	9
"Feel important/enjoy privileges"	5	3	3	5	8
"Feel respected/gain recognition"	2	6	4	4	8
"Serve the country"	2	1	1	2	3
"Ambition"	1	1	0	2	2
"For the money"	1	0	0	1	1
"It's a career"	1	0	1	0	1
"Interest in what's happening"	0	1	1	0	1
	n=14	n=21	n=19	n=16	n=35**

* Senior members are those with 10 years' or more service as of January 1971. Junior members are those with up to nine years' service.
**Some members gave more than one reason.

wise do. Traditional power requires a relationship between A and B and is a concept appropriate for an analysis of relationships within the legislature. But the legislators were talking about an amorphous sense of power, which did not involve a relationship *per se*. It was not personal power, but situational power; it was power they had by being part of a powerful institution, which gained its power by virtue of the situations into which it embedded itself.[39] The sense of power was inextricably linked to the purpose of the institution.

The members' orientation to power in this special way was further evident when they were asked to name three persons, living or dead, whom they most admired. The question was asked at the end of a long interview, in a way that suggested it was not part of the formal interview. For this reason the question may have caught the members unguarded, and the answers may be an accurate indication of the members' role models.

Presidents were the overwhelming favorite. Nearly two thirds of the respondents (62 percent) mentioned a president. Some mentioned only presidents. Thirty-five percent of the total responses were for presidents, with no difference between Democrats and Republicans in the sample.[40] Approximately one quarter of the sample (26 percent) mentioned a senator or representative, and 15 percent of the total responses were for legislators. (See Table 7–3.)

The choice of president would seem to reveal an admiration for power, for control, and for success. Notably, the presidents who scored highest are generally considered to be great leaders who directed the

TABLE 7–3 **Whom the Members Admire**

TYPE OF PERSON NAMED	FREQUENCY		
	Democrats (n=29)	Republicans (n=24)	Total
President*	26	24	50
Senator or representative	7	14	21
World leader	5	2	7
Parent	5	3	8
Cabinet secretary	3	3	6
Judge**	3	3	6
Teacher/educator	3	2	5
Friend/home-town acquaintance	3	2	5
Philosopher	3	2	5
General	0	4	4
Jesus Christ	0	4	4
Scientist	2	1	3
Clergyman	1	2	3
Spouse	2	0	2
Industrialist	2	0	2
Labor leader	2	0	2
Eleanor Roosevelt	2	0	2
Other	5	2	7
Total	74	68	142***

* Dwight Eisenhower was counted as a president, not a general.
**Earl Warren was counted as a judge, not as a governor.
***Not all of the 53 respondents provided 3 role models.

United States during critical periods. They are men who reached the pinnacle of the profession (politics) in which the respondents labor. While the choice of a President might not indicate that a member believes he or she is powerful, it might suggest that he or she yearns to be powerful and so might act in ways that are consistent with the ideal.

Similarly, in the choices of a general, a Supreme Court Justice, a Cabinet secretary, or a world leader, such as Churchill, Nehru, Gandhi, or Mao Zedong (all of whom were named), we might see an emulation of power, the capability of commanding large numbers of people and having them follow the orders. If we exclude the category of legislator so as not to confuse the analysis, we could reasonably say that 76 of the remaining 128 total responses (or 59 percent) were choices related to power.

This conservative assessment would exclude Jesus Christ, because it would be difficult to separate religious from leadership qualities. The assessment would exclude even scientists, though they might be seen as powerful because they shape our knowledge, as one member observed.

The reasons that members of Congress gave for choosing presidents tended to conform to our common-sense notion of what this response symbolizes: "a great leader," "decisive," "changed the direction of our country," "saved our country," "ability to move the government." These reasons paralleled those given for the others we have classified as symbolizing power, such as a world leader: "towering figure," "accomplished change against enormous odds," "a true leader," "produced results."

Members of Congress thus have two senses of power. They have a sense of power as rulers and a personal sense of power over particular people. It is the second sense about which they often talk, which makes it seem so important, because on a daily level this is what power does mean to them. By spending so much time doing favors for particular interests and by working within a fragmented institution in which each member is usually left to his or her own devices, they are encouraged to dwell on the power of individuals. This is power without history. It is power at a moment in time, unattached to struggles and structures that embody an institution with power.

However, there are other aspects of congressional life that encourage a broader perspective. As demonstrated in Chapters 3, 4, and 5, there are several reasons for a member to transcend parochial orientation. Institutional responsibilities, such as membership on the Foreign Affairs or Education and Labor committees, might force a member to take a broader view. In addition, the class background of some members might lead them to relate comfortably to other elites who take a national view of events. Finally, the sorts of problems with which Congress grapples force members to examine the larger context, because the larger context sets their agenda.

The critique of the power assumption earlier in this chapter did not dispute the prevalence of an individualistic orientation to power in Congress; its point was that individualistic power was not the only sort in the legislature. There are moments when members of Congress transcend their particularism to act like the rulers they think they are. These are moments of history, when the legislators view their institution as part of a broad social context and consequently see themselves as responsible for the society. In these moments of history, members feel powerful as leaders of the state, and in these moments they attempt to steer the ship of state.

Rulers of a Weak State

Even though they may think they are rulers, members of Congress cannot do whatever they wish. What they can do is limited by the nature of the state in the United States. Congress has few resources to use in trying to control society, because the very basis of society—the means by which most essential goods and services are produced and distributed—are owned privately. Congress must operate in accord with the owners of this wealth as it attempts to coerce or cajole them to put into effect the policies members of Congress might want. The decisions that owners of wealth have the right to make shape the lives of most Americans. These decisions include where to put a new factory, how many workers they will lay off in a slack period, whether the products they produce will serve the needs of the middle class or only those of the rich, what sorts of medicines and medical practices they will develop, and for whom they will build new houses. Through their investment decisions owners thus affect the policies members of Congress might want.[41]

Congress could gain greater resources by increasing corporate taxes or by nationalizing some of the privately held property, and the reasons it does not do this are important in understanding its limits. One explanation is that Congress is not really able to tax corporations, because by virtue of not producing its own wealth, the government in a capitalist country must nurture, not deplete, the private sector on which it depends. It follows from this view that by taking too much from corporations, the government dries up the profits that corporations would use for reinvestment, that is, for the source of future profits that the government will need for taxes. It also follows that with lower profits corporations might also reduce their workers' wages, thereby reducing the amount available to the government from personal income taxes. However, governments in other industrialized capitalist countries have taken the route of high taxes and nationalization.[42] These countries have remained essentially capitalist, and several have surpassed the United States in productivity, annual growth, and economic stability.

Indeed, the United States has one of the lowest tax rates in the industrialized capitalist world, and it is virtually alone in the extent to which it has permitted basic services such as health care to remain private. It would seem that the unique position of the United States in this regard cannot be explained by general assertions about the dependence of capitalist states on the owners of wealth. In effect, the federal government has attempted to influence the investment decisions of private owners of wealth principally through cajoling rather than coercion. It has picked up the costs for research and development in high technology, for the transportation networks (highways, canals, railway rights-of-way, aircraft design), for educating the work force, and for protecting private overseas facilities; it encourages investment in particular areas through "tax expenditures," that is, through loopholes that enable companies to reduce their tax burden.

The choice of the carrot instead of the stick suggests an explanation for the distinctive character of the state in the United States: it is a relatively weak state.[43] There are several factors that contribute to this condition. Taken together, the factors indicate why members of Congress cannot do whatever they wish.

Consider four factors that make the state—and so each of its component institutions, including Congress—unable to assert itself aggressively against private owners of wealth. While the four are not equally significant, it is important that they tend to complement and reinforce each other.

The state is not a unitary actor. There are formal and informal checks and balances that each of the three branches holds against the others. The formal checks are codified in the Constitution, in Court interpretations of the Constitution, and in statutes.[44] As an example of the informal checks at work, recall how the president was able to use the media in 1976 and 1978 to shift public opinion quickly about Cuba and so limit what congressional advocates of normalization felt they were free to do. The system of checks and balances works against initiatives that depart from a prevailing pattern. There needs to be agreement among the three branches, and only under extraordinary circumstances do the three agree on departures.[45]

The state is permeable. The wealthy have the greatest access to state managers. They provide the largest contributions to congressional campaigns and to a president's party, and they can offer jobs to retiring senior-level bureaucrats, fueling a "revolving door" of personnel between the government and the private sector. Corporations have the greatest capacity to lobby, and the interests of a large corporation may be represented by several trade associations, a Washington office of the corporation, a Washington law firm, and direct contacts by corporate officers through the Business Roundtable. Finally, most executive-branch policymakers and many members of Congress are themselves wealthy or have worked on behalf of large corporations. Their presence does not mean that the state is a mere instrument of the owners of property, nor are their backgrounds sufficient evidence to indicate how all of them will behave. But a climate of receptivity to the owners of wealth contributes to the state's reluctance to challenge property rights.

A weak working class offers little to balance the owning class. Were the working class well organized, it could act as an ally of a state that sought to challenge private property. At the least, if it were strong it would control aspects of private decision making. It could thus make demands on the state in the manner in which private owners of wealth now make them. To be sure, there has been and continues to be dedicated struggle, as workers resist increased exploitation and degradation and seek better working conditions, higher wages, and increased control over their lives.[46] As discussed in Chapter 2, these struggles are a source of disruption in the smooth process of accumulation and thus contribute to the setting of the congressional agenda. But the workers' movement itself remains weak. There are several explanations for what has been called "American exceptionalism," that is, the absence of a strong, class-conscious workers' movement in the United States.[47] Regardless of its source, the weakness may explain why the working class has tended to eschew either an alliance with the state or capture of the state. Instead, it has tended to view state power as inherently antagonistic to the interests of the working class, and indeed the state has often lived up to this expectation.[48] The working-class view of the state is part of an anti-state attitude, however, that goes beyond the actions of the state against the working class.

An anti-state tradition militates against state power. There has been an enduring belief in the United States that individual autonomy and democracy are necessary correlates.[49] Even in the face of giant trusts and corporations, there has persisted a fear of large government, a fear that only government can deprive us of liberty. In the current era, this spirit was appropriated by President Nixon when he created the New Federalism, though increasing liberty may not have been among his purposes, and by President Reagan when he championed de-regulation and block grants to state governments, supposedly in order to "get government off our backs." This tradition in part explains why much state activity unrelated to military preparedness—such as building the interstate highway system or funding higher education in the 1950s—has been conducted in the name of national security.[50] While defense is thus one of the few activities that has been a traditional exception to the anti-state tradition, it has been a point of weakness for Congress, because national security policy has been dictated largely by the executive.

The Dialectics of Congressional Decision-Making

The work of legislators reflects two conflicting structural features of Congress. On the one hand, there are the factors that lead members of Congress to take a broad, societal view, to take the perspective of national rulers. This structural feature coincides with the members' orientation to national power. The coincidence is undoubtedly no accident. People oriented to national power seek congressional office, and by working with national problems and making national decisions, a legislator develops such an orientation.

On the other hand, members of Congress confront limits to their rule. This structural feature is rooted in Congress's lack of resources, because productive wealth is privately owned in the United States and the state's weakness prevents it from claiming more of the privately held resources.

This fundamental conflict confronts each member of Congress and shapes the way he or she views the functioning of the legislature. The perspective of rulership provides members of Congress with a sense of responsibility for the system as a whole. The limits on their rule force them to take a conservative stance—improving the ongoing system, maintaining the system, reproducing the system. The interaction of the two features leads members of Congress to see themselves as rulers of this society; their purpose is to sustain this society in its essential nature, not to change it.

The resulting world outlook of members of Congress is reinforced by the media, by other national elites to whom the members relate, by other policymakers in the national government, and by intellectuals at leading universities. Each group tends to subscribe to this same outlook, which might be called the dominant ideology.[51] In the United States this perspective emphasizes the basic soundness of a system in which the means of production are privately owned and in which the relations between owners and workers are structured by the private ownership of productive wealth. Furthermore, the dominant ideology reduces politics to a process of gaining individualistic power for the narrow purpose of self-aggrandizement.[52]

This common world view that members of Congress share with other elites comes to act as a force itself, as it fixes for them a vision of the world. It is a vision in which the "apparent limits of the possible are defined by the existing order."[53] Such a vision is what the Italian scholar-activist Antonio Gramsci called a hegemonic view. As described by Gwyn Williams, hegemony is

> . . . an order in which a certain way of life and thought is dominant, in which one concept of reality is diffused throughout society in all its institutional and private manifestations, informing with its spirit all taste, morality, customs, religious and political principles, and all social relations, particularly in their intellectual and moral connotation. An element of direction and control, not necessarily conscious, is implied.[54]

Hegemony is an elaboration of Marx's contention that "the ideas of the ruling class are in every epoch the ruling ideas: i.e., the class which is the ruling *material* force of society, is at the same time its ruling *intellectual* force."[55]

Members of Congress do not see their own outlook in these terms. In making choices, they believe they are acting as free individuals. They believe that they freely choose the boundaries of their decisions, because these limits seem quite natural to them and do not need to be questioned. This was most evident, perhaps, in the case of the Higher Education Act, when members accepted blithely that their legislation would enable universities again to serve as mechanisms for reproducing status differentials. Status differentials that are related to the capitalist labor market, they believed, were part of a natural order.

Within the bounds of a hegemonic view, members of Congress are creative in the way they operate. But it is important to appreciate that the hegemonic view is not merely a set of ideas. As Gramsci observes, "The politician . . . neither creates out of nothing nor does he move in the emptiness of his wishes and dreams. His actions are grounded in factual reality."[56] That is, a legislator's actions are rooted in the reality of a society dominated by the private owners of wealth.

The longer members of Congress make decisions within the boundaries of the hegemonic view, the more this view itself acts as a real force on them and limits what they do. They do not see the links between the view and the material world. They know only how they perceive the world, without an appreciation for the origins of the perception. In this way, ultimately, they come to think what they think because they do what they do. The route to doing what they do is complex, and the particular activities are varied. But in practice their worldview and behavior outline a general function for Congress.

Functions of Congress

Whatever its original purposes were, and regardless of what its purposes should be, Congress today takes its function from the manner of its operation. It provides essential services—discussed in Chapter 2—for the private accumulation of wealth, accumulation that would not be possible in its present form without the intervention of the national government.[57] Congress is not involved in direct production. Its services, taken together, serve the purpose of *reproduction*.[58] The intersection of its two conflicting structural features, considered in the last section, generates a hegemonic view that leads Congress to reproduce the capitalist mode of production in the United States and the social relations that attend this mode of production.

The particular organization of our society for the production and distribution of goods and services is not a natural phenomenon. The private ownership of productive property, which gives the owners the right to do what they wish with the property, must be asserted every day, because non-owners also assert their claim to make decisions. These assertions are the struggles discussed in Chapter 2, which create problems in the accumulation process that in turn form the context for congressional decision making. The task of reproducing capitalism is a daily one, but reproduction is also a long-term process, which involves establishing conditions favorable to continuing domination by the owners of wealth. Access to foreign markets, for example, and widespread acceptance of the dominant ideology are important long-term factors that enable owners of wealth to reproduce the system. Reproduction, therefore, becomes an essential aspect of production itself.

When Congress attempts to reproduce the society, it does not try to recreate precisely what exists today.[59] Members of Congress appreciate that the relations of production are an ongoing process and involve changes. What works today to maintain the nature of production and the relations between classes may not work tomorrow in the face of demographic shifts, the concentration of capital, international conflicts, and previous struggles won by workers. Members of Congress confront the ever present problem of devising techniques that will work to maintain the society in its general form. The techniques are neither obvious nor certain to work. For this reason, Congress does make "mistakes"; that is, it may act in a way that exacerbates a problem in the accumulation process or that undermines the viability of private property. In fact, it is bound to make such mistakes, because the dominant ideology that leads Congress to fulfill the function of reproduction embodies the seeds of its own destruction.

The dominant ideology includes a belief in democracy, a belief in government by and for the people. We give Congress the right to make societal decisions because we believe Congress will act in everyone's interest, not merely in the interest of the few. But when Congress acts to maintain and reproduce the society, it is acting in the interests of the few who dominate this society—the owners of wealth. Members may claim that their actions are intended to serve the many, even as they serve the few. A tax loophole may be called a job-opportunity program; recreating status differentials may be called equal educational opportunity.[60] But members also may be forced to go beyond such claims, to provide benefits for non-owners by depriving owners of some power over their property, in order to secure Congress's right to rule.

Their effort to serve property and people at the same time creates an unrelieved tension for members of Congress, because the two efforts are contradictory.[61] How severe the tension is, and how well legislators can fashion techniques to walk the thin line, depends on the nature of the class struggle and the nature of problems in the accumulation process.

The more Congress acts to aid capital, the more people will demand (either directly, or indirectly at the polls) that Congress should help non-owners.[62] To the extent that helping non-owners weakens capital, Congress undermines its own reason for being, and it must redress its "mistake," which in turn may create new problems. That is, in the short run, despite its weaknesses, Congress may act in ways that are dysfunctional for the larger system.

This pattern can be seen generally by considering the military budget. In Europe, large governmental budgets have not "threatened the reproduction of capital," because the money has been largely channeled back into the economy through the purchase of goods and services from companies that employ people who then generate more wealth.[63] In the United States, the military budget has this immediate effect, too, which has made it popular with members of Congress as a way of relieving the tension of contradictory purposes. It seems to provide support for corporations and at the same time provide jobs for the middle class. But in the long run it weakens the accumulation process, because military expenditures absorb capital but do not generate new capital, distort investment decisions and undermine industrial efficiency, and have an inflationary impact that saps the strength of the dollar in international markets.[64] Large military budgets are therefore a "mistaken" strategy for resolving the contradiction between supporting the owners of wealth and providing benefits to the mass of citizens. This strategy fails to resolve the contradiction and also weakens the system of production.

In attempting to resolve the conflict between its principal functions, Congress takes on four subsidiary functions that are derived from both sides of the conflict. These subsidiary functions were evident in the case studies on United States Cuban policy and on the 1972 Higher Education Act. The four functions differ from those that scholars often ascribe to Congress and which are more appropriately conceived of as "tasks."[65] An activity is understood as a function when it can be related to the purposes it serves in a system. Indeed, the emphasis here has been that Congress can be best understood in terms of its relationship to the larger system. Consider, then, the four functions of Congress.

To check the executive branch when it is not acting in the interests of capital accumulation. Congress might do this by providing a forum for the dissemination of propaganda, to create either a favorable or hostile climate for a new policy or an existing one. From 1971 to 1975, congressional hearings, speeches, and, most importantly, trips to Cuba served this purpose with respect to changing United States policy. Congress might also develop and pursue a new policy, through legislation, when a problem arises that the president ignores. Though the president proposed a version of the 1972 Higher Education Act, the legislation was largely the product of congressional initiative.

To legitimate mechanisms of inequality in ways that enable them to gain broad public acceptance. Status differentials serve the purpose of dividing the working class and making it less able to struggle effectively against capital. Education in this century has become an accepted mechanism for generating such differences, because people believe that workers with different levels of education deserve different rewards. The Higher Education Act was drafted to be consistent with this view.

To provide benefits for the mass of people, in order to preserve Congress's right to rule. While the Higher Education Act served to divide the working class, it also authorized large sums of money to be given to non-owners of wealth. This was a clear and tangible benefit that overshadowed the more subtle anti-worker aspects of the legislation.

To provide access to the government for all groups, so that no one feels left out of the process. In the case of Cuba, both the pro- and anti-normalization sides had their advocates in Congress, and members of Congress gave both sides several opportunities to disseminate their views. Members themselves may not have spoken in the extremes of some groups, but the groups were heard.

Contradictions and Possibilities

As Congress attempts to fulfill these functions, it will create new problems, because there is a tendency for old solutions to become inappropriate for new circumstances. The old solutions act as "lags" and prevent the adequate consideration of new conditions. Thus the old solutions themselves become problems. This pattern, too, was evident in the case studies. The congressional initiative on Cuba ultimately weakened the legitimacy of Congress when quick shifts in 1976 and 1978—to a posture of hostility towards Cuba—made Congress seem frivolous. The Higher Education Act was an effort that was too little, too late, to serve the purposes of re-establishing the higher-education system as a mechanism for legitimating inequality. At private schools, tuitions alone by 1972 had doubled the $1,400 that Congress was offering, preventing the Basic Educational Opportunity Grants from being a source of full equal opportunity. And the mass of students could not be "cooled out" in community colleges, as some had envisioned, because many public four-year institutions had already been added on to existing universities and could not be abandoned. By reauthorizing the old programs, Congress also added their burden to the cost of the new ones. The costs became a drain that Congress could not justify, while the equal educational opportunity it promised was never realized.

The contradictions embedded in the four functions generate a congressional dynamic that is neither unchanging nor determined neatly by one set of forces. Congress's dynamic changes with the alterations in the society, and here lie the possibilities. While Congress may always attempt to reproduce the society, it can be forced to try to serve people's needs. Serving people and reproducing class is a balancing act likely to produce "mistakes," miscalculations that will benefit non-owners without reproducing class relations. The ultimate possibilities of Congress thus rest with our demands that Congress serve us, act in our interests, and be an institution by and for the people. The possibilities are not unlimited, because Congress will not deviate too far from the interests of the private owners of wealth. But within the limits we should pursue our demands to their fullest and not constrain ourselves by excuses that rationalize Congress's inaction.

NOTES

1. Roger H. Davidson, *The Role of the Congressman* (New York: Pegasus, 1969), p. 122.
2. Congressional Quarterly *Weekly Report,* 24 January 1981, p. 199.
3. David Vogler, *The Politics of Congress,* 3rd ed. (Boston: Allyn and Bacon, 1980), pp. 64–65. Randall B. Ripley and Grace A. Franklin, *Congress, the Bureaucracy and Public Policy,* rev. ed. (Homewood, Ill.: Dorsey Press, 1980), pp. 32–33, 35.
4. Harrison W. Fox, Jr., and Susan Webb Hammond, *Congressional Staffs: The Invisible Force in American Lawmaking* (New York: Free Press, 1977), pp. 33–46, 60–62; Michael Barone, "The Senate the Staff Built," *Washington Post,* 14 April 1981, p. A21; Michael J. Malbin, "Delegation, Deliberation, and the New Role of Congressional Staff," in Thomas E. Mann and Norman J. Ornstein, eds., *The New Congress* (Washington, D.C.: American Enterprise Institute, 1981), pp. 149–154.
5. Lawrence C. Dodd, "Congress, the Constitution, and the Crisis of Legitimation," in Lawrence C. Dodd and Bruce I. Oppenheimer, eds., *Congress Reconsidered,* 2nd ed. (Washington, D.C.: CQ Press, 1981), p. 411.
6. Norman Frohlich and Joe Oppenheimer, "Post-Election Redistributive Strategies of Representation: Part of a Theory of the Politics of Redistribution" (paper presented at the 1980 Annual Meeting of the American Political Science Association, Washington, D.C., September 1980).
7. Philip Brenner, "An Examination of Conflict in the U.S. House of Representatives" (Ph.D. diss, Johns Hopkins University, 1975), Chapter 2. Also see Ripley and Franklin, *Congress, The Bureaucracy and Public Policy,* Chapter 6.
8. Morton Mintz, "25 House Races Broke Spending Records, and the Meter's Running," *Washington Post,* 8 November 1980, p. A4.
9. Larry Light, "Business Giving Heavily to GOP: Democrats May Lose Edge in Contributions from PACs," Congressional Quarterly *Weekly Report,* 22 November 1980, pp. 3405–3409.
10. This was perhaps most striking in the loss by Senator Warren Magnuson (D-Wash), a renowned provider of federal projects for his state. See Larry Light, "Slade Gorton," Congressional Quarterly *Weekly Report,* 13 December 1980, p. 3560.
11. Vogler, *The Politics of Congress,* 3rd ed., p. 96.

12. Richard F. Fenno, Jr., *Home Style: House Members in Their Districts* (Boston: Little, Brown, 1978), pp. 211, 231–232; Timothy E. Cook, "Legislature vs. Legislator: A Note on the Paradox of Congressional Support," *Legislative Studies Quarterly*, 4, No. 1 (February 1979), 43–52; Glenn R. Parker and Roger H. Davidson, "Why Do Americans Love Their Congressmen So Much More Than Their Congress?", *Legislative Studies Quarterly* 4, No. 1 (February 1979), 53–61.

13. John W. Kingdon, *Congressmen's Voting Decisions*, 2nd ed. (New York: Harper & Row, 1981), pp. 30, 44–45.

14. Joseph Cooper and William West, "The Congressional Career in the 1970s," in Dodd and Oppenheimer, *Congress Reconsidered*, 2nd ed., pp. 86–91; Vogler, *The Politics of Congress*, 3rd ed., p. 3; Mark Green, *Who Runs Congress?*, 3rd ed. (New York: Bantam, 1979), pp. 242–243.

15. Alan Ehrenhalt, "Congress and the Country: The 'Juniority' System in Congress," *Congressional Quarterly Weekly Report*, 21 March 1981, p. 535.

16. "The Congressional Career in the 1970s," p. 84.

17. David R. Mayhew, *Congress: The Electoral Connection* (New Haven: Yale University Press, 1974), pp. 13–14.

18. Morris P. Fiorina, *Congress: Keystone of the Washington Establishment* (New Haven: Yale University Press, 1977), pp. 7–11; Fenno, *Home Style*, pp. 199–203.

19. Albert D. Cover and David R. Mayhew, "Congressional Dynamics and the Decline of Competitive Congressional Elections," in Dodd and Oppenheimer, *Congress Reconsidered*, 2nd ed., pp. 63, 75–76.

20. Charles S. Bullock III, "House Committee Assignments," in Leroy N. Rieselbach, ed., *The Congressional System: Notes and Readings*, 2nd ed. (North Scituate, Mass.: Duxbury, 1979), p. 83.

21. Mark Green and Jack Newfield, "Who Owns Congress: A Guide to Indentured Politicians," *Village Voice*, 21 April 1980, p. 1.

22. Gordon Adams, *The Iron Triangle: The Politics of Defense Contracting* (New York: Council on Economic Priorities, 1981), Chapters 1, 2.

23. For example, consider the following statement by then House Minority Leader Gerald Ford: "Mr. Chairman, I have lost before, and I probably will lose in the future, but it does not affect me personally because that is part of the ball game." *Congressional Record*, daily ed., 10 May 1973, p. H3593.

24. For example, see Lawrence C. Dodd, "Congress and the Quest for Power," in Lawrence C. Dodd and Bruce I. Oppenheimer, eds., *Congress Reconsidered* (New York: Praeger, 1977), pp. 270–271; Norman J. Ornstein, "Causes and Consequences of Congressional Change: Subcommittee Reforms in the House of Representatives, 1970–73," in Norman J. Ornstein, ed., *Congress in Change: Evolution and Reform* (New York: Praeger, 1975), p. 89.

25. Ralf Dahrendorf, *Class and Class Conflict in Industrial Society* (Stanford: Stanford University Press, 1959), Chapters 7, 8.

26. Robert L. Peabody, *Leadership in Congress: Stability, Succession and Change* (Boston: Little, Brown, 1976), p. 6.

27. Ibid., p. 470.

28. Powerful members were defined as follows: the four committee chairmen, the subcommittee chairmen on Appropriations and Ways and Means, task force chairmen on Budget, and all Democratic members on Rules. Ratings are from *Congressional Quarterly Weekly Report*, 21 March 1981, pp. 514–517.

29. Dan Rostenkowski (D-Ill.) is a case in point. When he became chairman of the Ways and Means Committee in 1981, his goals reportedly changed from being obsessed with power to writing tax legislation. He changed his behavior, too, and devoted more time to legislating. But it would be hard to say that before 1981 he neither cared about policy nor was uninvolved in making it. See Irwin B. Arieff, "As Ways and Means Chairman: New Role for Rostenkowski Gets Him Into the Thick of House Power-Playing," *Congressional Quarterly Weekly Report*, 16 May 1981, pp. 863–866.

30. Fenno, *Home Style*, pp. 245–246.

31. Ibid., p. 246; Parker and Davidson, "Why Do Americans Love Their Congressmen So Much More Than Their Congress?"; Cook, "Legislature vs. Legislator."

32. Philip E. Slater, *The Pursuit of Loneliness: American Culture at the Breaking Point* (Boston: Beacon Press, 1970), Chapter 1. Garry Wills, *Nixon Agonistes* (Boston: Houghton Mifflin, 1970).

33. This has been the thrust of several studies about presidents. See, for example, James David Barber, *Presidential Character*, 2nd ed. (Englewood Cliffs, N.J.: Prentice-Hall, 1977).

34. Jean-Paul Sartre, *Search for a Method*, trans. Hazel E. Barnes (New York: Vintage, 1968), pp. 85–90; Bertell Ollman, *Alienation: Marx's Conception of Man in Capitalist Society* (London: Cambridge University Press, 1971), Chapter 17; Karl Marx, *The German Ideology*, in Robert C. Tucker, ed., *The Marx-Engels Reader*, 2nd ed. (New York: Norton, 1978), p. 150.

35. For example, see Donald Matthews, *U.S. Senators and Their World* (New York: Vintage, 1961), Chapter 4; Richard F. Fenno, Jr., 'The House Appropriations Committee as a Political System: The Problem of Integration," *American Political Science Review*, 56 (1962), pp. 310–324.

36. Notably, constituents tend to see their representative as a local leader (Cook, "Legislature vs. Legislator"), but the members themselves prefer "not to become local political leaders" (Fenno, *Home Style*, p. 114).

37. For example, third-term Representative Don Riegle proudly described his attendance at the Bilderberg meetings, which "are designed to get about a hundred top people in business, government and education together." Donald Riegle, with Trevor Armbrister, *O Congress* (Garden City, N.Y.: Doubleday, 1972), p. 9.

38. See Table 5–1 for information on the sample.

39. Steven Lukes, *Power: A Radical View* (London: MacMillan, 1974), Chapter 5. Also see Göran Therborn, *What Does the Ruling Class Do When It Rules?* (London: Verso, 1980), pp. 132–135.

40. The presidents were mentioned with the following frequencies: Franklin Roosevelt (11), Lincoln (11), Truman (7), Jefferson (7), Nixon (3), Jackson (3), Eisenhower (3), Lyndon Johnson (2), Theodore Roosevelt (2), Wilson (1).

41. Fred Block, "The Ruling Class Does Not Rule: Notes on the Marxist Theory of the State," *Socialist Revolution*, No. 33 (May-June 1977), p. 15.

42. For example, see Arnold J. Heidenheimer, Hugh Heclo, and Carolyn Teich Adams, *Comparative Public Policy: The Politics of Social Choice in Europe and America* (New York: St. Martin's, 1975).

43. Ira Katznelson and Kenneth Prewitt, "Constitutionalism, Class, and the Limits of Choice in U.S. Foreign Policy," in Richard R. Fagen, ed., *Capitalism and the State in U.S.–Latin American Relations* (Stanford: Stanford University Press, 1979), pp. 30–33.

44. In *U.S.* v. *Nixon* (1974), for example, the Court established "national security" as grounds for the president to invoke "executive privilege." See Louis Fisher, *The Constitution Between Friends* (New York: St. Martin's, 1978), pp. 161–165. Also see Marcus Raskin, *Notes on the Old System* (New York: David McKay, 1974), pp. 86–91; Thomas M. Franck and Edward Weisband, *Foreign Policy by Congress* (New York: Oxford University Press, 1979), Chapter 3.

45. Arthur F. Bentley observed in 1908 that this phenomenon weakens the executive, because groups are able to play one branch off against the other to secure their ends. See *The Process of Government* (Cambridge, Mass.: Harvard University Press, 1967), pp. 344–345. For a modern formulation see David B. Truman, *The Governmental Process* (New York: Alfred A. Knopf, 1951), pp. 398–404.

46. Richard O. Boyer and Herbert M. Morais, *Labor's Untold Story* (New York: United Electrical, Radio and Machine Workers, 1972); Michael Parenti, *Democracy for the Few*, 3rd ed. (New York: St. Martin's, 1980), pp. 314–318; Gosta Esping-Anderson, Roger Friedland, and Erik Olin Wright, "Modes of Class Struggle and the Capitalist State," *Kapitalistate*, Nos. 4–5 (1976), pp. 198–212.

47. These range from the lack of a feudal heritage to the divisive role of racism, the mobility of the population, the brutal repression of militant organizers, and the con-

scious segmentation of the working class. See Katznelson and Prewitt, "Constitutionalism, Class and the Limits of Choice," pp. 28–30; Louis Hartz, *The Liberal Tradition in America* (New York: Harcourt Brace and World, 1955); Frances Fox Piven and Richard Cloward, *Poor People's Movements: Why They Succeed, How They Fail* (New York: Vintage, 1979); Daniel Bell, *The End of Ideology*, rev. ed. (New York: Collier, 1962), pp. 393–405.

48. Grant McConnell, *Private Power and American Democracy* (New York: Alfred A. Knopf, 1967), Chapter 9; Boyer and Morais, *Labor's Untold Story*, Chapter 14. However, the state may not always act against labor, even when labor avoids dealing with it. See Theda Skocpol, "Political Response to Capitalist Crisis: Neo-Marxist Theories of the State and the Case of the New Deal," *Politics & Society*, 10, No. 3 (1981).

49. McConnell, *Private Power and American Democracy*, Chapters 2, 3.

50. Marcus Raskin, *The Politics of National Security* (New Brunswick, N.J.: Transaction Books, 1979); Alan Wolfe, *The Rise and Fall of the 'Soviet Threat': Domestic Sources of the Cold War Consensus* (Washington, D.C.: Institute for Policy Studies, 1979), Chapter 7; Richard J. Barnet, *Roots of War* (New York: Atheneum, 1972), Chapters 6, 7.

51. Ira Katznelson and Mark Kesselman, *The Politics of Power*, 2nd ed. (New York: Harcourt Brace Jovanovich, 1979), pp. 29–32; Frank Parkin, *Class Inequality and Political Order* (New York: Praeger, 1971), pp. 82–83. Also see Bertram Gross, *Friendly Fascism: The New Face of Power in America* (New York: M. Evans, 1980), Chapter 12.

52. Alan Wolfe, *The Limits of Legitimacy* (New York: Free Press, 1977), Chapter 9.

53. Joseph Femia, "Hegemony and Consciousness in the Thought of Antonio Gramsci," *Political Studies*, 23, No. 1 (March 1975), p. 33. Also see Block, "The Ruling Class Does Not Rule," p. 14.

54. Gwyn A. Williams, "The Concept of 'Egemonia' in the Thought of Antonio Gramsci: Some Notes On Interpretation," *Journal of the History of Ideas*, 21, No. 4 (October–December, 1960), p. 587.

55. Marx, *The German Ideology*, p. 172.

56. Antonio Gramsci, "Notes on Machiavelli, Politics, and the Modern State," quoted in Femia, "Hegemony and Consciousness," p. 36. Claus Offe has explored this idea with the concept of "selective mechanisms." These are ideological filters that sensitize state elites to certain claims, leading them to exclude others and to respond to problems in ways that support the existing mode of production. See his "Structural Problems of the Capitalist State," *German Political Studies*, No. 1 (1974). Also see Alan Wolfe, *Limits of Legitimacy*, p. 270.

57. Fred Block, "Beyond Relative Autonomy: State Managers as Historical Subjects," in Ralph Miliband and John Saville, eds., *The Socialist Register, 1980* (London: Merlin Press, 1980), p. 231.

58. Therborn, *What Does The Ruling Class Do When It Rules?*, Chapter 3; Block, "The Ruling Class Does Not Rule," p. 10.

59. Therborn, *What Does The Ruling Class Do When It Rules?*, p. 63; Henri Lefebvre, *The Survival of Capitalism: Reproduction of the Relations of Production*, trans. Frank Bryant (New York: St. Martin's, 1976), pp. 42–46, 59–68.

60. Consider in this light the comments of liberal Senator Paul Sarbanes (D-Md.), during a meeting with constituents in 1981. After he explained at length how difficult he found his job, trying to please everyone, someone asked why if it were so exhausting he wanted to be a senator. He replied with an example of how he had helped to name a black and a woman to the federal bench. "This was an important symbol for two groups in our country, a living example of what the system can do," he exclaimed. 'I'm proud of that."

61. Wolfe, *The Limits of Legitimacy*, pp. 4–7.

62. For an alternative formulation of this problem, see Dodd, "Congress, the Constitution, and the Crisis of Legitimation," pp. 414–415.

63. Therborn, *What Does The Ruling Class Do When It Rules?*, p. 166.

64. Seymour Melman, *The Permanent War Economy* (New York: Simon and Schuster, 1974), Chapters 4, 5.

65. For example, see Vogler, *The Politics of Congress*, 3rd ed. pp. 10–18.

Index

Abourezk, James (Senator), 47, 49, 92
Adams, Gordon, 173
Administration Committee, House, 147
Africa, 84, 85
Agricultural Trade Development and Assistance Act of 1954, 44
Airborne Warning and Control Systems (AWACS), 84
Albert, Carl (Speaker), 142
Allen, James, 106, 107
Allende Gossens, Salvador, 70, 72
American Association of Junior Colleges, 103
American Association of State Colleges and Universities, 103
American Council on Education (ACE), 103, 112
"American exceptionalism," 186
American Federation of Labor, 25
Americans for Democratic Action, 55
Anderson, Jack, 136
Angola, 57, 58, 59, 79–80, 82, 84, 86, 89, 90, 92
Apathy, 29
Appropriations Committee
House, 150, 175, 176, 177
Senate, 150, 177
Argentina, 73, 74, 77
Aspin, Les (Representative), 49, 92
Association of American Colleges, 103
Association of American Universities, 103

Bafalis, L.A. (Representative), 81
Balance-of-payments deficit, 69
Banks

multinational corporations and, 27–28
1970 crisis and, 69
Basic Educational Opportunity Grants (BEOGs), 101–102, 114, 191
Batista, Fulgencio, 42
Bay of Pigs invasion, 41, 42
Behavior. See Congressional behavior; Legislators
Behaviorism, as approach to study of Congress, 15–16
Berg, Ivar, 123
Bibby, John, 143
Bingham, Jonathan (Representative), 47, 48, 49, 56, 92
Blacks
civil rights, 29
poverty of, 29
unemployment, 26–27
Block, Fred, 70
Blockade against Cuba, 43, 45, 46, 47, 61
Blumenthal, W. Michael, 75
Bolling, Richard (Representative), 137, 140–141, 142
Bolling Committee, 138
Bowles, Samuel, 114, 124
Brademas, John (Representative), 108, 110, 112–113
Brazil, multinational corporations in, 70
Breaux, John (Representative), 54, 78, 92
Britain, balance-of-payments problem in, 69
Brookings Institution, 105, 114
Brzezinski, Zbigniew, 51, 87
Budget, military, 190
Budgetary and Accounting Act (1921), 155

Budgetary process
  reforms of, 150, 155
  reform of congressional, 145–146
Budget Committee, House, 176
Budget Control and Impoundment
    Act, 150
Bullock, Charles, 172
Burns, James MacGregor, 141
Business Roundtable, 149, 185
Butler, Lewis, 106
Byrd, Robert (Majority Whip), 46

Campaign finances, 7
  contributions to, 30
  recruitment process and, 136–137
  reform of, 148–149
Carnegie Commission on Higher
    Education, 104–105, 106,
    113–114, 126, 173, 174
Carnegie Foundation, 115–117, 167
Carnegie-Rivlin perspective, 105
Carter, Jimmy, 84, 85–86, 87, 89, 93,
    169
Carter, Rosalynn, 85
Casework, for re-election of legisla-
    tors, 7
Castro Ruz, Fidel, 42, 43, 47, 49, 51,
    57, 73, 82
Celler, Emanuel (Representative),
    39, 166
Central Intelligence Agency (CIA),
    43
  Cuba and, 80–81
Centralizing reforms, 148–151, 156,
    158–159
Checks and balances, 185, 190–191
Cheit, Earl, 103
Chile, 72, 92
  multinational corporations in, 70
Chowder and Marching Society, 45
Christmas-tree bill, 101
  See also Higher Education Act of
    1972
Church, Frank (Senator), 45, 50, 51,.
    81, 149
Cities, fiscal crisis in, 26

Class conflicts, 189
  Higher Education Act of 1972
    and, 115–117
  labor movement and, 25
  legislators and
    awareness of, 128–129
    behavior of and, 34
Cloture, 149
Codes of ethics, 137
Cohen, David, 124
Collective experience, of legislators,
    179–180
Colleges, 167
  functions, 122–126
  See also Higher Education Act of
    1972
College Work-Study, 102
Committee on Committees, 142
Committees
  power and, 175, 176
  reform and
    rules, 139–140
    structure, 142–146, 150
  selection process and, 10, 14
  See also specific committees
Common Cause, 137
Communist countries, American re-
    lations with, 58
  See also Cuba; Soviet Union
Communist parties, in Western Eu-
    rope, 28
Community colleges, 119–121, 127,
    191
Congress, functions of, 188–192
Congress of Industrial Organizations,
    25
Congressional behavior, 33–35
  instrumentalist analysis of, 112–
    117
  interest groups and, 30–33, 34
  political and economic context of,
    24
    ideological base of, 28–29
    material base of, 24–28
  See also Legislators; Pluralism
Congressional Black Caucus, 46

Congressional Budget and Impound-
    ment Control Act of 1974,
    145–146
Congressional Budget Office (CBO),
    145, 148
Congressional initiative
    foreign policy and, 88–95, 177
    legitimacy crisis and, 128–129
Consensus, on foreign policy, 93
Constituents
    Cuba and, 54–55
    foreign policy and, 91
    pressures of, 35
    re-election and, 7–8
    significance of, 13, 171
Contact with Congress, as approach
    to study of Congress, 14–15
Cooper, Joseph, 172
Corporations, national, 24–25
    See also Multinational corporations
CORU, 80–81
Coser, Lewis, 15
Costanzo, G.A., 75
Cuba, American policy towards, 40,
    153, 167–168, 177, 190, 191
    background of, 40–44
    Congressional action on, 44
    international context of, 67–88
    1971–1975, 45–48
    1976, 48–49
    1977–1978, 49–52
    congressional initiative and, 88–95
    legislators' perceptions of, 52–63
Cuban Resolution of 1962, 44–45
Culver, John (Senator), 149

Dahl, Robert, 15, 16
Dahrendorf, Ralph, 174
Davidson, Roger, 13, 34, 169–170
Debate, curbing, 140
Decentralizing reforms, 151–152,
    156, 158
Decision-making, dialectics of, 186–
    188
Dellenback, John (Representative),
    110, 112, 113

Democratic Study Group, 46, 139
Dexter, Lewis Anthony, 144
Disposition of legislators, 17–18
Dodd, Lawrence, 8, 9
Dollar, multinational corporations
    and, 69
Domestic Council, 155
Domestic policy, Congress and. *See*
    Higher Education Act of 1972
Domestic transformations, congres-
    sional behavior and, 24–27
Domhoff, G. William, 30, 114
Dominant ideology, 187–188, 189
Dominguez, Jorge, 80
Dominican Republic, 72
Du Bridge, Lee, 106

East Africa, 86
Easton, David, 32, 67–68
Economy, 68–69
    Cuba and, 60–61, 68–72
    international, 69–72
    legitimacy crisis in, 154–155
Education. *See* Higher Education
    Act of 1972
Education Amendments (1968), 105,
    107
Education Amendments Act of 1972.
    See Higher Education Act of
    1972
Education and Labor Committee,
    House, 10, 109, 112
Education and Labor subcommittee on
    higher education, House, 113
Eisenhower, Dwight D., 42
Elections of legislators
    cost of, 170–171
    parochialism and, 7–8, 11
    See also Re-elections of legislators
Elites. *See* Policy elites
Employment Act of 1946, 36, 155
Energy crisis, 27
Ethics
    campaign-finance reform and,
        148–149
    codes of, 137

Ethiopia, 86
Eulau, Heinz, 116
Euro-Communism, 28
Executive branch
  Congress checking on, 190–191
  Higher Education Act of 1972
    and, 105–107
  legislators' relationship with, 8
Export Control Act of 1949, 44

Fascell, Dante (Representative), 46,
  47
Fenno, Richard, 34, 57, 68, 136
Ferre, Maurice, 49
Filibuster, 149
Finance Committee
  House, 177
  Senate, 81
Finn, Chester, 104, 106, 113
Fiorina, Morris, 7, 8
Fisher, Louis, 145
Ford, Gerald, 9, 46, 73–74
Foreign Affairs Committee, House,
  10
  Cuba and, 46, 47, 55, 56, 57
Foreign Assistance Act of 1961, 44
Foreign policy, 40
  Congress and, 88–95, 177
  See also Cuba, American policy
    towards
Foreign Relations Committee (Sen-
  ate), Cuba and, 44, 45, 50,
  54, 55, 56, 81, 86, 89
Franck, Thomas, 90, 93
Frye, Alton, 94
Fulbright, J. William (Senator), 45
Fund for New Priorities, 45

Gardner, John, 104
Garn, Jake (Senator), 173
General Accounting Office, 147–148
Gibbons, Sam (Representative), 81
Gintis, Herbert, 114, 124
Gladieux, Lawrence, 103, 105, 119
Gleysteen, Culver, 86
Gorelick, Sherry, 123

Government Affairs Committee,
  Senate, 27–28
Graham, Otis, 154
Gramn, Phil (Representative), 73
Gramsci, Antonio, 187
Green, Edith (Representative), 101,
  107–108, 109, 110, 112, 113,
  116, 127
Green, Mark, 136, 173
Greider, William, 148–149
Gross, Bertram, 75, 153, 155
Group of 77, 83
Grubb, W. Norton, 120
Guantanamo Base, 41
Gulf Oil, 79
Guyana, 72

Halberstam, David, 41
Halleck, Charles (House Minority
  Leader), 46
Hamilton, Lee (Representative), 90,
  91
Hansen Committee, 145
Harkin, John (Representative), 92
Harrington, Michael (Representa-
  tive), 46
Haskell, Floyd (Senator), 92
Hays, Wayne, 137
Hegemonic view, 187–188
Hegemony, 187
Heinz, Henry J., 75
Herbert, Edward F. (Repre-
  sentative), 138
Higher education, 177–178
  legitimacy crisis and, 121–126,
    127–128
  See also Colleges; Higher Educa-
    tion Act of 1972
Higher Education Act of 1972, 31,
  100–102, 153, 167, 172, 173,
  177–178, 188, 190, 191
  executive branch and, 105–107
  instrumental analysis of, 112–117
  interest groups and, 102–104, 111–
    112
  legislators' perceptions of, 117–121

personal interests of legislators
and, 107–111
policy elites and, 104–105, 113–
117
Hijacking agreement with Cuba
(1973), 73, 78, 81
Holt, Pat, 73
Hostility among legislators, Higher
Education Act of 1972 and,
109–110
Huitt, Ralph, 103
Humphrey, Hubert (Senator), 50
Huntington, Samuel P., 6
Hurwitch, Robert, 73

Ideology
dominant, 187–188, 189
Higher Education Act of 1972
and, 115–117
Industry
competitive, 26, 32
oligopolistic, 25–26, 32
Inequality
Congressional legitimacy and, 191
of power, 174–175
See also Class conflict
Inflation, 26–27
Information resources, reform of,
146–148, 150–151
Information Systems staff, House,
147
Initiative of Congress. *See* Congressional initiative
Institutional interests
Cuba and, 56–57
legislators' behavior and, 35–36,
179, 180
"Instrumentalist" analysis
of congressional behavior, 30
of Higher Education Act of 1972,
112–117
Interest groups, 34
congressional behavior and, 30–
33
Higher Education Act of 1972
and, 102–104, 111–112

Internal Security Subcommittee, Sen-
ate, 18
International financial institutions
(IFIs), Cuba and, 51, 75
International Monetary Fund, 51, 75
International Operations Subcommit-
tee, 50
International Organizations Subcom-
mittee, 47
International Relations Committee
(House), Cuba and, 47, 54,
55, 80, 81, 92
International Relations Subcommit-
tee on International Trade
and Commerce, 92
International Security Assistance and
Arms Control Act of 1976, 48
International Trade and Commerce
Subcommittee, 48, 56, 57
International transformations, con-
gressional behavior and, 27–28

Jamaica, 84–85
Janda, Kenneth, 147
Japan, 71
Javits, Jacob (Senator), 47, 50, 74,
78
Johnson, Lyndon, 169
Joint Study Committee on Budget
Control, 145
Judiciary Committee, House, 139

Karabel, Jerome, 127
Keefe, William, 12
Kennedy, Edward (Senator), 45, 56,
92
Kennedy, John, 43, 44
Kerr, Clark, 104, 116
Kerr Commission, 29, 104–105, 106,
113, 115–117
Khrushchev, Nikita, 44
Kissinger, Henry, 58, 73, 76, 80, 90

Labor movement, conflict in (1932),
25
See also Unions

Labor and Public Welfare education subcommittee, 113
Lane, Lyle, 87
Latin America, 59–60, 72, 168
See also specific countries
Lazerson, Marvin, 120, 124
Legislative Reorganization Act
of 1946, 35–36, 143
of 1970, 147
Legislative Research Service, 147
Legislators
behavior assumptions, 4–5, 168–169, 178–179 (See also Congressional behavior)
approaches to studying, 14–17
institutional shaping, 12–13, 14, 35–36
interest groups and, 173–174
parochialism, 6–7, 11, 169–171, 183
personal interests and, 8–9, 11, 13–14, 35
power and, 9–10, 11–12, 174–175, 176
public policy concern and, 10–11, 12, 175, 177–178
re-election, 7–8, 11, 171–173
self-perception and, 179–183
wealth influencing, 173
ideology of, 187–188
limits of, 183–186
possibilities of, 166–183
reasons for being, 181
Legitimacy crisis, 19, 126–127
Congress and, 167
Congressional initiative and, 128–129
economic planning and, 29, 154–155
government and, 29
higher education and, 121–126, 127–128
reforms and, 156–157, 158
Less developed countries. See Third World
Liberalism, decline of, 28–29

Library of Congress, 147
Linowitz Commission Report, 59, 75
Litton Industries, 74
Lobbyists, registration of, 137
Long, Russell (Senator), 81
Losano, Hernan Ricardo, 81
Lowi, Theodore, 28, 143, 144
Lugo, Freddy, 81

McGee, Gale (Senator), 46, 48
McGovern, George (Senator), 47, 49, 50, 55, 86, 149
Majak, Roger, 47
Manley, John, 93
Manley, Michael, 85
Marcos, Ferdinand, 70
Marx, Karl, 187
Masses, Congress and, 191
See also Class conflict
Mathias, Charles McC. (Senator), 45
Matsunaga, Spark (Senator), 81
Matthews, Herbert, 42
Mayaguez incident, 90
Mayhew, David, 13, 172
Members of Congress. See Legislators
Mexico, multinational corporations in, 70
Meyer, Charles, 75
Miliband, Ralph, 30
Military budget, 190
Miller, Warren, 13
Mills, C. Wright, 8
Missile crisis, 43–44
Monetary crisis, 69
Morgan, Edward, 106
Morrill Land Grant Act of 1862, 102
Moynihan, Daniel Patrick, 29, 105, 106, 107, 116
Multinational corporations, 27
Cuba and, 60–61, 81
in Latin America, 77–78
speculation on the dollar by, 69
Third World and, 69–71

Mutual Defense Assistance Control
Act of 1951, 44

Nader, Ralph, 136, 137, 139, 147
Nathan, Richard, 106
National Association of State Uni-
versities and Land-Grant
Colleges (NASULGC), 103
National Committee for an Effective
Congress, 137
National Conservative Political Ac-
tion Committee, 149
National Direct Student Loans, 102
National Front for the Liberation of
Angola (FNLA), 79, 80
National (public) interests, 32–33
Cuba and, 57–63
foreign policy and, 71
National Security Act of 1947, 155
National Security Council, Cuba and,
48
National Security Memorandum, 68,
155
National Union for the Total Libera-
tion of Angola (UNITA), 79,
80
New Federalism, 186
Newfield, Jack, 173
New international economic order,
71, 83
Nigeria, 84
Nixon, Richard, 73, 105, 107, 155,
186
Noblesse oblige, of legislators, 128,
129
Nunn, Sam (Senator), 173

O'Connor, James, 154
Offe, Claus, 5
Office of Management and Budget,
155
Office of Technology Assessment,
147–148
Ogaden War, 86
Oil, 69, 83
Omnibus legislation, 109, 172

See also Higher Education Act of
1972
O'Neill, Thomas P. (Speaker), 142
Organization of African Unity, 84,
86
Organizational reforms. See Reform
Organization of American States
(OAS), 43, 48, 59, 72, 79, 88,
89
Organization of Petroleum Exporting
Countries (OPEC), 27, 71, 84
Organizations. See Institutional
interests
Ornstein, Norman, 14

Panama, 82
Panama Canal treaties, 82
Park, Tongsun, 137
Parochialism, of legislators, 6–7, 11,
169–171, 183
Party discipline, reform of, 140–142,
144–150
Pastor, Robert, 51
Patman, Wright (Representative),
138
Peabody, Robert, 12, 137, 141, 175
Pearson, Drew, 136
Peers, desire of legislators for respect
by, 55
Pell, Claiborne (Senator), 47, 55, 74,
78, 101, 109, 110, 113, 172
Perkins, Carl (Representative), 110
Personal interests of legislators, 8–9,
11, 13–14, 35
Cuba and, 54–55
Higher Education Act of 1972
and, 107–111
reforms and, 158
See also Constituents; Re-election
of legislators
Personal reforms. See Reform
Peterson, Peter, 75
Philippines, multinational corpora-
tions in, 70
Pifer, Alan, 105
Pincus, Walter, 142

Pinochet, Augusto, 70
Platt Amendment of 1901, 41
Pluralism, 33
  as approach to study of Congress,
    16–17, 30–31
  public interest and, 32
Poage, W.R. (Representative), 138
Policy. *See* Public policy
Policy elite
  dominant ideology of, 187
  Higher Education Act of 1972
    and, 104–105, 113–117
  legislators' self-perception as, 180
Political Action Committees (PACs),
  149
Political and Military Affairs, Sub-
  committee on, 47
Popular Movement for the Libera-
  tion of Angola (MPLA), 79–
  80
Portugal, 79, 84
Poverty, blacks and, 29
Power, 16–17
  legislators' quest for, 9–10, 11–12
  legislators' self-perception of, 180–
    181, 183
  purpose of, 174–175, 176
  state of, 186
President, legislators' choice of, 181-
  182, 183
Pride of legislators, Higher Education Act of 1972 and, 107–109
Public interest. *See* National interests
Public opinion, 76
  Cuba and, 75–76
Public policy
  legislators' commitment to, 10–11,
    12, 175, 177–178
  power and, 175, 176
  See also Higher Education Act of
    1972

Quie, Albert (Representative), 110,
  112, 113
Quigley, Harold, 116

Rawlins, V. Lane, 122–123
Rayburn, Sam, 166
Reagan, Ronald, 82, 150, 186
Rebozo, Bebe, 73
Recession, 79
Recruitment to committees, bias in,
  136–137
Re-election of legislators, 7–8, 11,
  13, 19, 171–173
  Higher Education Act of 1972
    and, 109
  power and, 175
Reform, 134, 157–158, 166–167
  context for, 152–157
  goals of, 134–135
  institutional consequences of, 148–
    152
    centralization, 148–151, 156, 158
    decentralization and, 151–152,
      156, 158–159
  organizational, 134, 137–148
    committee structure, 142–146,
      150
    information resources, 146–148,
      150–151
    party discipline, 140–142, 149–
      150
    rules, 139–140, 149
    seniority, 138–139, 149
  personal, 134, 135–137
Reification of Congress, 17–18
Reorganization, of government, 154–
  155
Reorganization Act (1970), 171
Reproduction, Congress and, 188–
  189
Rhodesia, 84, 87, 90
Richardson, Bill, 56
Richmond, Frederick (Representa-
  tive), 92
Ripley, Randall, 9, 135–136
Rivlin, Alice, 105
Robinson, James, 90
Rogers, William D., 74
Rules Committee, House, 139, 141,
  142, 150, 175, 176

Rules of Congress, reform of, 139–140, 149

Safire, William, 140
Schattschneider, E.E., 89, 149
Schick, Allen, 145
Schott, Richard, 8
Secrecy, reform of, 140
Select Committee on Committees (House), 137–138
Select Committee to Study the Senate Committee System (Senate), 143
Seniority system, reform of, 138–139, 149
Servicemen's Readjustment Act (1940), 102
Shaba, 87
Smith, Ian, 84
Solarz, Stephen (Representative), 47
South Africa, 79–80, 84, 87
Soviet Union, 62, 73, 80, 91
Sparkman, John (Senator), 46, 49
Speaker, reform of powers of, 141–142
Stanton, William (Representative), 173
State
  Congressional behavior and, 32
  limitations of, 183–186
Steering and Policy Committee, Democratic, 142, 149
Stern, Paula, 91
Stokes, Donald, 13
Stone, Richard (Senator), 48, 81
"Subcommittee bill of rights," 158, 159
  See also specific subcommittees
Subgovernment decision making, 154, 155
Suburbs, growth of, 26
Supplemental Educational Opportunity Grants, 102
Symms, Steve (Senator), 173

Tacit agreement, 17–18
Taft-Hartley Act, 25

Task Force on International Relations, 49
Third World, 71, 177
  multinational corporations in, 69–71
  new international economic order, 71, 83
  OPEC and, 84
  United States and, 28, 63, 82, 85, 88
Thomas, Norman C., 104
Thompson, Frank (Representative), 112
Todman, Terence, 85
Tonkin Gulf Resolution, 44
Tower, John (Senator), 173
Trade Reform Act, Jackson amendment to, 91
Transnational corporations. See Multinational corporations
Treaties, 45
Truman, David, 32
26th of July Movement, 42
Two-year colleges, 119–121, 127, 191

Ulman, Lloyd, 122–123
Un-American Activities Committee, 18
Unions
  inflation and, 27
  in 1930's, 31–32
  workers' rights to form, 29
United Nations, Israel and, 81
United Nations Conference on Trade and Development (UNCTAD), 83
United States Foreign Claims Settlement Commission, 81–82
Universities, 167
  functions, 122–126
  See also Higher Education Act of 1972

Vance, Cyrus, 85
Van Dusen, Michael, 91
Vietnam War, 28, 69, 72, 88, 92, 93, 126

Wachtel, Howard, 70
Waggoner, Joseph (Representative), 81
Walters, Barbara, 55
War on Poverty, 29
War Powers Resolution (1973), 90
Ways and Means Committee, House, 81, 142, 175, 176, 177
Wealth
  Congress assisting, 188–189, 191
  influence of, 173, 185–186, 188–189
Weaver, Warren Jr., 136
Wednesday Group, 45, 46, 62
Weisband, Edward, 90, 93
West, William, 172
Whalen, Charles (Representative), 47, 55, 56, 119

Wildavsky, Aaron, 145, 154
Wills, Garry, 28
Wilson, Woodrow, 14, 142
Wolanin, Thomas, 103, 105
Wolfe, Alan, 126
Women, civil rights and, 129
Woodcock, Leonard, 75.
Working class, 185–186
  See also Class conflict
Working Group on Higher Education, 105–107
World power, United States as a, 61–63
Wright, James (Majority Leader), 142

Young, Andrew, 84, 85, 87